The Expositor's Bible
The Pastoral Epistles

By

Alfred Plummer

The Expositor's Bible
The Pastoral Epistles
by Alfred Plummer

Copyright © 2024

All Rights reserved.

No part of this publication may be reproduced, stored in a retrieval system, or transmitted in any form or by any means, electronic, mechanical, photocopying or Otherwise, without the written permission of the publisher.
The author/editor asserts the moral right to be identified as the author/editor of this work.

ISBN: 978-93-61157-58-5

Published by
DOUBLE 9 BOOKS
2/13-B, Ansari Road
Daryaganj, New Delhi – 110002
info@double9books.com
www.double9books.com
Tel. 011-40042856

This book is under public domain

ABOUT THE AUTHOR

Alfred Plummer became an outstanding English theologian and biblical pupil regarded for his large contributions to biblical statement and exegesis. Plummer served as a prominent instructional, retaining the placement of Master of University College, Durham, and later because the Master of Balliol College, Oxford. His knowledge in biblical studies and his commitment to sound scholarship made him a reputable determine in theological circles. One of Alfred Plummer's incredible works is "The Expositor's Bible: The Pastoral Epistles," where he centered on offering insightful remark at the New Testament books of one Timothy, 2 Timothy, and Titus. The Pastoral Epistles are letters traditionally attributed to the Apostle Paul and addressed to early Christian leaders, offering steering on matters of doctrine and church employer. In "The Expositor's Bible: The Pastoral Epistles," Plummer brings his erudition to endure, imparting readers a thorough and scholarly exam of these critical biblical texts. His statement delves into ancient context, linguistic nuances, and theological implications, presenting pastors, scholars, and widespread readers with a precious useful resource for know-how and interpreting those epistles.

CONTENTS

INTRODUCTORY

CHAPTER I
    THE CHARACTER AND THE
    GENUINENESS OF THE PASTORAL EPISTLES 11

THE FIRST EPISTLE TO TIMOTHY

CHAPTER II
    TIMOTHY THE BELOVED DISCIPLE OF
    ST. PAUL. HIS LIFE AND CHARACTER 20

CHAPTER III
    THE DOCTRINE CONDEMNED IN
    THE PASTORAL EPISTLES A JEWISH FORM
    OF GNOSTICISM.—THE GNOSTIC'S PROBLEM 28

CHAPTER IV
    THE MORAL TEACHING OF THE
    GNOSTICS.—ITS MODERN COUNTERPART 35

CHAPTER V
    THE LORD'S COMPASSION IN ENABLING
    A BLASPHEMER AND A PERSECUTOR TO
    BECOME A SERVANT OF CHRIST JESUS
    AND A PREACHER OF THE GOSPEL 42

CHAPTER VI
    THE PROPHECIES ON TIMOTHY.—THE
    PROPHETS OF THE NEW TESTAMENT, AN
    EXCEPTIONAL INSTRUMENT OF EDIFICATION 48

CHAPTER VII
    THE PUNISHMENT OF HYMENÆUS AND
    ALEXANDER.—DELIVERING TO SATAN AN
    EXCEPTIONAL INSTRUMENT OF PURIFICATION.—
    THE PERSONALITY OF SATAN 54

CHAPTER VIII
    ELEMENTS OF CHRISTIAN WORSHIP;
    INTERCESSORY PRAYER AND THANKSGIVING.—
    THE SOLIDARITY OF CHRISTENDOM
    AND OF THE HUMAN RACE 60

CHAPTER IX
BEHAVIOUR IN CHRISTIAN WORSHIP:
MEN'S ATTITUDE OF BODY AND MIND:
WOMEN'S ATTIRE AND ORNAMENT 68

CHAPTER X
ORIGIN OF THE CHRISTIAN MINISTRY;
VARIOUS CERTAINTIES AND
PROBABILITIES DISTINGUISHED.. 74

CHAPTER XI
THE APOSTLE'S RULE RESPECTING
SECOND MARRIAGES; ITS MEANING
AND PRESENT OBLIGATION 83

CHAPTER XII
THE RELATION OF HUMAN CONDUCT
TO THE MYSTERY OF GODLINESS.. 91

CHAPTER XIII
THE COMPARATIVE VALUE OF BODILY
EXERCISE AND OF GODLINESS... 98

CHAPTER XIV
THE PASTOR'S BEHAVIOUR TOWARDS
WOMEN.—THE CHURCH WIDOW 104

CHAPTER XV
THE PASTOR'S RESPONSIBILITIES
IN ORDAINING AND JUDGING
PRESBYTERS.—THE WORKS THAT GO
BEFORE AND THAT FOLLOW US... 112

CHAPTER XVI
THE NATURE OF ROMAN SLAVERY
AND THE APOSTLE'S ATTITUDE TOWARDS
IT.—A MODERN PARALLEL 119

CHAPTER XVII
THE GAIN OF A LOVE OF GODLINESS, AND
THE UNGODLINESS OF A LOVE OF GAIN 127

THE EPISTLE TO TITUS
CHAPTER XVIII
THE EPISTLE TO TITUS.—
HIS LIFE AND CHARACTER 134

CHAPTER XIX
THE CHURCH IN CRETE AND ITS
ORGANIZATION.—THE APOSTLE'S
DIRECTIONS FOR APPOINTING ELDERS.................................. 141

CHAPTER XX
CHRISTIANITY AND
UNCHRISTIAN LITERATURE 148

CHAPTER XXI
THE MEANING AND VALUE OF
SOBERMINDEDNESS.—THE USE AND
ABUSE OF RELIGIOUS EMOTION.. 156

CHAPTER XXII
THE MORAL CONDITION OF
SLAVES.—THEIR ADORNMENT
OF THE DOCTRINE OF GOD... 163

CHAPTER XXIII
HOPE AS A MOTIVE POWER.—
THE PRESENT HOPES OF CHRISTIANS 170

CHAPTER XXIV
THE DUTY OF OBEDIENCE TO
AUTHORITY, WITH ITS LIMITS; THE
DUTY OF COURTESY WITHOUT LIMITS 177

CHAPTER XXV
THE CO-OPERATION OF THE DIVINE
PERSONS IN EFFECTING THE NEW BIRTH.—
THE LAVER OF REGENERATION 184

CHAPTER XXVI
THE MEANING OF HERESY IN THE
NEW TESTAMENT, AND THE APOSTLE'S
DIRECTIONS RESPECTING THE TREATMENT
OF HERETICAL PERSONS.. 192

THE SECOND EPISTLE TO TIMOTHY
CHAPTER XXVII
THE CHARACTER AND CONTENTS OF
THE LAST EPISTLE OF ST. PAUL.—THE
NEMESIS OF NEGLECTED GIFTS... 200

CHAPTER XXVIII
THE HEARTLESSNESS OF PHYGELUS AND HERMOGENES.—THE DEVOTION OF ONESIPHORUS.—PRAYERS FOR THE DEAD............................ 206

CHAPTER XXIX
THE NEED OF MACHINERY FOR THE PRESERVATION AND TRANSMISSION OF THE FAITH.—THE MACHINERY OF THE PRIMITIVE CHURCH 214

CHAPTER XXX
THE CHRISTIAN'S LIFE AS MILITARY SERVICE; AS AN ATHLETIC CONTEST; AS HUSBANDRY 221

CHAPTER XXXI
THE POWER OF A BELIEF IN THE RESURRECTION AND THE INCARNATION.—THE GOSPEL OF ST. PAUL 227

CHAPTER XXXII
THE NEED OF A SOLEMN CHARGE AGAINST A CONTROVERSIAL SPIRIT, OF DILIGENCE FREE FROM SHAME, AND OF A HATRED OF THE PROFANITY WHICH WRAPS UP ERROR IN THE LANGUAGE OF TRUTH 234

CHAPTER XXXIII
THE LAST DAYS.—THE BEARING OF THE MENTION OF JANNES AND JAMBRES ON THE QUESTION OF INSPIRATION AND THE ERRORS CURRENT IN EPHESUS 241

CHAPTER XXXIV
THE PERILS OF RATIONALISM AND THE RESPONSIBILITIES OF A LIFELONG CONTACT WITH TRUTH.—THE PROPERTIES OF INSPIRED WRITINGS 247

CHAPTER XXXV
THE PARADOXICAL EXULTATION OF
THE APOSTLE.—HIS APPARENT FAILURE
AND THE APPARENT FAILURE OF THE
CHURCH.—THE GREAT TEST OF SINCERITY 255

CHAPTER XXXVI
THE PERSONAL DETAILS
A GUARANTEE OF GENUINENESS 261

CHAPTER XXXVII
THE APOSTLE FORSAKEN BY MEN
BUT STRENGTHENED BY THE LORD.—
THE MISSION TO THE GENTILES
COMPLETED.—THE SURE HOPE, AND
THE FINAL HYMN OF PRAISE 268

INDEX 276

INTRODUCTORY

CHAPTER I
THE CHARACTER AND THE GENUINENESS OF THE PASTORAL EPISTLES

"Paul, an Apostle of Christ Jesus."—1 Tim. i; 2 Tim. i. 1.
"Paul, a servant of God, and an Apostle of Jesus Christ."—Titus i. 1.

The first question which confronts us on entering upon the study of the Pastoral Epistles is that of their authenticity, which of late has been confidently denied. In reading them are we reading the farewell words of the great Apostle to the ministers of Christ? Or are we reading only the well-meant but far less weighty counsels of one who in a later age assumed the name and imitated the style of St. Paul? It seems necessary to devote the first of these expositions to a discussion of this question.

The title "Pastoral Epistles" could hardly be improved, but it might easily be misunderstood as implying more than is actually the case. It calls attention to what is the most conspicuous, but by no means the only characteristic in these Epistles. Although the words which most directly signify the pastor's office, such as "shepherd," "feed," "tend," and "flock," do not occur in these letters and do occur elsewhere in Scripture, yet in no other books in the Bible do we find so many directions respecting the pastoral care of Churches. The title is much less appropriate to 2 Timothy than to the other two Epistles. All three are both pastoral and personal; but while 1 Timothy and Titus are mainly the former, 2 Timothy is mainly the latter. The three taken together stand between the other Epistles of St. Paul and the one to Philemon. Like the latter, they are personal; like the rest, they treat of large questions of Church doctrine, practice, and government, rather than of private and personal matters. Like that to Philemon, they are addressed, not to Churches, but to individuals; yet they are written to them, not as private friends, but as delegates, though not mere delegates, of the Apostle, and as officers of the Church. Moreover the important Church matters of which they treat are regarded, not, as in the other Epistles, from the point of view of the congregation or of the Church at large, but rather from that of the overseer or minister. And, as being official rather than private letters, they are evidently intended to be read by other persons besides Timothy and Titus.

Among the Epistles which bear the name of St. Paul none have excited so much controversy as these, especially as regards their genuineness. But the controversy is entirely a modern one. It is little or no exaggeration to say that from the first century to the nineteenth no one ever denied or doubted that they were written by St. Paul. It is true that certain heretics of the second century rejected some or all of them. Marcion, and perhaps Basilides, rejected all three. Tatian, while maintaining the Apostolicity of the Epistle to Titus, repudiated those to Timothy. And Origen tells us that some people doubted about 2 Timothy because it contained the names of Jannes and Jambres, which do not occur in the Old Testament. But it is well known that Marcion in framing his mutilated and meagre canon of the Scriptures, did not profess to do so on critical grounds. He rejected everything excepting an expurgated edition of St. Luke and certain Epistles of St. Paul,—not because he doubted their authenticity, but because he disliked their contents. They did not fit into his system. And the few others who rejected one or more of these Epistles did so in a similar spirit. They did not profess to find that these documents were not properly authenticated, but they were displeased with passages in them. The evidence, therefore, justifies us in asserting that, with some very slight exception in the second century, these three Epistles were, until quite recent times, universally accepted as written by St. Paul.

This large fact is greatly emphasized by two considerations. (1) The repudiation of them by Marcion and others directed attention to them. They were evidently not accepted by an oversight, because no one thought anything about them. (2) The evidence respecting the general acceptance of them as St. Paul's is full and positive, and reaches back to the earliest times. It does not consist merely or mainly in the absence of evidence to the contrary. Tertullian[1] wonders what can have induced Marcion, while accepting the Epistle to Philemon, to reject those to Timothy and Titus: and of course those who repudiated them would have pointed out weak places in their claim to be canonical, if such had existed. And even if we do not insist upon the passages in which these Epistles are almost certainly quoted by Clement[2] of Rome (c. a.d. 95), Ignatius of Antioch (c. a.d. 112), Polycarp of Smyrna (c. a.d. 112), and Theophilus of Antioch (c. a.d. 180), we have direct evidence of a very convincing kind. They are found in the Peshitto, or early Syriac Version, which was made in the second century. They are contained in the Muratorian canon, the date of which may still be placed as not later than a.d. 170. Irenæus, the disciple of Polycarp, states that

"Paul mentions Linus in the Epistle to Timothy," and he quotes Titus iii. 10 with the introduction "as Paul also says." Eusebius renders it probable that both Justin Martyr and Hegesippus quoted from 1 Timothy; and he himself places all three Epistles among the universally accepted books and not among the disputable writings: *i.e.*, he places them with the Gospels, Acts, 1 Peter, 1 John, and the other Epistles of St. Paul, and not with James, 2 Peter, 2 and 3 John, and Jude. In this arrangement he is preceded by Clement of Alexandria and Tertullian, both of whom quote frequently from all three Epistles, sometimes as the words of Scripture, sometimes as of "the Apostle," sometimes as of Paul, sometimes as of the Spirit. Occasionally it is expressly stated that the words quoted are addressed to Timothy or to Titus.

It would take us too far afield to examine in detail the various considerations which have induced some eminent critics to set aside this strong array of external evidence and reject one or more of these Epistles. They fall in the main under four heads. (1) The difficulty of finding a place for these letters in the life of St. Paul as given us in the Acts and in his own writings. (2) The large amount of peculiar phraseology not found in any other Pauline Epistles. (3) The Church organization indicated in these letters which is alleged to be of a later date than St. Paul's time. (4) The erroneous doctrines and practices attacked, which are also said to be those of a later age. To most of these points we shall have to return on some future occasion: but for the present this much may be asserted with confidence. (1) In the Acts and in the other Epistles of St. Paul the Apostle's life is left incomplete. There is nothing to forbid us from supposing that the remaining portion amounted to several years, during which these three letters were written. The Second Epistle to Timothy in any case has the unique interest of being the last extant utterance of the Apostle St. Paul. (2) The phraseology which is peculiar to each of these Epistles is not greater in amount than the phraseology which is peculiar to the Epistle to the Galatians, which even Baur admits to be of unquestionable genuineness. The peculiar diction which is common to all three Epistles is well accounted for by the peculiarity of the common subject, and by the fact that these letters are separated by several years from even the latest among the other writings of St. Paul.[3] (3, 4) There is good reason for believing that during the lifetime of St. Paul the organization of the Church corresponded to that which is sketched in these letters, and that errors were already in existence such as these letters denounce.

Although the controversy is by no means over, two results of it are very generally accepted as practically certain. (1) The three Epistles must stand or fall together. It is impossible to accept two, or one, or any portion of one of them, and reject the rest. (2) They stand or fall with the hypothesis of St.

Paul's second imprisonment. If the Apostle was imprisoned at Rome only once, and was put to death at the end of that imprisonment, then these three letters were not written by him.

(1) The Epistles stand or fall together: they are all three genuine, or all three spurious. We must either with the scholars of the Early Church, of the Middle Ages, and of the Renaissance, whether Roman or Protestant, and with a clear majority of modern critics,[4] accept all three letters; or else with Marcion, Basilides, Eichhorn, Bauer, and their followers,[5] reject all three. As Credner himself had to acknowledge, after having at first advocated the theory, it is impossible to follow Tatian in retaining Titus as apostolic, while repudiating the other two as forgeries. Nor have the two scholars[6] who originated the modern controversy found more than one critic of eminence to accept their conclusion that both Titus and 2 Timothy are genuine, but 1 Timothy not. Yet another suggestion is made by Reuss, that 2 Timothy is unquestionably genuine, while the other two are doubtful. And lastly we have Pfleiderer admitting that 2 Timothy contains at least two sections which have with good reason been recognized as genuine (i. 15–18 and iv. 9–21), and Renan asking whether the forger of these three Epistles did not possess some authentic letters of St. Paul which he has enshrined in his composition.[7]

It will be seen, therefore, that those who impugn the authenticity of the Pastoral Epistles are by no means agreed among themselves. The evidence in some places is so strong, that many of the objectors are compelled to admit that the Epistles are at least in part the work of St. Paul. That is, certain portions, which admit of being severely tested, are found to stand the test, and are passed as genuine, in spite of surrounding difficulties. The rest, which does not admit of such testing, is repudiated on account of the difficulties. No one can reasonably object to the application of whatever tests are available, nor to the demand for explanations of difficulties. But we must not treat what cannot be satisfactorily tested as if it had been tested and found wanting; nor must we refuse to take account of the support which those parts which can be thoroughly sifted lend to those for which no decisive criterion can be found. Still less must we proceed on the assumption that to reject these Epistles or any portion of them is a proceeding which gets rid of difficulties. It is merely an exchange of one set of difficulties for another. To unbiassed minds it will perhaps appear that the difficulties involved in the assumption that the Pastoral Epistles are wholly or partly a forgery, are not less serious than those which have been urged against the well-established tradition of their genuineness. The very strong external evidence in their favour has to be accounted for. It is already full, clear, and decided, as soon as we could at all expect to find it, viz., in Irenæus, Clement of Alexandria, and Tertullian. And it must be noticed that these witnesses give us the traditional beliefs of several chief centres in Christendom. Irenæus speaks with full knowledge of what was accepted in Asia Minor, Rome, and Gaul; Clement witnesses for Egypt, and Tertullian for North Africa. And although the absence of such support would not have caused serious perplexity, their direct evidence is very materially supported by passages closely parallel to the words of the Pastoral Epistles found in writers still earlier than Irenæus. Renan admits the relationship between 2 Timothy and the Epistle of Clement of Rome, and suggests that each writer has borrowed from a common source. Pfleiderer admits that the Epistle of Ignatius to Polycarp "displays striking points of contact with 2 Timothy." Bauer's theory, that all three letters are as late as a.d. 150, and are an attack on Marcion, finds little support now. But we are still asked to believe that 2 Timothy was forged in the reign of Trajan (98–117) and the other two Epistles in the reign of Hadrian (117–138). Is it credible that a forgery perpetrated a.d. 120–135 would in less than fifty years be accepted in Asia Minor, Rome, Gaul, Egypt, and North Africa, as a genuine letter of the Apostle St. Paul? And yet this is what must have happened in the case of 1 Timothy, if the hypothesis just stated is correct. Nor is this all, Marcion, as we know, rejected all three of the Pastoral Epistles; and Tertullian cannot think why Marcion should do so. But, when Marcion was framing his canon, about the reign of Hadrian, 2 Timothy according to these dates, would be scarcely twenty years old, and 1 Timothy would be brand-new. If this had been so, would Marcion, with his intimate knowledge of St. Paul's writings, have been in ignorance of the fact; and if he had known it, would he have failed to denounce the forgery? Or again, if we assume that he merely treated this group of Epistles with silent contempt, would not his rejection of them, which was well-known, have directed attention to them, and caused their recent origin to be quickly discovered? From all which it is manifest that the theory of forgery by no means frees us from grave obstacles.

It will be observed that the external evidence is large in amount and overwhelmingly in favour of the Apostolic authorship. The objections are based on internal evidence. But some of the leading opponents admit that even the internal evidence is in favour of certain portions of the Epistles. Let us, then, with Renan, Pfleiderer, and others admit that parts of 2 Timothy were written by St. Paul; then there is strong presumption that the whole letter is by him; for even the suspected portions have the external evidence in their favour, together with the support lent to them by those parts for which the internal evidence is also satisfactory. Add to which the improbability that any one would store up genuine letters of St. Paul for fifty years and then use parts of them to give substance to a fabrication.

Or let us with Reuss contend that in 2 Timothy "the whole Epistle is so completely the natural expression of the actual situation of the author, and contains, unsought and for the most part in the form of mere allusions, such a mass of minute[8] and unessential particulars, that even did the name of the writer not chance to be mentioned at the beginning it would be easy to discover it." Then there is strong presumption that the other two letters are genuine also; for they have the external evidence on their side, together with the good character reflected upon them by their brother Epistle. This result is of course greatly strengthened, if, quite independently of 2 Timothy, the claims of Titus to be Apostolic are considered to be adequate. With two of the three letters admitted to be genuine, the case for the remaining letter becomes a strong one. It has the powerful external evidence on its side, backed up by the support lent to it by its two more manifestly authentic companions. Thus far, therefore, we may agree with Baur: "The three Epistles are so much alike that none of them can be separated from the others; and from this circumstance the identity of their authorship may be confidently inferred."[9] But when he asserts that whichever of this family of letters be examined will appear as the betrayer of his brethren, he just reverses the truth. Each letter, upon examination, lends support to the other two; "and a threefold cord is not easily broken." The strongest member of the family is 2 Timothy: the external evidence in its favour is ample, and no Epistle in the New Testament is more characteristic of St. Paul. It would be scarcely less reasonable to dispute 2 Corinthians. And if 2 Timothy be admitted, there is no tenable ground for excluding the other two.

II. But not only do the three Epistles stand or fall together, they stand or fall with the hypothesis of the release and second imprisonment of the Apostle. The contention that no place can be found for the Pastoral Epistles in the narrative of the Acts is valid; but it is no objection to the authenticity of the Epistles. The conclusion of the Acts implies that the end of St. Paul's life is not reached in the narrative. "He abode two whole years in his own hired dwelling," implies that after that time a change took place. If that change was his death, how unnatural not to mention it! The conclusion is closely parallel to that of St Luke's Gospel; and we might almost as reasonably contend that "they were continually in the temple," proves that they were never "clothed with power from on high," because they were told to "tarry in the city" until they were so clothed, as contend that "abode two whole years in his own hired dwelling," proves that at the end of the two years came the end of St. Paul's life. Let us grant that the conclusion of the Acts is unexpectedly abrupt, and that this abruptness constitutes a difficulty. Then we have our choice of two alternatives. Either the two years of imprisonment were followed by a period of renewed labour, or they were cut short by the Apostle's martyrdom. Is it not more easy to believe that the writer did not consider that this new period of work, which would have filled many chapters, fell within the scope of his narrative, than that he omitted so obvious a conclusion as St. Paul's death, for which a single verse would have sufficed? But let us admit that to assert that St. Paul was released at the end of two years is to maintain a mere hypothesis: yet to assert that he was *not* released is equally to maintain a mere hypothesis. If we exclude the Pastoral Epistles, Scripture gives no means of deciding the question, and whichever alternative we adopt we are making a conjecture. But which hypothesis has most evidence on its side? Certainly the hypothesis of the release. (1) The Pastoral Epistles, even if not by St. Paul, are by some one who believed that the Apostle did a good deal after the close of the Acts. (2) The famous passage in Clement of Rome (*Cor.* v.) tells that St. Paul "won the noble renown which was the reward of his faith, having taught righteousness unto the whole world, and *having reached the furthest bound of the West* (τὸ τέρμα τῆς δύσεως)." This probably means Spain;[10] and if St. Paul ever went to Spain as he hoped to do (Rom. xv. 24, 28), it was after the imprisonment narrated in the Acts. Clement gives us the tradition in Rome (c. a.d. 95). (3) The Muratorian fragment (c. a.d. 170) mentions the "departure of Paul from the city to Spain." (4) Eusebius (*H.E.*, II. xxii. 2) says that at the end of the two years of imprisonment, according to tradition, the Apostle went forth again upon the ministry of preaching, and on a second visit to the city ended his career by martyrdom under Nero; and that during this imprisonment he composed the Second Epistle to Timothy. All this does not amount to proof; but it raises the hypothesis of the release to a high degree of probability. Nothing of this kind can be urged in favour of the counter hypothesis. To urge the improbability that the labours of these last few years of St. Paul's life would be left unrecorded is no argument. (1) They are partly recorded in the Pastoral Epistles. (2) The entire labours of most of the Twelve are left unrecorded. Even of St. Paul's life, whole years are left a blank. How fragmentary the narrative in the Acts must be is proved by the autobiography in 2 Corinthians. That we have very scanty notice of St. Paul's doings between the two imprisonments does not render the existence of such an interval at all doubtful.

The result of this preliminary discussion seems to show that the objections which have been urged against these Epistles are not such as to compel us to doubt that in studying them we are studying the last writings of the Apostle of the Gentiles. If any doubts still survive, a closer examination of the details will, it is hoped, tend to remove rather than to strengthen them. When we have completed our survey, we may be able to add our testimony to those who through many centuries have found these writings a source of Divine guidance, warning, and encouragement, especially in ministerial work. The experience of countless numbers of pastors attests the wisdom of the Church, or in other words the good Providence of God, in causing these Epistles to be included among the sacred Scriptures.

"It is an established fact," as Bernhard Weiss rightly points out (*Introduction to the New Testament,* vol. i., p. 410), "that the essential, fundamental features of the Pauline doctrine of salvation are even in their specific expression reproduced in our Epistles with a clearness such as we do not find in any Pauline disciple, excepting perhaps Luke or the Roman Clement." Whoever composed them had at his command, not only St. Paul's forms of doctrine and expression, but large funds of Apostolic zeal and discretion, such as have proved capable of warming the hearts and guiding the judgments of a long line of successors. Those who are conscious of these effects upon themselves will probably find it easier to believe that they have derived these benefits from the great Apostle himself, rather than from one who, with however good intentions, assumed his name and disguised himself in his mantle. Henceforward, until we find serious reason for doubt, it will be assumed that in these Epistles we have the farewell counsels of none other than St Paul.

FOOTNOTES:

[1] *Adv. Marc.,* V. xxi.

[2] *Clem. Rom.* I. ii., xxix., lxi.; Ign. *Magn.* viii., *Pol. passim*; Polycarp, iv; Theoph. *Autol.,* III., xiv,; Iren., *Hær.,* III. iii. 3, 4; Euseb. *H. E.,* III. xxv., 2., xxvi. 4., xxxii. 8.

[3] "The wealth and mobility of the Pauline intellect ... must not be fettered in mode of teaching or expression by a rule taken from a number of older epistles arbitrarily selected." — Bernhard Weiss, *Introduction to the N. T.,* i. p. 410 (Hodder: 1887).

[4] Among them Alford, Baumgarten, Beck, Döllinger, Fairbairn, Farrar, Guericke, Herzog, Hofmann, Huther, Kölling, Lange, Lightfoot, Neander, Oosterzee, Otto, Plumptre, Salmon, Schaff, Thiersch, Wace, Wieseler, Wiesinger, Wordsworth.

[5] Among them Credner, S. Davidson, Ewald, Hausrath, Hilgenfeld, Holtzmann, Mangold, Schenkel, and on the whole De Wette.

[6] Schmidt and Schleiermacher followed by Bleek.

[7] Similar admissions, which are quite fatal to the view that the three Epistles are not genuine, are made by Hausrath, Immer and Lemme; while Ewald, Hitzig, Krenkel, and Weisse think that Titus contains authentic fragments. See the exposition of 2 Tim. iv. 9–21.

[8] What forger would have thought of the cloak (or bookcase) left at Troas with Carpus, or would have been careful to speak only of "the *house* of Onesiphorus," and not of himself, in two places?

[9] *Paul, his Life and Works*, Pt. II., ch. viii. Eng. Trans., p. 105.

[10] It cannot possibly mean Rome; least of all in a document written in Rome. Rome was a centre, not a frontier.

THE FIRST EPISTLE TO TIMOTHY

CHAPTER II
TIMOTHY THE BELOVED DISCIPLE OF ST. PAUL. HIS LIFE AND CHARACTER

"Timothy, my true child in faith."—1 Tim. i. 2.
"Timothy, my beloved child."—2 Tim. i. 2.

In the relation of St. Paul to Timothy we have one of those beautiful friendships between an older and a younger man which are commonly so helpful to both. It is in such cases, rather than where the friends are equals in age, that each can be the real complement of the other. Each by his abundance can supply the other's want, whereas men of equal age would have common wants and common supplies. In this respect the friendship between St. Paul and Timothy reminds us of that between St. Peter and St. John. In each case the friend who took the lead was much older than the other; and (what is less in harmony with ordinary experience) in each case it was the older friend who had the impulse and the enthusiasm, the younger who had the reflectiveness and the reserve. These latter qualities are perhaps less marked in St. Timothy than in St. John, but nevertheless they are there, and they are among the leading traits of his character. St. Paul leans on him while he guides him, and relies upon his thoughtfulness and circumspection in cases requiring firmness, delicacy, and tact. Of the affection with which he regarded Timothy we have evidence in the whole tone of the two letters to him. In the sphere of faith Timothy is his *"own true* child" (not merely adopted, still less supposititious), and his "beloved child." St. Paul tells the Corinthians that as the best means of making them imitators of himself he has sent unto them "Timothy, who is my beloved and faithful child in the Lord, who shall put you in remembrance of my ways which be in Christ, even as I teach everywhere in every Church" (1 Cor. iv. 17). And a few years later he tells the Philippians that he hopes to send Timothy shortly unto them, that he may know how they fare. For he has no one like him, who will have a genuine anxiety about their welfare. The rest care only for their own interests. "But the proof of him ye know, that, as a child a father, so he slaved with me for the Gospel" (ii. 22). Of all whom he ever converted to the faith Timothy seems to have been to St. Paul the disciple who was most beloved and most trusted. Following the example of the fourth Evangelist, Timothy might have called himself "The disciple whom Paul loved." He shared his spiritual father's outward labours and most intimate thoughts. He was with him when the Apostle could not or would not have the companionship of others. He was sent on the most delicate and confidential missions. He had charge of the most important congregations. When the Apostle was in his last and almost lonely imprisonment it was Timothy whom he summoned to console him and receive his last injunctions.

There is another point in which the beloved disciple of the Pastoral Epistles resembles the beloved disciple of the Fourth Gospel. We are apt to think of both of them as always young. Christian art nearly invariably represents St. John as a man of youthful and almost feminine appearance. And, although in Timothy's case, painters and sculptors have not done much to influence our imagination, yet the picture which we form for ourselves of him is very similar to that which we commonly receive of St. John. With strange logic this has actually been made an argument against the authenticity of the Pastoral Epistles. Myth, we are told, has given to this Christian Achilles the attributes of eternal youth. Timothy was a lad of about fifteen when St. Paul converted him at Lystra, in or near a.d. 45; and he was probably not yet thirty-five when St. Paul wrote the First Epistle to him. Even if he had been much older there would be nothing surprising in the tone of St. Paul's letters to him. It is one of the commonest experiences to find elderly parents speaking of their middle-aged children as if they were still boys and girls. This trait, as being so entirely natural, ought to count as a touch beyond the reach of a forger rather than as a circumstance that ought to rouse our suspicions, in the letters of "Paul the aged"[11] to a friend who was thirty years younger than himself.

Once more, the notices of Timothy which have come down to us, like those which we have respecting the beloved disciple, are very fragmentary; but they form a beautiful and consistent sketch of one whose full portrait we long to possess.

Timothy was a native, possibly of Derbe, but more probably of the neighbouring town of Lystra, where he was piously brought up in a knowledge of the Jewish Scriptures by his grandmother Lois and his mother Eunice. It was probably during St Paul's first visit to Lystra, on his first missionary journey, that he became the boy's spiritual father, by converting him to the Christian faith. It was at Lystra that the Apostle was stoned by the mob and dragged outside the city as dead: and there is no improbability in the suggestion that, when he recovered consciousness and re-entered the town, it was in the home of Timothy that he found shelter. In any case Lystra was to the Apostle a place of strangely mixed associations; the brutality of the pagan multitude side by side with the tender friendship of the young Timothy. When St. Paul on his next missionary journey again visited Lystra he found Timothy already enjoying a good report among the Christians of that place and of Iconium for his zeal and devotion during the six or seven years which had elapsed since his first visit. Perhaps he had been engaged in missionary work in both places. The voices of the prophets had singled him out as one worthy of bearing office in the Church; and the Apostle, still grieving over the departure of Barnabas with John Mark, recognized in him one who with Silas could fill the double vacancy. The conduct of the Apostle of the Gentiles on this occasion has sometimes excited surprise. Previously to the ordination, Paul, the great proclaimer of the abrogation of the Law by the Gospel, circumcised the young evangelist. The inconsistency is more apparent than real. It was an instance of his becoming "all things to all men" for the salvation of souls, and of his sacrificing his own convictions in matters that were not essential, rather than cause others to offend. Timothy's father had been a Gentile, and the son, though brought up in his mother's faith, had never been circumcised. To St. Paul circumcision was a worthless rite. The question was, whether it was a harmless one. This depended upon circumstances. If, as among the Galatians, it caused people to rely upon the Law and neglect the Gospel, it was a superstitious obstacle with which no compromise could be made. But if it was a passport whereby preachers, who would otherwise be excluded, might gain access to Jewish congregations, then it was not only a harmless but a useful ceremony. In the synagogue Timothy as an uncircumcised Jew would have been an intolerable abomination, and would never have obtained a hearing. To free him from this crippling disadvantage, St. Paul subjected him to a rite which he himself knew to be obsolete. Then followed the ordination, performed with great solemnity by the laying on of the hands of all the elders of the congregation: and the newly ordained Evangelist forthwith set out to accompany Paul and Silas in their labours for the Gospel. Wherever they went they distributed copies of the decrees of the Apostolic Council at Jerusalem, which declared circumcision to be unnecessary for Gentiles. Their true position with regard to circumcision was thus made abundantly evident. For the sake of others they had abstained from availing themselves of the very liberty which they proclaimed.

In the Troad they met Luke the beloved physician (as indicated by the sudden use of the first person plural in the Acts), and took him on with them to Philippi. Here probably, as certainly afterwards at Berœa, Timothy was left behind by Paul and Silas to consolidate their work. He rejoined the

Apostle at Athens, but was thence sent back on a mission to Thessalonica, and on his return found St. Paul at Corinth. The two Epistles written from Corinth to the Thessalonians are in the joint names of Paul and Timothy. At Corinth, as at Lystra, Iconium, and Philippi, Timothy became prominent for his zeal as an evangelist; and then for about five years we lose sight of him. We may think of him as generally at the side of St. Paul, and as always working with him; but of the details of the work we are ignorant. About A.D. 57 he was sent by St. Paul on a delicate mission to Corinth. This was before 1 Corinthians was written; for in that letter St. Paul states that he has sent Timothy to Corinth, but writes as if he expected that the letter would reach Corinth before him. He charges the Corinthians not to aggravate the young evangelist's natural timidity, and not to let his youth prejudice them against him. When St. Paul wrote 2 Corinthians from Macedonia later in the year, Timothy was again with him, for his name is coupled with Paul's: and he is still with him when the Apostle wrote to the Romans from Corinth, for he joins in sending salutations to the Roman Christians. We find him still at St. Paul's side on his way back to Jerusalem through Philippi, the Troad, Tyre, and Cæsarea. And here we once more lose trace of him for some years. We do not know what he was doing during St. Paul's two years' imprisonment at Cæsarea; but he joined him during the first imprisonment at Rome, for the Epistles to the Philippians, the Colossians, and Philemon are written in the names of Paul and Timothy. From the passage already quoted from Philippians we may conjecture that Timothy went to Philippi and returned again before the Apostle was released. At the close of the Epistle to the Hebrews we read, "Know ye that our brother Timothy hath been set at liberty." It is possible that the imprisonment to which this notice refers was contemporaneous with the first imprisonment of St. Paul, and that it is again referred to in 1 Timothy (vi. 12) as "the good confession" which he "confessed in the sight of many witnesses."

The few additional facts respecting Timothy are given us in the two letters to him. Some time after St. Paul's release the two were together in Ephesus; and when the Apostle went on into Macedonia he left his companion behind him to warn and exhort certain holders of erroneous doctrine to desist from teaching it. There were tears, on the younger friend's side at any rate, to which St. Paul alludes at the opening of the Second Epistle; and they were natural enough. The task imposed upon Timothy was no easy one; and after the dangers and sufferings to which the Apostle had been exposed, and which his increasing infirmities continually augmented, it was only too possible that the friends would never meet again. So far as we know, these gloomy apprehensions may have been realized. In his first letter, written from Macedonia, St. Paul expresses a hope of returning very soon to Timothy; but, like some other hopes expressed in St. Paul's Epistles, it was perhaps never fulfilled. The second letter, written from Rome, contains no allusion to any intermediate meeting. In this second letter he twice implores Timothy to do all he can to come to him without delay, for he is left almost alone in his imprisonment. But whether Timothy was able to comply with this wish we have no means of knowing. We like to think of the beloved disciple as comforting the last hours of his master; but, although the conjecture may be a right one, we must remember that it is conjecture and no more. With the Second Epistle to him ends all that we really know of Timothy. Tradition and ingenious guesswork add a little more which can be neither proved nor disproved. More than two hundred years after his death, Eusebius tells us that he is related to have held the office of overseer of the diocese of Ephesus; and five centuries later Nicephorus tells us, that he was beaten to death by the Ephesian mob for protesting against the licentiousness of their worship of Artemis. It has been conjectured that Timothy may be the "Angel" of the Church of Ephesus, who is partly praised and partly blamed in the Apocalypse, and parallels have been drawn between the words of blame in Rev. ii. 4, 5, and the uneasiness which seems to underlie one or two passages in the Second Epistle to Timothy. But the resemblances are too slight to be relied upon. All we can say is, that even if the later date be taken for the Apocalypse, Timothy may have been overseer of the Church of Ephesus at the time when the book was written.

But of all the scattered memorials that have come down to us respecting this beautiful friendship between the great Apostle and his chief disciple, the two letters of the older friend to the younger are by far the chief. And there is so much in them that fits with exquisite nicety into the known conditions of the case, that it is hard to imagine how any forger of the second century could so have thrown himself into the situation. Where else in that age have we evidence of any such literary and historical skill? The tenderness and affection, the anxiety and sadness, the tact and discretion, the strength and large-mindedness of St. Paul are all there; and his relation to his younger but much-trusted disciple is quite naturally sustained throughout. Against this it is not much to urge that there are some forty words and phrases in these Epistles which do not occur in the other Epistles of St. Paul. The explanation of that fact is easy. Partly they are words which in his other Epistles he had no need to use; partly they are words which the circumstances of these later letters suggested to him, and which those of the earlier letters did not. The vocabulary of every man of active mind who reads and mixes with other men, especially if he travels much, is perpetually changing. He comes across new metaphors, new figures of speech, remembers them, and uses them. The reading of such a work as Darwin's *Origin of Species* gives a man command of a new sphere of thought and expression. The conversation of such a man as "Luke the beloved physician" would have a similar effect on St. Paul. We shall never know the minds or the circumstances which suggested to him the language which has now become our own possession; and it is unreasonable to suppose that the process of assimilation came to a dead stop in the Apostle's mind when he finished the Epistles of the first imprisonment. The result, therefore, of this brief survey of the life of Timothy is to confirm rather than to shake our belief that the letters which are addressed to him were really written by his friend St. Paul.

The friendship between these two men of different gifts and very different ages is full of interest. It is difficult to estimate which of the two friends gained most from the affection and devotion of the other. No doubt Timothy's debt to St. Paul was immense: and which of us would not think himself amply paid for any amount of service and sacrifice, in having the privilege of being the chosen friend of such a man as St. Paul? But on the other hand, few men could have supplied the Apostle's peculiar needs as Timothy did. That intense craving for sympathy which breathes so strongly throughout the writings of St. Paul, found its chief human satisfaction in Timothy. To be alone in a crowd is a trial to most men; and few men have felt the oppressiveness of it more keenly than St. Paul. To have some one, therefore, who loved and reverenced him, who knew his "ways" and could impress them on others, who cared for those for whom Paul cared and was ever willing to minister to them as his friend's missioner and delegate— all this and much more was inexpressibly comforting to St. Paul. It gave him strength in his weaknesses, hope in his many disappointments, and solid help in his daily burden of "anxiety for all the Churches." Specially consoling was the clinging affection of his young friend at those times when the Apostle was suffering from the coldness and neglect of others. At the time of his first imprisonment the respect or curiosity of the Roman Christians had moved many of them to come out thirty miles to meet him on his journey from Cæsarea to Rome; yet as soon as he was safely lodged in the house of his gaoler they almost ceased to minister to him. But the faithful disciple seems to have been ever at his side. And when the Romans treated Paul with similar indifference during his second imprisonment, it was this same disciple that he earnestly besought to come with all speed to comfort him. It was not merely that he loved and trusted Timothy as one upon whose devotion and discretion he could always rely: but Timothy was the one among his many disciples who had sacrificed everything for St. Paul and his Master. He had left a loving mother and a pleasant home in order to share with the Apostle a task which involved ceaseless labour, untold anxiety, not a little shame and obloquy, and at times even danger to life and limb. When he might have continued to live on as the favourite of his family, enjoying the respect of the presbyters and prophets of Lycaonia, he chose to wander abroad with the man to whom, humanly speaking, he owed his salvation, "in journeyings often," in perils of every kind from the powers of nature, and from the violence or treachery of man, and in all those countless afflictions and necessities, of which St. Paul gives us such a touching summary in the second letter to the Corinthians. All this St. Paul knew, and he knew the value of it to himself and the Church; and hence the warm affection with which the Apostle always speaks of him and to him.

But what did not Timothy owe to his friend, his father in the faith, old enough to be his father in the flesh? Not merely his conversion and his building up in Christian doctrine, though that was much, and the chief item of his debt. But St. Paul had tenderly watched over him among the difficulties to which a person of his temperament would be specially exposed. Timothy was young, enthusiastic, sensitive, and at times showed signs of timidity. If his enthusiasm were not met with a generous sympathy, there was danger lest the sensitive nature would shrivel up on contact with an unfeeling world, and the enthusiasm driven in upon itself would be soured into a resentful cynicism. St. Paul not only himself gave to his young disciple the sympathy that he needed; he encouraged others also to do the same. "Now if Timothy come," he writes to the Corinthians, "see that he be with you without fear; for he worketh the work of the Lord, as I also do: let no man therefore despise him." He warned these factious and fastidious Greeks against chilling the generous impulses of a youthful evangelist by their sarcastic criticisms. Timothy might be wanting in the brilliant gifts which Corinthians adored: in knowledge of the world, in address, in oratory. But he was real. He was working God's work with a single heart and with genuine fervour. It would be a cruel thing to mar that simplicity or quench that fervour, and thus turn a genuine enthusiast into a cold-blooded man of the world. On their treatment of him might depend whether he raised them to his own zeal for Christ, or they dragged him down to the level of their own paralysing superciliousness.

The dangers from which St. Paul thus generously endeavoured to shield Timothy, are those which beset many an ardent spirit, especially in England at the present day. Everywhere there is a cynical disbelief in human nature and a cold contempt for all noble impulses, which throw a damp and chilling atmosphere over society. At school and at the university, in family life and in domestic service, young men and young women are encouraged to believe that there is no such thing as unselfishness or holiness, and that enthusiasm is always either silly or hypocritical. By sarcastic jests and contemptuous smiles they are taught the fatal lesson of speaking slightingly, and at last of thinking slightingly, of their own best feelings. To be dutiful and affectionate is supposed to be childish, while reverence and trust are regarded as mere ignorance of the world. The mischief is a grave one, for it poisons life at its very springs. Every young man and woman at times has aspirations which at first are only romantic and sentimental, and as such are neither right nor wrong. But they are nature's material for higher and better things. They are capable of being developed into a zeal for God and for man, such as will ennoble the characters of all who come under its influence. The sentimentalist may become an enthusiast, and the enthusiast a hero or a saint. Woe to him who gives to such precious material a wrong turn, and by offering cynicism instead of sympathy turns all its freshness sour. The loss does not end with the blight of an exuberant and earnest character. There are huge masses of evil in the world, which seem to defy the good influences that from time to time are brought to bear upon them. Humanly speaking, there seems to be only one hope of overcoming these strongholds of Satan,—and that is by the combined efforts of many enthusiasts. "This is the victory which overcometh the world, even our faith." It will be a grievous prospect for mankind, if faith in God, in ourselves, and in our fellow-men becomes so unfashionable as to be impossible. And this is the faith which makes enthusiasts. If we have not this faith ourselves, we can at least respect it in others. If we cannot play the part of Timothy, and go forth with glowing hearts to whatever difficult and distasteful work may be placed before us, we can at least avoid chilling and disheartening others; and sometimes at least we may so far follow in the footsteps of St. Paul as to protect from the world's cynicism those who, with hearts more warm perhaps than wise, are labouring manfully to leave the world purer and happier than they found it.

FOOTNOTES:

[11] "Paul an ambassador, and now also a prisoner of Jesus Christ" is probably right in Philemon; but even there "Paul the aged" would be true.

CHAPTER III
THE DOCTRINE CONDEMNED IN THE PASTORAL EPISTLES A JEWISH FORM OF GNOSTICISM.—THE GNOSTIC'S PROBLEM

"As I exhorted thee to tarry at Ephesus, when I was going into Macedonia, that thou mightest charge certain men not to teach a different doctrine, neither to give heed to fables and endless genealogies, the which minister questionings, rather than a dispensation of God which is in faith; so do I now"—*1 Tim.* i. 2, 3.

This Epistle falls into two main divisions, of which the first continues down to the 13th verse of chap. iii. It treats of three different subjects: Christian doctrine; Christian worship; and the Christian ministry. The first of these three subjects is introduced in the words of the text, which in the original form an incomplete sentence. The last four words, "so do I now," are not expressed in the Greek. But something must be supplied to complete the sense; and it is more natural to understand with the Revisers "So do I now exhort thee," than with the A. V. "So do thou tarry at Ephesus." But the question is not of great moment and cannot be decided with absolute certainty. It is of more importance to enquire what was the nature of the "different doctrine" which Timothy was to endeavour to counteract. And on this point we are not left in serious doubt. There are various expressions used respecting it in these two letters to Timothy which seem to point to two factors in the heterodoxy about which St. Paul is anxious. It is clear that the error is Jewish in origin; and it is almost equally clear that it is Gnostic as well. The evidence of the letter to Titus tends materially to confirm these conclusions.

(1) The heresy is *Jewish* in character. Its promoters "desire to be teachers of the Law" (ver. 7). Some of them are "they of the circumcision" (Tit. i. 10). It consists in "Jewish fables" (Tit. i. 14). The questions which it raises are "fightings about the Law" (Tit. iii. 9).

(2) Its *Gnostic* character is also indicated. We are told both in the text and in the Epistle to Titus (i. 14; iii. 9) that it deals in "fables and genealogies."

It is "empty talking" (ver. 6), "disputes of words" (vi. 4), and "profane babblings" (vi. 20). It teaches, an unscriptural and unnatural asceticism (iv. 3, 8). It is "Gnosis falsely so called" (vi. 20).

A heresy containing these two elements, Judaism and Gnosticism, meets us both before and after the period covered by the Pastoral Epistles: before in the Epistle to the Colossians; afterwards in the Epistles of Ignatius. The evidence gathered from these three sources is entirely in harmony with what we learn elsewhere—that the earliest forms of Christian Gnosticism were Jewish in character. It will be observed that this is indirect confirmation of the genuineness of the Pastoral Epistles. The Gnosticism condemned in them is Jewish; and any form of Gnosticism that was in existence in St. Paul's time would almost certainly be Jewish.[12]

Professor Godet has pointed out how entirely the relation of Judaism to Christianity which is implied in these Epistles, fits in with their being the last group of Epistles written by St. Paul. At first, Judaism was entirely outside the Church, opposing and blaspheming. Then it entered the Church and tried to make the Church Jewish, by foisting the Mosaic Law upon it. Lastly, it becomes a fantastic heresy inside the Church, and sinks into profane frivolity. "Pretended revelations are given as to the names and genealogies of angels; absurd ascetic rules are laid down as counsels of perfection, while daring immorality defaces the actual life."[13] This is the phase which is confronted in the Pastoral Epistles: and St. Paul meets it with a simple appeal to faith and morality.

It is quite possible that the "fables," or "myths," and "genealogies" ought to be transferred from the Gnostic to the Jewish side of the account. And thus Chrysostom interprets the passage. "By fables he does not mean the Law; far from it; but inventions and forgeries, and counterfeit doctrines. For, it seems, the Jews wasted their whole discourse on these unprofitable points. They numbered up their fathers and grandfathers, that they might have the reputation of historical knowledge and research." The "fables" then, may be understood to be those numerous legends which the Jews added to the Old Testament, specimens of which abound in the Talmud. But similar myths abound in Gnostic systems, and therefore "fables" may represent *both* elements of the heterodox teaching. So also with the "endless genealogies." These cannot well refer to the genealogies in Genesis, for they are not endless, each of them being arranged in tens. But it is quite possible that Jewish speculations about the genealogies of angels may be meant. Such things, being purely imaginary, would be endless. Or the Gnostic doctrine of emanations, in its earlier and cruder forms, may be intended. By genealogies in this sense early thinkers, especially in the East, tried to bridge the chasm between the Infinite and the Finite, between God and creation.

In various systems it is assumed that matter is inherently evil. The material universe has been from the beginning not "very good" but very bad. How then can it be believed that the Supreme Being, infinite in goodness, would create such a thing? This is incredible: the world must be the creature of some inferior and perhaps evil being. But when this was conceded, the distance between this inferior power and the supreme God still remained to be bridged. This, it was supposed, might be done by an indefinite number of generations, each lower in dignity than the preceding one, until at last a being capable of creating the universe was found. From the Supreme God emanated an inferior deity, and from this lower power a third still more inferior; and so on, until the Creator of the world was reached. These ideas are found in the Jewish philosopher Philo; and it is to these that St. Paul probably alludes in the "endless genealogies which minister questionings rather than a dispensation of God." The idea that matter is evil dominates the whole philosophy of Philo. He endeavoured to reconcile this with the Old Testament, by supposing that matter is eternal; and that it was out of pre-existing material that God, acting through His creative powers, made the world which He pronounced to be "very good." These powers are sometimes regarded as the angels, sometimes as existences scarcely personal. But they have no existence apart from their source, any more than a ray apart from the sun. They are now the instruments of God's Providence, as formerly of His creative power.

St. Paul condemns such speculations on four grounds. (1) They are *fables*, myths, mere imaginings of the human intellect in its attempt to account for the origin of the world and the origin of evil. (2) They are *endless* and interminable. From the nature of things there is no limit to mere guesswork of this kind. Every new speculator may invent a fresh genealogy of emanations in his theory of creation, and may make it any length that he pleases. If hypotheses need never be verified,—need not even be *capable* of verification,—one may go on constructing them *ad infinitum*. (3) As a natural consequence of this (αἵτινες) they *minister questionings* and nothing better. It is all barren speculation and fruitless controversy. Where any one may assert without proof, any one else may contradict without proof; and nothing comes of this see-saw of affirmation and negation. (4) Lastly, these vain imaginings are *a different doctrine*. They are not only empty but untrue, and are a hindrance to the truth. They occupy the ground which ought to be filled with the *dispensation of God which is in faith*. Human minds are limited in their capacity, and, even if these empty hypotheses were innocent, minds that were filled with them would have little room left for the truth. But they are not innocent: and those who are attracted by them become disaffected towards the truth. It is impossible to love both, for the two are opposed to one another. These fables are baseless; they have no foundation either in revelation or in human life. Moreover they are vague, shifting, and incoherent. They ramble on without end. But the Gospel is based on a Divine Revelation, tested by human experience. It is an economy, a system, an organic whole, a dispensation of means to ends. Its sphere is not unbridled imagination or audacious curiosity, but faith.

The history of the next hundred and fifty years amply justifies the anxiety and severity of St. Paul. The germs of Gnostic error, which were in the air when Christianity was first preached, fructified with amazing rapidity. It would be hard to find a parallel in the history of philosophy to the speed with which Gnostic views spread in and around Christendom between a.d. 70 and 220. Eusebius tells us that, as soon as the Apostles and those who had listened "with their own ears to their inspired wisdom had passed away, then the conspiracy of godless error took its rise through the deceit of false teachers, who (now that none of the Apostles was any longer left) henceforth endeavoured with brazen face to preach their *knowledge falsely so called* in opposition to the preaching of the truth."[14] Throughout the Christian world, and especially in intellectual centres such as Ephesus, Alexandria and Rome, there was perhaps not a single educated congregation which did not contain persons who were infected with some form of Gnosticism. Jerome's famous hyperbole respecting Arianism might be transferred to this earlier form of error, perhaps the most perilous that the Church has ever known: "The whole world groaned and was amazed to find itself *Gnostic.*"

However severely we may condemn these speculations, we cannot but sympathize with the perplexities which produced them. The origin of the universe, and still more the origin of evil, still remain unsolved problems. No one in this life is ever likely to reach a complete solution of either. What is the origin of the material universe? To assume that it is not a creature, but that matter is eternal, is to make two first principles, one spiritual and one material; and this is perilously near making two Gods. But the belief that God made the world is by no means free from difficulty. What was His motive in making the world? Was His perfection increased by it? Then God was once not fully perfect. Was His perfection diminished by the act of creation? Then God is now not fully perfect; and how can we suppose that He would voluntarily surrender anything of His absolute perfection? Was God neither the better nor the worse for the creation of the universe? Then the original question returns with its full force: What induced Him to create it? We cannot suppose that creation was an act of caprice. No complete answer to this enigma is possible for us. One thing we know;—that *God is light* and that *God is love.* And we may be sure that in exercising His creative power He was manifesting His perfect wisdom and His exhaustless affection.

But will the knowledge that *God is light* and that *God is love* help us to even a partial solution of that problem which has wrung the souls of countless saints and thinkers with anguish—the problem of the origin of evil? How could a God who is perfectly wise and perfectly good, make it possible for evil to arise, and allow it to continue after it had arisen? Once more the suggestion that there are two First Principles presents itself, but in a more terrible form. Before, it was the thought that there are two co-eternal Existences, God and Matter. Now, it is the suggestion that there are two co-eternal, and perhaps co-equal Powers, Good and Evil. This hypothesis, impossible for a Christian and rejected by John Stuart Mill,[15] creates more difficulties than it solves. But, if this is the wrong answer, what is the right one? Cardinal Newman, in one of the most striking passages even in his works, has told us how the problem presents itself to him. "Starting then with the being of God (which, as I have said, is as certain to me as the certainty of my own existence, though when I try to put the grounds of that certainty into logical shape, I find difficulty in doing so in mood and figure to my satisfaction), I look out of myself into the world of men, and there I see a sight which fills me with unspeakable distress. The world seems simply to give the lie to that great truth, of which my whole being is so full; and the effect upon me is, in consequence, as a matter of necessity, as confusing as if it denied that I am in existence myself. *If I looked into a mirror, and did not see my face, I should have the sort of feeling which actually comes upon me, when I look into this living busy world and see no reflection of its Creator.* This is, to me, one of the great difficulties of this absolute primary truth, to which I referred just now. Were it not for this voice, speaking so clearly in my conscience and my heart, I should be an atheist, or a pantheist, or a polytheist, when I looked into the world. I am speaking for myself only; and I am far from denying the real force of the arguments in proof of a God, drawn from the general facts of human society, but these do not warm me or enlighten me; they do not take away the winter of my desolation, or make the buds unfold and the leaves grow within me, and my moral being rejoice. The sight of the world is nothing else than the prophet's scroll full of 'lamentations, and mourning, and woe.' ... What shall be said to this heart-piercing, reason-bewildering fact? I can only answer, that either there is no Creator, or this living society of men is in a true sense discarded from His presence. Did I see a boy of good make and mind, with the tokens on him of a refined nature, cast upon the world without provision, unable to say whence he came, his birthplace or his family connexions, I should conclude that there was some mystery connected with his history, and that he was one, of whom, from one cause or other, his parents were ashamed. Thus only should I be able to account for the contrast between the promise and condition of his being. And so I argue about the world;—*if* there be a God, *since* there is a God, the human race is implicated in some terrible aboriginal calamity. It is out of joint with the purposes of its Creator. This is a fact, a fact as true as the fact of its existence; and thus the doctrine of what is theologically called original sin becomes to me almost as certain as that the world exists, and as the existence of God."[16]

But this only carries us a short way towards a solution. Why did God allow the "aboriginal calamity" of sin to be possible? This was the Gnostic's difficulty, and it is our difficulty still. Can we say more than this by way of an answer? God willed that angels and men should honour Him with a voluntary and not a mechanical service. If they obeyed Him, it should be of their own free will, and not of necessity. It should be possible to them to refuse service and obedience. In short, God willed to be reverenced and worshipped, and not merely served and obeyed. A machine can render service; and a person under the influence of mesmerism may be forced to obey. But do we not all feel that the voluntary service of a conscious and willing agent, who prefers to render rather than to withhold his service, is a nobler thing both for him who gives, and him who receives it? Compulsory labour is apt to turn the servant into a slave and the master into a tyrant. We see, therefore, a reason why the Creator in creating conscious beings made them also moral; made them capable of obeying Him of their own free will, and therefore also capable of disobeying Him. In other words, He made sin, with all its consequences, possible. Then it became merely a question of historical fact whether any angelic or human being would ever abuse his freedom by choosing to disobey. That "aboriginal calamity," we know, has taken place; and all the moral and physical evil which now exists in the world, is the natural consequence of it.

This is, perhaps, the best solution that the human mind is likely to discover, respecting this primeval and terrible mystery. But it is only a partial solution; and the knowledge that we have still not attained to a complete answer to the question which perplexed the early Gnostics, ought to banish from our minds anything like arrogance or contempt, when we condemn their answer as unchristian and inadequate. "The end of the charge" which has been given to us is not the condemnation of others, but "love out of a pure heart and a good conscience and faith unfeigned."

FOOTNOTES:

[12] F. C. Baur himself contends that the false teachers here condemned are "Judaizing Gnostics, who put forth their figurative interpretation of the Law as true knowledge of the Law. Such were the earlier Gnostics, such as the Ophites and Saturninus" (*Protestant Commentary*, note on 1 Tim. i. 7).

[13] *Expositor*, July, 1888, p. 42.

[14] *H. E.*, VI, xxxii. 8.

[15] *Three Essays on Religion*, pp. 185, 186.

[16] *Apologia pro Vita Sua* (Longmans, 1864), pp. 376–379.

CHAPTER IV
THE MORAL TEACHING OF THE GNOSTICS.—
ITS MODERN COUNTERPART

"But we know that the law is good if a man use it lawfully, as knowing this, that law is not made for a righteous man, but for the lawless and unruly, for the ungodly and sinners, for the unholy and profane, for murderers of fathers and murderers of mothers, for man-slayers, for fornicators, for abusers of themselves with men, for men-stealers, for liars, for false swearers, and if there be any other thing contrary to the sound doctrine; according to the gospel of the glory of the blessed God, which was committed to my trust"—1 Tim. i. 8–11.

The speculations of the Gnostics in their attempts to explain the origin of the universe and the origin of evil, were wild and unprofitable enough; and in some respects involved a fundamental contradiction of the plain statements of Scripture. But it was not so much their metaphysical as their moral teaching, which seemed so perilous to St. Paul. Their "endless genealogies" might have been left to fall with their own dead weight, so dull and uninteresting were they. Specimens of them still survive, in what is known to us of the systems of Basilides and Valentinus; and which of us, after having laboriously worked through them, ever wished to read them a second time? But it is impossible to keep one's philosophy in one compartment in one's mind, and one's religion and morality quite separate from it in another. However unpractical metaphysical speculations may appear, it is beyond question that the views which we hold respecting such things may have momentous influence upon our life. It was so with the early Gnostics, whom St. Paul urges Timothy to keep in check. Their doctrine respecting the nature of the material world and its relation to God, led to two opposite forms of ethical teaching, each of them radically opposed to Christianity.

This fact fits in very well with the character of the Pastoral Epistles, all of which deal with this early form of error. They insist upon discipline and morality, more than upon doctrine. These last solemn charges of the great

Apostle aim rather at making Christian ministers, and their congregations, lead pure and holy lives, than at constructing any system of theology. Erroneous teaching must be resisted; the plain truths of the Gospel must be upheld; but the main thing is holiness of life. By prayer and thanksgiving, by quiet and grave conduct, by modesty and temperance, by self-denial and benevolence, by reverence for the sanctity of home life, Christians will furnish the best antidote to the intellectual and moral poison which the false teachers are propagating. "The sound doctrine" has its fruit in a healthy, moral life, as surely as the "different doctrine" leads to spiritual pride and lawless sensuality.

The belief that Matter and everything material is inherently evil, involved necessarily a contempt for the human body. This body was a vile thing; and it was a dire calamity to the human mind to be joined to such a mass of evil. From this premise various conclusions, some doctrinal and some ethical, were drawn.

On the doctrinal side it was urged that the resurrection of the body was incredible. It was disastrous enough to the soul that it should be burdened with a body in this world. That this degrading alliance would be continued in the world to come, was a monstrous belief. Equally incredible was the doctrine of the Incarnation. How could the Divine Word consent to be united with so evil a thing as a material frame? Either the Son of Mary was a mere man, or the body which the Christ assumed was not real. It is with these errors that St. John deals, some twelve or fifteen years later, in his Gospel and Epistles.

On the ethical side the tenet that the human body is utterly evil produced two opposite errors,—asceticism and antinomian sensuality. And both of these are aimed at in these Epistles. If the enlightenment of the soul is everything, and the body is utterly worthless, then this vile clog to the movement of the soul must be beaten under and crushed, in order that the higher nature may rise to higher things. The body must be denied all indulgence, in order that it may be starved into submission (iv. 3). On the other hand, if enlightenment is everything and the body is worthless, then every kind of experience, no matter how shameless, is of value, in order to enlarge knowledge. Nothing that a man can do can make his body more vile than it is by nature, and the soul of the enlightened is incapable of pollution. Gold still remains gold, however often it is plunged in the mire.

The words of the three verses taken as a text, look as if St. Paul was aiming at evil of this kind. These Judaizing Gnostics "desired to be teachers of the Law." They wished to enforce the Mosaic Law, or rather their fantastic interpretations of it, upon Christians. They insisted upon its excellence, and would not allow that it has been in many respects superseded. "We know quite well," says the Apostle, "and readily admit, that the Mosaic Law is an excellent thing; provided that those who undertake to expound it make a legitimate use of it. They must remember that, just as law in general is not made for those whose own good principles keep them in the right, so also the restrictions of the Mosaic Law are not meant for Christians who obey the Divine will in the free spirit of the Gospel." Legal restrictions are intended to control those who will not control themselves; in short, for the very men who by their strange doctrines are endeavouring to curtail the liberties of others. What they preach as "the Law" is really a code of their own, "commandments of men who turn away from the truth.... They profess that they know God; but by their works they deny Him, being abominable, and disobedient, and unto every good work reprobate" (Tit. i. 14, 16). In rehearsing the various kinds of sinners for whom law exists, and who are to be found (he hints) among these false teachers, he goes roughly through the Decalogue. The four commandments of the First Table are indicated in general and comprehensive terms; the first five commandments of the Second Table are taken one by one, flagrant violators being specified in each case. Thus the stealing of a human being in order to make him a slave, is mentioned as the most outrageous breach of the eighth commandment. The tenth commandment is not distinctly indicated, possibly because the breaches of it are not so easily detected. The overt acts of these men were quite sufficient to convict them of gross immorality, without enquiring as to their secret wishes and desires. In a word, the very persons who in their teaching were endeavouring to burden men with the ceremonial ordinances, which had been done away in Christ, were in their own lives violating the moral laws, to which Christ had given a new sanction. They tried to keep alive, in new and strange forms, what had been provisional and was now obsolete, while they trampled under foot what was eternal and Divine.

"If there be any other thing contrary to the sound doctrine." In these words St. Paul sums up all the forms of transgression not specified in his catalogue. The sound, healthy teaching of the Gospel is opposed to the morbid and corrupt teaching of the Gnostics, who are sickly in their speculations (vi. 4), and whose word is like an eating sore (2 Tim. ii. 17). Of course healthy teaching is also *health-giving*, and corrupt teaching is *corrupting*; but it is the primary and not the derived quality that is stated here. It is the healthiness of the doctrine in itself, and its freedom from what is diseased or distorted, that is insisted upon. Its wholesome character is a consequence of this.

This word "sound" or "healthy" (ὑγιαίνων, ὑγιής), as applied to doctrine,[17] is one of a group of expressions which are peculiar to the Pastoral Epistles, and which have been condemned as not belonging to St. Paul's style of language. He never uses "healthy" in his other Epistles; therefore these three Epistles, in which the phrase occurs eight or nine times, are not by him.

This kind of argument has been discussed already, in the first of these expositions. It assumes the manifest untruth, that as life goes on men make little or no change in the stock of words and phrases which they habitually use. With regard to this particular phrase, the source of it has been conjectured with a fair amount of probability. It may have come from "the beloved physician," who, at the time when St. Paul wrote the Second Epistle to Timothy, was the Apostle's sole companion. It is worth remarking that the word here used for "sound" (with the exception of one passage in the Third Epistle of St. John) occurs nowhere in the New Testament in the literal sense of being in sound bodily health, except in the Gospel of St. Luke. And it occurs nowhere in a figurative sense, except in the Pastoral Epistles. It is obviously a medical metaphor; a metaphor which any one who had never had anything to do with medicine might easily use, but which is specially likely to be used by a man who had lived much in the society of a physician. Before we call such a phrase un-Pauline we must ask: (1) Is there any passage in the earlier Epistles of St. Paul where he would certainly have used this word "sound," had he been familiar with it? (2) Is there any word in the earlier Epistles which would have expressed his meaning here equally well? If either of these questions is answered in the negative, then we are going beyond our knowledge in pronouncing the phrase "sound doctrine"[18] to be un-Pauline.

"Contrary to the sound doctrine." It sums up in a comprehensive phrase the doctrinal and moral teaching of the Gnostics. What they taught was unsound and morbid, and as a consequence poisonous and pestilential. While professing to accept and expound the Gospel, they really disintegrated it and explained it away. They destroyed the very basis of the Gospel message; for they denied the reality of sin. And they equally destroyed the contents of the message; for they denied the reality of the Incarnation. Nor were they less revolutionary on the moral side than on the doctrinal. The foundations of morality are sapped when intellectual enlightenment is accounted as the one thing needful, while conduct is treated as a thing of no value. Principles of morality are turned upside down when it is maintained that any act which adds to one's knowledge is not only allowable, but a duty. It is necessary to remember these fatal characteristics of this early form of error, in order to appreciate the stern language used by St. Paul and St. John respecting it, as also by St. Jude and the author of the Second Epistle of Peter.

St. John in his Epistles deals mainly with the doctrinal side of the heresy,—the denial of the reality of sin and of the reality of the Incarnation:[19] although the moral results of doctrinal error are also indicated and condemned.[20] In the Apocalypse, as in St. Paul and in the Catholic Epistles, it is mainly the moral side of the false teaching that is denounced, and that in both its opposite phases. The Epistle to the Colossians deals with the *ascetic* tendencies of early gnosticism.[21] The Apocalypse and the Catholic Epistles deal with its *licentious* tendencies.[22] The Pastoral Epistles treat of both asceticism and licentiousness, but chiefly of the latter, as is seen from the passage before us and from the first part of chapter iii. in the Second Epistle. As we might expect, St. Paul uses stronger language in the Pastoral Epistles than he does in writing to the Colossians; and in St. John and the Catholic Epistles we find stronger language still. Antinomian licentiousness is a far worse evil than misguided asceticism, and in the interval between St. Paul and the other writers the profligacy of the antinomian Gnostics had increased. St. Paul warns the Colossians against delusive "persuasiveness of speech," against "vain deceit," "the rudiments of the world," "the precepts and doctrines of men." He cautions Timothy and Titus respecting "seducing spirits and doctrines of devils," "profane and old wives' fables," "profane babblings" and teachings that "will eat as doth a gangrene," "vain talkers and deceivers" whose "mind and conscience is deceived," and the like. St. John denounces these false teachers as "liars," "seducers," "false prophets," "deceivers," and "antichrists;" and in Jude and the Second Epistle of Peter we have the profligate lives of these false teachers condemned in equally severe terms.

It should be observed that here again everything falls into its proper place if we assume that the Pastoral Epistles were written some years later than the Epistle to the Colossians and some years earlier than those of St. Jude and St. John. The ascetic tendencies of Gnosticism developed first. And though they still continued in teachers like Tatian and Marcion, yet from the close of the first century the licentious conclusions drawn from the premises that the human body is worthless and that all knowledge is divine, became more and more prevalent; as is seen in the teaching of Carpocrates and Epiphanes, and in the monstrous sect of the Cainites. It was quite natural, therefore, that St. Paul should attack Gnostic asceticism first in writing to the Colossians, and afterwards both it and Gnostic licentiousness in writing to Timothy and Titus. It was equally natural that his language should grow stronger as he saw the second evil developing, and that those who saw this second evil at a more advanced stage should use sterner language still.

The extravagant theories of the Gnostics to account for the origin of the universe and the origin of evil are gone and are past recall. It would be impossible to induce people to believe them, and only a comparatively small number of students ever even read them. But the heresy that knowledge is more important than conduct, that brilliant intellectual gifts render a man superior to the moral law, and that much of the moral law itself is the tyrannical bondage of an obsolete tradition, is as dangerous as ever it was. It is openly preached and frequently acted upon. The great Florentine artist, Benvenuto Cellini, tells us in his autobiography that when Pope Paul III. expressed his willingness to forgive him an outrageous murder committed in the streets of Rome, one of the gentlemen at the Papal Court ventured to remonstrate with the Pope for condoning so heinous a crime. "You do not understand the matter as well as I do," replied Paul III.: "I would have you to know that men like Benvenuto, unique in their profession, *are not bound by the laws.*" Cellini is a braggart, and it is possible that in this particular he is romancing. But, even if the story is his invention, he merely attributes to the Pope the sentiments which he cherished himself, and upon which (as experience taught him) other people acted. Over and over again his murderous violence was overlooked by those in authority, because they admired and wished to make use of his genius as an artist. "Ability before honesty" was a common creed in the sixteenth century, and it is abundantly prevalent in our own. The most notorious scandals in a man's private life are condoned if only he is recognized as having talent. It is the old Gnostic error in a modern and sometimes agnostic form. It is becoming daily more clear that the one thing needful for the regeneration of society, whether upper, middle, or lower, is the creation of a "sound" public opinion. And so long as this is so, God's ministers and all who have the duty of instructing others will need to lay to heart the warnings which St. Paul gives to his followers Timothy and Titus.

FOOTNOTES:

[17] 1 Tim. vi. 3; 2 Tim. i. 13, iv. 3; Tit. i. 9, 13, ii. 1, 2, 8.

[18] The Revisers as a rule render διδασκαλία by "doctrine," as here, iv. 6, vi. 1, 3; 2 Tim. iv. 3; Tit. i. 9, ii. 1, 7, 10 (but not in iv. 13, 16, v. 17; 2 Tim. iii. 10, 16), while they render διδαχή by "teaching," as 2 Tim. iv. 2; Tit. i. 9, and frequently in the Gospels. But διδασκαλία, as being closer to διδάσκαλος "a teacher," is "teaching" rather than "doctrine," and διδαχή is "doctrine" rather than "teaching."

[19] 1 John i. 8–10, ii. 22, 23, iii. 4, 8, iv. 2, 3, 15, v. 1, 5, 16, 17; 2 John 7.

[20] ii. 9, 11, iii. 15, 17.

[21] ii. 16, 21, 23.

[22] Rev. ii. 14, 20–22; 2 Peter ii. 10–22; Jude 8, 10, 13, 16, 18.

CHAPTER V
THE LORD'S COMPASSION IN ENABLING A BLASPHEMER AND A PERSECUTOR TO BECOME A SERVANT OF CHRIST JESUS AND A PREACHER OF THE GOSPEL

"I thank Him that enabled me, even Christ Jesus our Lord, for that He counted me faithful, appointing me to His service; though I was before a blasphemer, and a persecutor, and injurious: howbeit I obtained mercy, because I did it ignorantly in unbelief; and the grace of our Lord abounded exceedingly with faith and love which is in Christ Jesus."—1 Tim. i. 12–14.

In the concluding sentence of the preceding paragraph (vv. 3, 11) the Apostle points out that what he has been saying respecting the erroneous teaching and practice of the heterodox innovators is entirely in harmony with the spirit of the Gospel which had been committed to his trust.[23] This mention of his own high commission to preach "the Gospel of the glory of the blessed God" suggests at once to him some thoughts both of thankfulness and humility, to which he now gives expression. His own experience of the Gospel, especially in connexion with his conversion from being a persecutor to becoming a preacher, offer further points of contrast between Gnosticism and Christianity.

The false teachers wasted thought and attention upon barren speculations, which, even if they could under any conceivable circumstances be proved true, would have supplied no guidance to mankind in regulating conduct. And whenever Gnostic teaching became practical, it frittered away morality in servile observances, based on capricious interpretations of the Mosaic Law. Of true morality there was an utter disregard, and frequently an open violation. Of the one thing for which the self-accusing conscience was yearning—the forgiveness of sin—it knew nothing, because it had no appreciation of the reality of sin. Sin was only part of the evil which was inherent in the material universe, and therefore in the human body. A system which had no place for the forgiveness of sin had also no place for the Divine compassion, which it is the purpose of the Gospel to reveal. How very real this compassion and forgiveness are, and how much human beings stand in need of them, St. Paul testifies from his own experience, the remembrance of which makes him burst out into thanksgiving.

The Apostle offers thanks to Jesus Christ, the source of all his strength, for having confidence in him as a person worthy of trust. This confidence He proved by "appointing Paul to His service;" a confidence all the more marvellous and worthy of gratitude because Paul had before been "a blasphemer, and a persecutor, and injurious." He had been a blasphemer, for he had thought that he "ought to do many things contrary to the name of Jesus of Nazareth;" and he had been a persecutor for he had punished believers "often-times in all the synagogues," and "strove to make them blaspheme." That is ever the persecutor's aim;—to make those who differ from him speak evil of what they reverence but he abhors; to say they renounce what in their heart of hearts they believe. There is, therefore, thus far an ascending scale in the iniquity which the Apostle confesses. He not only blasphemed the Divine Name himself, but he endeavoured to compel others to do the same. The third word, although the English Version obscures the fact, continues the ascending scale of self-condemnation. "Injurious" does scant justice to the force of the Greek word used by the Apostle (ὑβριστής), although it is not easy to suggest a better rendering. The word is very common in classical authors, but in the New Testament occurs only here and in Rom. i. 30, where the A.V. translates it "despiteful" and the R.V. "insolent." It is frequent in the Septuagint. It indicates one who takes an insolent and wanton delight in violence, one whose pleasure lies in outraging the feelings of others. The most conspicuous instance of it in the New Testament, and perhaps anywhere, would be the Roman soldiers mocking and torturing Jesus Christ with the crown of thorns and the royal robe. Of such conduct St. Paul himself since his conversion had been the victim, and he here confesses that before his conversion he had been guilty of it himself. In his misguided zeal he had punished innocent people, and he had inflicted punishment, not with pitying reluctance, but with arrogant delight.

It is worth pointing out that in this third charge against himself, as well as in the first, St. Paul goes beyond what he states in the similar passages in the Epistles to the Corinthians, Philippians, and Galatians. There he simply draws attention to the fact that he had been a persecutor who had made havoc of the Church.[24] He says nothing about blaspheming or taking an insolent satisfaction in the pain which he inflicted. This has some bearing on the genuineness of this Epistle. (1) It shows that St. Paul was in the habit of alluding to the fact that he had been a persecutor. It was part of his preaching, for it proved that his conversion was directly and immediately God's work. He did not owe the Gospel which he preached to any persuasion on the part of man. It is, therefore, quite in harmony with St. Paul's practice to insist on his former misconduct. But it may be urged that a forger might notice this and imitate it. That of course is true. But if these Epistles are a forgery, they are certainly not forged with any intention of injuring St. Paul's memory. Is it likely, then, that a forger in imitating the self-accusation of the Apostle, would use stronger language than the Apostle himself uses in those Epistles which are indisputably his? Would he go out of his way to use such strong language as "blasphemer," and "insolent oppressor"? But, if St. Paul wrote these Epistles, this exceptionally strong language is thoroughly natural in a passage in which the Apostle wishes to place in as strong a light as may be the greatness of the Divine compassion in forgiving sins, as manifested in his own case. He had been foremost as a bitter and arrogant opponent of the Gospel; and yet God had singled him out to be foremost in preaching it. Here was a proof that no sinner need despair. What comfort for a fallen race could the false teachers offer in comparison with this?

Like St. Peter's sin in denying His Lord, St. Paul's sin in persecuting Him was overruled for good. The Divine process of bringing good out of evil was strongly exemplified in it. The Gnostic teachers had tried to show how, by a gradual degradation, evil might proceed from the Supreme Good. There is nothing Divine in such a process as that. The fall from good to evil is rather a devilish one, as when an angel of light became the evil one and involved mankind in his own fall. Divinity is shown in the converse process of making what is evil work towards what is good. Under Divine guidance St. Paul's self-righteous confidence and arrogant intolerance were turned into a blessing to himself and others. The recollection of his sin kept him humble, intensified his gratitude, and gave him a strong additional motive to devote himself to the work of bringing others to the Master who had been so gracious to himself. St. Chrysostom in commenting on this passage in his Homilies on the Pastoral Epistles points out how it illustrates St. Paul's humility, a virtue which is more often praised than practised. "This quality was so cultivated by the blessed Paul, that he is ever looking out for inducements to be humble. They who are conscious to themselves of great merits must struggle much with themselves if they would be humble. And he too was one likely to be under violent temptations, his own good conscience swelling him up like a gathering tumour.... Being filled, therefore, with high thoughts, and having used magnificent expressions, he at once depresses himself, and engages others also to do the like. Having said, then, that *the Gospel was committed to his trust*, lest this should seem to be said with pride, he checks himself at once, adding by way of correction, *I thank Him that enabled me, Christ Jesus our Lord, for that He counted me faithful, appointing me to His service.* Thus everywhere, we see, he conceals his own merit and ascribes everything to God, yet so far only as not to take away free will."

These concluding words are an important qualification. The Apostle constantly insists on his conversion as the result of a special revelation of Jesus Christ to himself, in other words a miracle: he nowhere hints that his conversion in itself was miraculous. No psychological miracle was wrought, forcing him to accept Christ against his will. God converts no one by magic. It is a free and reasonable service that he asks for from beings whom He has created free and reasonable. Men were made moral beings, and He who made them such does not treat them as machines. In his defence at Cæsarea St. Paul tells Herod Agrippa that he "was not *disobedient* to the heavenly vision." He might have been. He might, like Judas, have resisted all the miraculous power displayed before him and have continued to persecute Christ. If he had no choice whatever in the matter, it was an abuse of language to affirm that he "was not disobedient." And in that case we should need some other metaphor than "kicking against the goads." It is impossible to kick against the goads if one has no control over one's own limbs. The limbs and the strength to use them were God's gifts, without which he could have done nothing. But with these gifts it was open to him either to obey the Divine commands or "even to fight against God"—a senseless and wicked thing, no doubt, but still possible. In this passage the Divine and the human sides are plainly indicated. On the one hand, Christ enabled him and showed confidence in him: on the other, Paul accepted the service and was faithful. He might have refused the service; or, having accepted it, he might have shown himself unfaithful to his trust.

"Howbeit, I obtained mercy because I did it ignorantly in unbelief." These words are sometimes misunderstood. They are not intended as an excuse, any more than St. John's designation of himself as "the disciple whom Jesus loved" are intended as a boast. St. John had been the recipient of very exceptional favours. Along with only St. Peter and St. James he had been present at the raising of Jairus's daughter, at the Transfiguration, and at the Agony in the Gethsemane. From even these chosen three he had been singled out to be told who was the traitor; to have the lifelong charge of providing for the Mother of the Lord; to be the first to recognize the risen Lord at the sea of Tiberias.[25] What was the explanation of all these honours? The recipient of them had only one to give. He had no merits, no claim to anything of the kind; but Jesus loved him.

So also with St. Paul. There were multitudes of Jews who, like himself, had had, as he tells the Romans, "a zeal for God, but not according to knowledge."[26] There were many who, like himself, had opposed the truth and persecuted the Christ. Why did any of them obtain mercy? Why did he receive such marked favour and honour? Not because of any merit on their part or his: but because they had sinned ignorantly (*i.e.*, without knowing the enormity of their sin), and because "the grace of the Lord abounded exceedingly." The Apostle is not endeavouring to extenuate his own culpability, but to justify and magnify the Divine compassion. Of the whole Jewish nation it was true that "they knew not what they did" in crucifying Jesus of Nazareth; but it was true in very various degrees. "Even of the rulers many believed on Him; but because of the Pharisees they did not confess, lest they should be put out of the synagogue: for they loved the glory of men more than the glory of God." It was because St. Paul did not in this way sin against light that he found mercy, not merely in being forgiven the sin of persecuting Christ, but in being enabled to accept and be faithful in the service of Him whom he had persecuted.

Two of the changes made by the Revisers in this passage seem to call for notice: they both occur in the same phrase and have a similar tendency. Instead of "*putting* me into the *ministry*" the R.V. gives us "*appointing* me to His *service*." A similar change has been made in *v*. 7 of the next chapter, where "I was *appointed* a preacher" takes the place of "I am ordained a preacher," and in John xv. 16 where "I chose you and *appointed* you" has been substituted for "I have chosen you and *ordained* you."[27] In these alterations the Revisers are only following the example set by the A.V. itself in other passages. In 2 Tim. i. 11, as in Luke x. 1, and 1 Thess. v. 9, both versions have "appointed." The alterations are manifest improvements. In the passage before us it is possible that the Greek has the special signification of "putting me into the ministry," but it is by no means certain, and perhaps not even probable, that it does so. Therefore the more comprehensive and general translation, "appointing me to His service," is to be preferred. The wider rendering includes and covers the other; and this is a further advantage. To translate the Greek words used in these passages (τιθέναι, ποιεῖν, κ.τ.λ.) by such a very definite word as "ordain" leads the reader to suppose these texts refer to the ecclesiastical act of ordination; of which there is no evidence. The idea conveyed by the Greek in this passage, as in John xv. 16, is that of placing a man at a particular post, and would be as applicable to civil as to ministerial duties. We are not, therefore, justified in translating it by a phrase which has distinct ecclesiastical associations.

The question is not one of mere linguistic accuracy. There are larger issues involved than those of correct translation from Greek to English. If we adopt the wider rendering, then it is evident that the blessing for which St. Paul expresses heartfelt gratitude, and which he cites as evidence of Divine compassion and forgiveness, is not the call to be an Apostle, in which none of us can share, nor *exclusively* the call to be a minister of the Gospel, in which only a limited number of us can share; but also the being appointed to any service in Christ's kingdom, which is an honour to which all Christians are called. Every earnest Christian knows from personal experience this evidence of the Divine character of the Gospel. It is full of compassion for those who have sinned; not because, like the Gnostic teachers, it glosses over the malignity and culpability of sin, but because, unlike Gnosticism, it recognizes the preciousness of each human soul, and the difficulties which beset it. Every Christian knows that he has inherited an evil nature:—so far he and the Gnostic are agreed. But he also knows that to the sin which he has inherited he has added sin for which he is personally responsible, and which his conscience does not excuse as if it were something which is a misfortune and not a fault. Yet he is not left without remedy under the burden of these self-accusations. He knows that, if he seeks for it, he can find forgiveness, and forgiveness of a singularly generous kind. He is not only forgiven, but restored to favour and treated with respect. He is at once placed in a position of trust. In spite of the past, it is assumed that he will be a faithful servant, and he is allowed to minister to his Master and his Master's followers. To him also "the grace of our Lord" has "abounded exceedingly with faith and love which is in Christ Jesus." The generous compassion shown to St. Paul is not unique or exceptional; it is typical. And it is a type, not to the few, but to many; not to clergy only, but to all. "For this cause I obtained mercy, that in me as chief might Jesus Christ show forth all His long-suffering, for an ensample of *them which should hereafter believe on Him* unto eternal life."

FOOTNOTES:

[23] It is worth while pointing out that the peculiar construction ὃ ἐπιστεύθην ἐγώ occurs in the New Testament, only in the Pastoral Epistles and in other Pauline Epistles, the genuineness of which is now scarcely disputed—1 Thess. ii. 4; 1 Cor. ix. 17; Rom. iii. 2; Gal. ii. 7.

[24] 1 Cor. xv. 8, 10; Gal. i. 13, 23; Phil. iii. 6; comp. Acts xxii. 4, 5, 19.

[25] St. John xiii. 23, xix. 26, xxi. 7.

[26] Rom. x. 2.

[27] Comp. Acts xxii. 14 and 2 Cor. viii. 19; also Mark iii. 14 and Acts xiv. 23. See on Tit. i. 5–7.

CHAPTER VI
THE PROPHECIES ON TIMOTHY.—THE PROPHETS OF THE NEW TESTAMENT, AN EXCEPTIONAL INSTRUMENT OF EDIFICATION

"This charge I commit unto thee, my own child Timothy, according to the prophecies which went before on thee, that by them thou mayest war the good warfare; holding faith and a good conscience; which some having thrust from them made shipwreck concerning the faith: of whom is Hymenæus and Alexander; whom I delivered unto Satan, that they might be taught not to blaspheme."—1 Tim. i. 18–20.

In this section St. Paul returns from the subject of the false teachers against whom Timothy has to contend (vv. 3–11), and the contrast to their teaching exhibited by the Gospel in the Apostle's own case (vv. 12–17), to the main purpose of the letter, viz., the instructions to be given to Timothy for the due performance of his difficult duties as overseer of the Church of Ephesus. The section contains two subjects of special interest, each of which requires consideration;—the prophecies respecting Timothy and the punishment of Hymenæus and Alexander.

1. "This charge I commit unto thee, my child Timothy, *according to the prophecies which went before on thee.*" As the margin of the R.V. points out, this last phrase might also be read "according to the prophecies which *led the way to thee,*" for the Greek may mean either. The question is, whether St. Paul is referring to certain prophecies which "led the way to" Timothy, *i.e.*, which designated him as specially suited for the ministry, and led to his ordination by St. Paul and the presbyters; or whether he is referring to certain prophecies which were uttered *over* Timothy (ἐπὶ σέ) either at the time of his conversion or of his admission to the ministry. Both the A.V. and the R.V. give the preference to the latter rendering, which (without excluding such a view) does not commit us to the opinion that St. Paul was in any sense led to Timothy by these prophecies, a thought which is not clearly intimated in the original. All that we are certain of is, that long before the writing of this letter prophecies of which Timothy was the object were

uttered over him, and that they were of such a nature as to be an incentive and support to him in his ministry.

But if we look on to the fourteenth verse of the fourth chapter in this Epistle and to the sixth of the first chapter in the Second, we shall not have much doubt when these prophecies were uttered. There we read, "Neglect not the gift that is in thee, which was given thee *by prophecy*, with the laying on of the hands of the presbytery!" and "For which cause I put thee in remembrance that thou stir up the gift of God, which is in thee through the laying on of my hands." Must we not believe that these two passages and the passage before us all refer to the same occasion—the same crisis in Timothy's life? In all three of them St. Paul appeals to the spiritual gift that was bestowed upon his disciple *"by means of* prophecy" and *"by means of* the laying on of hands." The same preposition and case ((διά with the genitive) is used in each case. Clearly, then, we are to understand that the prophesying and the laying on of hands accompanied one another. Here only the prophesying is mentioned. In chapter iv. the prophesying, accompanied by the imposition of the presbyters' hands, is the means by which the grace is conferred. In the Second Epistle only the laying on of the Apostle's hands is mentioned, and it is spoken of as the means by which the grace is conferred. Therefore, although the present passage by itself leaves the question open, yet when we take the other two into consideration along with it, we may safely neglect the possibility of prophecies which *led the way* to the ordination of Timothy, and understand the Apostle as referring to those sacred utterances which were a marked element in his disciple's ordination and formed a prelude and earnest of his ministry. These sacred utterances indicated a Divine commission and Divine approbation publicly expressed respecting the choice of Timothy for this special work. They were also a means of grace; for by means of them a spiritual blessing was bestowed upon the young minister. In alluding to them here, therefore, St. Paul reminds him *Who* it was by whom he was really chosen and ordained. It is as if he said, "We laid our hands upon you; but it was no ordinary election made by human votes. It was God who elected you; God who gave you your commission, and with it the power to fulfil it. Beware, therefore, of disgracing His appointment and of neglecting or abusing His gift."[28]

The voice of prophecy, therefore, either pointed out Timothy as a chosen vessel for the ministry, or publicly ratified the choice which had already been made by St. Paul and others. But by whom was this voice of prophecy uttered? By a special order of prophets? Or by St. Paul and the presbyters specially inspired to act as such? The answer to this question involves some consideration of the office, or rather *function*, of a prophet, especially in the New Testament.

The word "prophet" is frequently understood in far too limited a sense. It is commonly restricted to the one function of predicting the future. But, if we may venture to coin words in order to bring out points of differences, there are three main ideas involved in the title "prophet." (1) A *for*-teller; one who speaks *for* or instead of another, especially one who speaks *for* or in the name of God; a Divine messenger, ambassador, interpreter, or *spokesman*. (2) A *forth*-teller; one who has a special message to deliver *forth* to the world; a proclaimer, harbinger, or herald. (3) A *fore*-teller; one who tells *beforehand* what is coming; a predicter of future events. To be the bearer or interpreter of a Divine message is the fundamental conception of the prophet in classical Greek; and to a large extent this conception prevails in both the Old and the New Testament. To be in immediate intercourse with Jehovah, and to be His spokesman to Israel, was what the Hebrews understood by the gift of prophecy. It was by no means necessary that the Divine communication which the prophet had to make known to the people should relate to the future. It might be a denunciation of past sins, or an exhortation respecting present conduct, quite as naturally as a prediction of what was coming. And in the Acts and Pauline Epistles the idea of a prophet remains much the same. He is one to whom has been granted special insight into God's counsels, and who communicates these mysteries to others. Both in the Jewish and primitive Christian dispensations, the prophets are the means of communication between God and His Church. Eight persons are mentioned by name in the Acts of the Apostles as exercising this gift of prophecy: Agabus, Barnabas, Symeon called Niger, Lucius of Cyrene, Manaen the foster-brother of Herod the tetrarch, Judas, Silas, and St. Paul himself. On certain occasions the Divine communication made to them by the Spirit included a knowledge of the future; as when Agabus foretold the great famine (xi. 28) and the imprisonment of St. Paul (xxi. 11), and when St. Paul told that the Holy Spirit testified to him in every city, that bonds and afflictions awaited him at Jerusalem (xx. 23). But this is the exception rather than the rule. It is in their character of prophets that Judas and Silas exhort and confirm the brethren. And, what is of special interest in reference to the prophecies uttered over Timothy, we find a group of prophets having special influence in the selection and ordination of Apostolic evangelists. "And as they ministered to the Lord, and fasted, the Holy Ghost said, Separate Me Barnabas and Saul, for the work whereunto I have called them. Then when they had fasted and prayed and laid their hands on them, they sent them away" (xiii. 2, 3).

We see, therefore, that these New Testament prophets were not a regularly constituted order, like apostles, with whom they are joined both in the First Epistle to the Corinthians (xii. 28) and in that to the Ephesians

(iv. 11). Yet they have this in common with apostles, that the work of both lies rather in founding Churches than in governing them. They have to convert and edify rather than to rule. They might or might not be apostles or presbyters as well as prophets; but as prophets they were men or women (such as the daughters of Philip) on whom a special gift of the Holy Spirit had been conferred: and this gift enabled them to understand and expound Divine mysteries with inspired authority, and at times also to foretell the future.

So long as we bear these characteristics in mind, it matters little how we answer the question as to who it was that uttered the prophecies over Timothy at the time of his ordination. It may have been St. Paul and the presbyters who laid their hands upon him, and who on this occasion at any rate were endowed with the spirit of prophecy. Or it may have been that besides the presbyters there were prophets also present, who, at this solemn ceremony, exercised their gift of inspiration. The former seems more probable. It is clear from chap. iv. 14, that prophecy and imposition of hands were two concomitant acts by means of which spiritual grace was bestowed upon Timothy; and it is more reasonable to suppose that these two instrumental acts were performed by the same group of persons, than that one group prophesied, while another laid their hands on the young minister's head.

This gift of prophecy, St. Paul tells the Corinthians (1 Cor. xiv.), was one specially to be desired; and evidently it was by no means a rare one in the primitive Church. As we might expect, it was most frequently exercised in the public services of the congregation. "When ye come together, each one hath a psalm, hath a teaching, hath a revelation, hath a tongue, hath an interpretation.... Let the prophets speak by two or three, and let the others discern. But if a revelation be made to another sitting by, let the first keep silence. For *ye all can prophesy one by one*, that all may learn and all may be comforted; and the spirits of the prophets are subject to the prophets." The chief object of the gift, therefore, was instruction and consolation, for the conversion of unbelievers (24, 25), and for the building up of the faithful.

But we shall probably be right in making a distinction between the prophesying which frequently took place in the first Christian congregations, and those special interventions of the Holy Spirit of which we read occasionally. In these latter cases it is not so much spiritual instruction in an inspired form that is communicated, as a revelation of God's will with regard to some particular course of action. Such was the case when Paul and Silas were "forbidden of the Holy Ghost to speak the word in Asia," and when "they assayed to go into Bithynia, and the Spirit of Jesus suffered them not:" or when on his voyage to Rome Paul was assured that he would stand before Cæsar, and that God had given him the lives of all those who sailed with him.[29]

Some have supposed that the Revelation of St. John was intended to mark the close of New Testament prophecy and to protect the Church against unwarrantable attempts at prophecy until the return of Christ to judge the world. This view would be more probable if the later date for the Apocalypse could be established. But if, as is far more probable, the Revelation was written c. a.d. 68, it is hardly likely that St. John, during the lifetime of Apostles, would think of taking any such decisive step. In his First Epistle, written probably fifteen or twenty years after the Revelation, he gives a test for distinguishing true from false prophets (iv. 1–4); and this he would not have done, if he had believed that all true prophecy had ceased.

In the newly discovered "Doctrine of the Twelve Apostles" we find prophets among the ministers of the Church, just as in the Epistles to the Corinthians, Ephesians, and Philippians. The date of this interesting treatise has yet to be ascertained; but it seems to belong to the period between the Epistles of St. Paul and those of Ignatius. We may safely place it between the writings of St. Paul and those of Justin Martyr. In the Epistle to the Corinthians (1 Cor. xii. 28) we have "First apostles, secondly prophets, thirdly teachers, then" those who had special gifts, such as healing or speaking with tongues. In Ephes. iv. 11 we are told that Christ "gave some to be apostles; and some evangelists; and some, pastors and teachers." The Epistle to the Philippians is addressed "to all the saints in Christ Jesus which are at Philippi, with the bishops and deacons," where the plural shows that "bishop" cannot be used in the later diocesan sense; otherwise there would be only one bishop at Philippi. Prophets, therefore, in St. Paul's time are a common and important branch of the ministry. They rank next to apostles, and a single congregation may possess several of them. In Ignatius and later writers the ministers who are so conspicuous in the Acts and in St. Paul's Epistles disappear, and their place is taken by other ministers whose offices, at any rate in their later forms, are scarcely found in the New Testament at all. These are the bishops, presbyters, and deacons; to whom were soon added a number of subordinate officials, such as readers, exorcists, and the like. The ministry, as we find it in the "Doctrine of the Twelve Apostles," is in a state of transition from the Apostolic to the latter stage. As in the time of St. Paul we have both itinerant and local ministers; the itinerant ministers being chiefly apostles and prophets, whose functions do not seem to be marked off from one another very distinctly; and the local ministry consisting of two orders only, bishops and deacons, as in the address to the Church of Philippi. When we reach the Epistles of Ignatius and other documents of a date later than a.d. 110, we lose distinct traces of these itinerant apostles and prophets. The title "Apostle" is becoming confined to St. Paul and the Twelve, and the title of "Prophet" to the Old Testament prophets.

The gradual cessation or discredit of the function of the Christian prophet is thoroughly intelligible. Possibly the spiritual gift which rendered it possible was withdrawn from the Church. In any case the extravagances of enthusiasts who deluded themselves into the belief that they possessed the gift, or of impostors who deliberately assumed it, would bring the office into suspicion and disrepute. Such things were possible even in Apostolic times, for both St. Paul and St. John give cautions about it, and directions for dealing with the abuse and the false assumption of prophecy. In the next century the eccentric delusions of Montanus and his followers, and their vehement attempts to force their supposed revelations upon the whole Church, completed the discredit of all profession to prophetical power. This discredit has been intensified from time to time whenever such professions have been renewed; as, for example, by the extravagances of the Zwickau Prophets or Abecedarians in Luther's time, or of the Irvingites in our own day. Since the death of St. John and the close of the Canon, Christians have sought for illumination in the written word of Scripture rather than in the utterances of prophets. It is there that each one of us may find "the prophecies that went before on" us, exhorting us and enabling us to "war the good warfare, holding faith and a good conscience." There will always be those who crave for something more definite and personal; who long for, and perhaps create for themselves and believe in, some living authority to whom they can perpetually appeal. Scripture seems to them unsatisfying, and they erect for themselves an infallible pope, or a spiritual director, whose word is to be to them as the inspired utterances of a prophet. But we have to fall back on our own consciences at last: and whether we take Scripture or some other authority as our infallible guide, the responsibility of the choice still rests with ourselves. If a man will not hear Christ and His Apostles, neither will he be persuaded though a prophet was granted to him. If we believe not their writings, how shall we believe his words?

FOOTNOTES:

[28] Chrysostom *in loco. Hom.* v. *sub init.*
[29] Acts xvi. 6, 7, xxvii. 24; comp. xviii. 9, xx. 23, xxi. 4, 11, xxii. 17–21.

CHAPTER VII
THE PUNISHMENT OF HYMENÆUS AND ALEXANDER.—DELIVERING TO SATAN AN EXCEPTIONAL INSTRUMENT OF PURIFICATION.—THE PERSONALITY OF SATAN

> "Holding faith and a good conscience; which some having thrust from them made shipwreck: of whom is Hymenæus and Alexander; whom I delivered unto Satan, that they might be taught not to blaspheme."—1 Tim. i. 19, 20.

In the preceding discourse one of the special *charismata* which distinguish the Church of the Apostolic age was considered,—the gift of prophecy. It seems to have been an exceptional boon to enable the first Christians to perform very exceptional work. On the present occasion we have to consider a very different subject—the heavy penalty inflicted on two grievous offenders. This again would seem to be something exceptional. And the special gift and the special punishment have this much in common, that both of them were extraordinary means for promoting and preserving the holiness of the Church. The one existed for the edification, the other for the purification, of the members of the Christian community.

The necessity of strict discipline both for the individual and for the community had been declared by Christ from the outset. The eye that caused offence was to be plucked out, the hand and the foot that caused offence were to be cut off, and the hardened offender who refused to listen to the solemn remonstrances of the congregation was to be treated as a heathen and an outcast. The experience of the primitive Church had proved the wisdom of this. The fall of Judas had shown that the Apostolic band itself was not secure from evil of the very worst kind. The parent Church of Jerusalem was no sooner founded than a dark stain was brought upon it by the conduct of two of its members. In the very first glow of its youthful enthusiasm Ananias and Sapphira conspired together to pervert the general unselfishness to their own selfish end, by attempting to gain the credit for equal generosity with the rest, while keeping back something for themselves. The Church of Corinth was scarcely five years old, and the Apostle had been absent from it only about three years, when he learnt that in this Christian community, the firstfruits of the heathen world, a sin which even the heathen regarded as a monstrous pollution had been committed, and that the congregation were glorying in it. Christians were boasting that the incestuous union of a man with his father's wife during his father's lifetime was a splendid illustration of Christian liberty. No stronger proof of the dangers of lax discipline could have been given. In the verses before us we have instances of similar peril on the doctrinal side. And in the insolent opposition which Diotrephes offered to St. John we have an illustration of the dangers of insubordination. If the Christian Church was to be saved from speedy collapse, strict discipline in morals, in doctrine, and in government, was plainly necessary.

The punishment of the incestuous person at Corinth should be placed side by side with the punishment of Hymenæus and Alexander, as recorded here. The two cases mutually explain one another. In each of them there occurs the remarkable formula of *delivering* or *handing over to Satan*. The meaning of it is not indisputable, and in the main two views are held respecting it. Some interpret it as being merely a synonym for excommunication. Others maintain that it indicates a much more exceptional penalty, which might or might not accompany excommunication.

1. On the one hand it is argued that the expression "deliver unto Satan" is a very intelligible periphrasis for "excommunicate." Excommunication involved "exclusion from all Christian fellowship, and consequently banishment to the society of those among whom Satan dwelt, and from which the offender had publicly severed himself."[30] It is admitted that "handing over to Satan" is strong language to use in order to express ejection from the congregation and exclusion from all acts of worship, but it is thought that the acuteness of the crisis makes the strength of language intelligible.

2. But the strength of language needs no apology, if the "delivering unto Satan" means something extraordinary, over and above excommunication. This, therefore, is an advantage which the second mode of interpreting the expression has at the outset. Excommunication was a punishment which the congregation itself could inflict; but this handing over to Satan was an Apostolic act, to accomplish which the community without the Apostle had no power. It was a supernatural infliction of bodily infirmity, or disease, or death, as a penalty for grievous sin. We know this in the cases of Ananias and Sapphira and of Elymas. The incestuous person at Corinth is probably another instance: for "the destruction of the flesh" seems to mean some painful malady inflicted on that part of his nature which had been the instrument of his fall, in order that by its chastisement the higher part of his

nature might be saved. And, if this be correct, then we seem to be justified in assuming the same respecting Hymenæus and Alexander. For although nothing is said in their case respecting "the destruction of the flesh," yet the expression "that they may be *taught* not to blaspheme," implies something of a similar kind. The word for "taught" παιδευθῶσι implies discipline and chastisement, sometimes in Classical Greek, frequently in the New Testament, a meaning which the word "teach" also not unfrequently has in English (Judges viii. 16). In illustration of this it is sufficient to point to the passage in Heb. xii., in which the writer insists that "whom the Lord loveth He *chasteneth*." Throughout the section this very word (παιδεύειν) and its cognate (παιδεία) are used.[31] It is, therefore, scarcely doubtful that St. Paul delivered Hymenæus and Alexander to Satan, in order that Satan might have power to afflict their bodies (just as he was allowed power over the body of Job), with a view to their spiritual amelioration. This personal suffering, following close upon their sin and declared by the Apostle to be a punishment for it, would teach them to abandon it. St. Paul himself, as he has just told us, had been a blasphemer and by a supernatural visitation had been converted: why should not these two follow in both respects in his steps? Satan's willingness to co-operate in such measures need not surprise us. He is always ready to inflict suffering; and the fact that suffering sometimes draws the sufferer away from him and nearer to God, does not deter him from inflicting it. He knows well that suffering not unfrequently has the very opposite effect. It hardens and exasperates some men, while it humbles and purifies others. It makes one man say "I abhor myself, and repent in dust and ashes." It makes another will to "renounce God and die." Satan hoped in Job's case to be able to provoke him to "renounce God to His face." In the case of these two blasphemers he would hope to induce them to blaspheme all the more.

We may pass by the question, "In what way did Hymenæus and Alexander blaspheme?" We can only conjecture that it was by publicly opposing some article of the Christian faith. But conjectures without evidence are not very profitable. If we were certain that the Hymenæus here mentioned with Alexander is identical with the one who is condemned with Philetus in 2 Tim. ii. 18 for virtually denying the resurrection, we should have some evidence. But this identification, although probable, is not certain. Still less certain is the identification of the Alexander condemned here with "Alexander the coppersmith," who in 2 Tim. iv. 14 is said to have done the Apostle much evil. But none of these questions is of great moment. What is of importance to notice is the Apostolic sentence upon the two blasphemers. And in it we have to notice four points. (1) It is almost certainly not identical with excommunication by the congregation, although it very probably was accompanied by this other penalty. (2) It is of a very extraordinary character, being a handing over into the power of the evil one. (3) Its object is the reformation of the offenders, while at the same time (4) it serves as a warning to others, lest they by similar offences should suffer so awful a punishment. To all alike it brought home the serious nature of such sins. Even at the cost of cutting off the right hand, or plucking out the right eye, the Christian community must be kept pure in doctrine as in life.

These two passages,—the one before us, and the one respecting the case of incest at Corinth,—are conclusive as to St. Paul's teaching respecting the existence and personality of the devil. They are supported and illustrated by a number of other passages in his writings; as when he tells the Thessalonians that "Satan hindered" his work, or warns the Corinthians that "even Satan fashioneth himself into an angel of light," and tells them that his own sore trouble in the flesh was, like Job's, "a messenger of Satan to buffet" him. Not less clear is the teaching of St. Peter and St. John in Epistles which, with those of St. Paul to the Corinthians, are among the best authenticated works in ancient literature. "Your adversary the devil as a roaring lion, walketh about, seeking whom he may devour," says the one: "He that doeth sin is of the devil; for the devil sinneth from the beginning," says the other. And, if we need higher authority, there is the declaration of Christ to the malignant and unbelieving Jews. "Ye are of your father the devil, and the lusts of your father it is your will to do. He was a murderer from the beginning, and stood not in the truth, because there is no truth in him. When he speaketh a lie, he speaketh of his own: for he is a liar, and the father thereof."[32] With regard to this last passage, those who deny the personal existence of Satan must maintain either (1) that the Evangelist here attributes to Christ words which He never used; or (2) that Christ was willing to make use of a monstrous superstition in order to denounce his opponents with emphasis; or (3) that He Himself erroneously believed in the existence of a being who was a mere figment of an unenlightened imagination: in other words, that "the Son of God was manifested that He might destroy the works of the devil," when all the while there was no devil and no works of his to be destroyed.

The first of these views cuts at the root of all trust in the Gospels as historical documents. Words which imply that Satan is a person are attributed to Christ by the Synoptists no less than by St. John; and if the Evangelists are not to be believed in their report of Christ's sayings on this topic, what security have we that they are to be believed as to their reports of the rest of His teaching; or indeed as to anything which they narrate? Again, how are we to account for the very strong statements made by the Apostles themselves respecting the evil one, if they had never heard anything of the kind from Christ.

The second view has been adopted by Schleiermacher, who thinks that Christ accommodated His teaching to the ideas then prevalent among the Jews respecting Satan without sharing them Himself. He knew that Satan was a mere personification of the moral evil which every man finds in his own nature and in that of his fellow-men: but the Jews believed in the personality of this evil principle, and He acquiesced in the belief, not as being true, but as offering no fundamental opposition to His teaching. But is this consistent with the truthfulness of Christ? If a personal devil is an empty superstition, He went out of his way to confirm men in their belief in it. Why teach that the enemy who sowed the tares is the devil? Why interpret the birds that snatch away the freshly sown seed as Satan? It would have been so easy in each case to have spoken of impersonal temptations. Again, what motive can Christ have had for telling His *Apostles* (not the ignorant and superstitious multitude), that He Himself had endured the repeated solicitations of a personal tempter, who had conversed and argued with Him?

Those who, like Strauss and Renan, believe Jesus of Nazareth to have been a mere man, would naturally adopt the third view. In believing in the personality of Satan Jesus merely shared the superstitions of His age. To all those who wish to discuss with him whether we are still Christians, Strauss declares that "the belief in a devil is one of the most hideous sides of the ancient Christian faith," and that "the extent to which this dangerous delusion still controls men's ideas or has been banished from them is the very thing to regard as a measure of culture." But at the same time he admits that "to remove so fundamental a stone is dangerous for the whole edifice of the Christian faith. It was the young Goethe who remarked against Bahrdt that if ever an idea was biblical, this one [of the existence of a personal Satan] was such."[33] And elsewhere Strauss declares that the conception of the Messiah and His kingdom without the antithesis of an infernal kingdom with a personal chief is as impossible as that of North pole without a South pole.[34]

To refuse to believe in an evil power external to ourselves is to believe that human nature itself is diabolical. Whence come the devilish thoughts that vex us even at the most sacred and solemn moments? If they do not come from the evil one and his myrmidons, they come from ourselves:—they are our own offspring. Such a belief might well drive us to despair. So far from being a "hideous" element in the Christian faith, the belief in a power, "*not ourselves*, that makes for" wickedness, is a most consoling one. It has been said that, if there were no God, we should have to invent one: and with almost equal truth we might say that, if there were no devil, we should have to invent one. Without a belief in God bad men would have little to induce them to conquer their evil passions. Without a belief in a devil good men would have little hope of ever being able to do so.

The passage before us supplies us with another consoling thought with regard to this terrible adversary, who is always invisibly plotting against us. It is often *for our own good* that God allows him to have an advantage over us. He is permitted to inflict loss upon us through our persons and our property, as in the case of Job, and the woman whom he bowed down for eighteen years, in order to chasten us and teach us that "we have not here an abiding city." And he is permitted even to lead us into sin, in order to save us from spiritual pride, and to convince us that apart from Christ and in our own strength we can do nothing. These are not Satan's motives, but they are God's motives in allowing him to be "the ruler of this world," and to have much power over human affairs. Satan inflicts suffering from love of inflicting it, and leads into sin from love of sin: but God knows how to bring good out of evil by making the evil one frustrate his own wiles. The devil malignantly afflicts souls that come within his power; but the affliction leads to those souls being "saved in the day of the Lord." It had that blessed effect in the case of the incestuous person at Corinth. Whether the same is true of Hymenæus and Alexander, there is nothing in Scripture to tell us. It is for us to take care that in our case the chastisements which inevitably follow upon sin do not drive us further and further into it, but teach us to sin no more.

FOOTNOTES:

[30] Dr. David Brown in Schaff's *Popular Commentary*, iii., p. 180.

[31] Heb. xii. 5, 11; comp. 1 Cor. xi. 32; 2 Cor. vi. 9; 2 Tim. ii. 25; Luke xxiii. 16, 22: Soph., *Ajax* 595; Xen., *Mem*. I. iii. 5.

[32] 1 Thess. ii. 18; 2 Cor. xi. 14, xii. 7; 1 Pet. v. 8; 1 John iii. 8; John viii. 44.

[33] Strauss, *Der alte und der neue Glaube*, p. 22.

[34] Herzog und Plitt, XV. p. 361.

CHAPTER VIII
ELEMENTS OF CHRISTIAN WORSHIP; INTERCESSORY PRAYER AND THANKSGIVING.—THE SOLIDARITY OF CHRISTENDOM AND OF THE HUMAN RACE

"I exhort, therefore, first of all, that supplications, prayers, intercessions, thanksgivings, be made for all men: for kings and all that are in high places; that we may lead a tranquil and quiet life in all godliness and gravity"—1 Tim. ii. 1.

The first chapter of the Epistle is more or less introductory. It repeats what St. Paul had already said to his beloved disciple by word of mouth, on the subject of Christian doctrine, and the necessity of keeping it pure. It makes a digression respecting the Apostle's own conversion. It reminds Timothy of the hopeful prophecies uttered over him at his ordination; and it points out the terrible consequences of driving conscience from the helm and placing oneself in antagonism to the Almighty. In this second chapter St Paul goes on to mention in order the subjects which led to the writing of the letter; and the very first exhortation which he has to give is that respecting Christian worship and the duty of intercessory prayer and thanksgiving.

There are two things very worthy of remark in the treatment of the subject of worship in the Pastoral Epistles. First, these letters bring before us a more developed form of worship than we find indicated in the earlier writings of St. Paul. It is still very primitive, but it has grown. And this is exactly what we ought to expect, especially when we remember how rapidly the Christian Church developed its powers during the first century and a half. Secondly, the indications of this more developed form of worship occur only in the letters to Timothy, which deal with the condition of things in the Church of Ephesus, a Church which had already been founded for a considerable time, and was in a comparatively advanced stage of organization. Hence we are not surprised to find in these two Epistles fragments of what appear to be primitive liturgical forms. In the First Epistle we have two grand doxologies, which may be the outcome of the Apostle's devotion at the moment, but are quite as likely to be quotations of formulas well known to Timothy (i. 17; vi.

15, 16). Between these two we have what looks like a portion of a hymn in praise of Jesus Christ, suitable for singing antiphonally (iii. 16; comp. Pliny, *Epp.* x. 96): and also what may be a baptismal exhortation (vi. 12). In the Second Epistle we have traces of another liturgical formula (ii. 11–13).

St. Paul of course does not mean, as the A.V. might lead us to suppose, that in all Christian worship intercession ought to come first; still less that intercession is the first duty of a Christian. But he does place it first among those subjects about which he has to give directions in this Epistle. He makes sure that it shall not be forgotten by himself in writing to his delegate at Ephesus; and he wishes to make sure that it shall not be forgotten by Timothy in his ministration. To offer prayers and thanksgivings on behalf of all men is a duty of such high importance that the Apostle places it first among the topics of his pastoral charge.

Was it a duty which Timothy and the congregation committed to his care had been neglecting, or were in serious danger of neglecting? It may well have been so. In the difficulties of the overseer's own personal position, and in the varied dangers to which his little flock were so unceasingly exposed, the claims of others upon their united prayer and praise may sometimes have been forgotten. When the Apostle had left Timothy to take his place for a time in Ephesus he had hoped to return very soon, and consequently had given him only brief and somewhat hasty directions as to his course of action during his absence. He had been prevented from returning; and there was a probability that Timothy would have to be his representative for an indefinite period. Meanwhile the difficulties of Timothy's position had not diminished. Many of his flock were much older men than himself, and some of them had been elders in the Church of Ephesus long before the Apostle's beloved disciple was placed in charge of them. Some of the leaders in the congregation had become tainted with the Gnostic errors with which the intellectual atmosphere of Ephesus was charged, and were endeavouring to make compromise and confusion between heathen lawlessness and Christian liberty. Besides which, there was the bitter hostility of the Jews, who regarded both Paul and Timothy as renegades from the faith of their ancestors, and who never lost an opportunity of thwarting and reviling them. Above all there was the ever-present danger of heathenism, which confronted the Christians every time they left the shelter of their own houses. In the city which counted it as its chief glory that it was the "Temple-keeper of the great Artemis" (Acts xix. 35), every street through which the Christians walked, and every heathen house which they entered, was full of pagan abominations; to say nothing of the magnificent temples, beautiful groves, and seductive idolatrous rites, which were among the main features that attracted such motley crowds to Ephesus. Amid difficulties and perils such as these, it would not be wonderful if Timothy and those committed to his care had been somewhat oblivious of the fact that "behind the mountains also there are people;" that beyond the narrow limits of their contracted horizon there were interests as weighty as their own—Christians who were as dear to God as themselves, whose needs were as great as their own, and to whom the Lord had been equally gracious; and moreover countless hosts of heathen, who also were God's children, needing His help and receiving His blessings; for all of whom, as well as for themselves, the Church in Ephesus was bound to offer prayer and thanksgiving.

But there is no need to assume that Timothy, and those committed to his care, had been specially neglectful of this duty. To keep clearly in view our responsibilities towards the whole human race, or even towards the whole Church, is so difficult a thing for all of us, that the prominent place which St. Paul gives to the obligation to offer prayers and thanksgivings for all men is quite intelligible, without the supposition that the disciple whom he addresses was more in need of such a charge than other ministers in the Churches under St. Paul's care.

The Apostle uses three different words for prayer, the second of which is a general term and covers all kinds of prayer to God, and the first a still more general term, including petitions addressed to man. Either of the first two would embrace the third, which indicates a bold and earnest approach to the Almighty to implore some great benefit. None of the three words necessarily means intercession in the sense of prayer *on behalf of others*. This idea comes from the context. St. Paul says plainly that it is prayers and thanksgivings "for all men" that he desires to have made: and in all probability he did not carefully distinguish in his mind the shades of meaning which are proper to the three terms which he uses. Whatever various kinds of supplication there may be which are offered by man at the throne of grace, he urges that the whole human race are to have the benefit of them. Obviously, as Chrysostom long ago pointed out, we cannot limit the Apostle's "all men" to all believers. Directly he enters into detail he mentions "kings and all that are in high place;" and in St. Paul's day not a single king, and we may almost say not a single person in high place, was a believer. The scope of a Christian's desires and gratitude, when he appears before the Lord, must have no narrower limit than that which embraces the whole human race. This important principle, the Apostle charges his representative, must be exhibited in the public worship of the Church in Ephesus.

The solidarity of the whole body of Christians, however distant from one another in space and time, however different from one another in nationality, in discipline, and even in creed, is a magnificent fact, of which we all of us need from time to time to be reminded, and which, even when we are reminded of it, we find it somewhat difficult to grasp. Members of sects that we never heard of, dwelling in remote regions of which we do not even know the names, are nevertheless united to us by the eternal ties of a common baptism and a common belief in God and in Jesus Christ. The eastern sectarian in the wilds of Asia, and the western sectarian in the backwoods of North America, are members of Christ and our brethren; and as such have spiritual interests identical with our own, for which it is not only our duty but our advantage to pray. "Whether one member suffereth, all the members suffer with it; or one member is honoured, all the members rejoice with it." The ties which bind Christians to one another are at once so subtle and so real, that it is impossible for one Christian to remain unaffected by the progress or retrogression of any other. Therefore, not only does the law of Christian charity require us to aid all our fellow-Christians by praying for them, but the law of self-interest leads us to do so also; for their advance will assuredly help us forward, and their relapse will assuredly keep us back. All this is plain matter of fact, revealed to us by Christ and His apostles, and confirmed by our own experience, so far as our feeble powers of observation are able to supply a test. Nevertheless, it is a fact of such enormous proportions (even without taking into account our close relationship with those who have passed away from this world), that even with our best efforts we fail to realize it in its immensity.

What shall we say, then, about the difficulty of realizing the solidarity of the whole human race? For they also are God's offspring, and as such are of one family with ourselves. If it is hard to remember that the welfare of the humblest member of a remote and obscure community in Christendom intimately concerns ourselves, how shall we keep in view the fact that we have both interests and obligations in reference to the wildest and most degraded heathens in the heart of Africa or in the islands of the Pacific? Here is a fact on a far more stupendous scale; for in the population of the globe, those who are not even in name Christians, outnumber us by at least three to one. And yet let us never forget that our interest in these countless multitudes, whom we have never seen and never shall see in this life, is not a mere graceful sentiment or empty flourish of rhetoric, but a sober and solid fact. The hackneyed phrase, "a man and a brother," represents a vital truth. Every human being is one of our brethren, and, whether we like the responsibility or not, we are still our "brother's keeper." In our keeping, to a very real extent, lie the supreme issues of his spiritual life, and we have to look to it that we discharge our trust faithfully. We read with horror, and it may be with compassion, of the monstrous outrages committed by savage chiefs upon their subjects, their wives, or their enemies. We forget that the guilt of these things may lie partly at our door, because we have not done our part in helping forward civilizing influences which would have prevented such horrors, above all because we have not prayed as we ought for those who commit them. There are few of us who have not some opportunities of giving assistance in various ways to missionary enterprise and humanizing efforts. But all of us can at least pray for God's blessing upon such things, and for His mercy upon those who are in need of it. Of those who, having nothing else to give, give their struggles after holiness and their prayers for their fellow-men, the blessed commendation stands written, "They have done what they could."

"For kings and all that are in high place." It is quite a mistake to suppose that "kings" here means the Roman Emperors. This has been asserted, and from this misinterpretation has been deduced the erroneous conclusion that the letter must have been written at a time when it was customary for the Emperor to associate another prince with him in the empire, with a view to securing the succession. As Hadrian was the first to do this, and that near to the close of his reign, this letter (it is urged) cannot be earlier than a.d. 138. But this interpretation is impossible, for "kings" in the Greek has no article. Had the writer meant the two reigning Emperors, whether Hadrian and Antoninus, or M. Aurelius and Verus, he would inevitably have written "for *the* kings and for all in high place." The expression "for kings," obviously means "for monarchs of all descriptions," including the Roman Emperor, but including many other potentates also. Such persons, as having the heaviest responsibilities and the greatest power of doing good and evil, have an especial claim upon the prayers of Christians. It gives us a striking illustration of the transforming powers of Christianity when we think of St. Paul giving urgent directions that among the persons to be remembered first in the intercessions of the Church are Nero and the men whom he put "in high place," such as Otho and Vitellius, who afterwards became Emperor: and this, too, after Nero's peculiarly cruel and wanton persecution of the Christians a.d. 64. How firmly this beautiful practice became established among Christians, is shown from their writings in the second and third centuries. Tertullian, who lived through the reigns of such monsters as Commodus and Elagabalus, who remembered the persecution under M. Aurelius, and witnessed that under Septimius Severus, can nevertheless write thus of the Emperor of Rome: "A Christian is the enemy of no one, least of all of the Emperor, whom he knows to have been appointed by his God, and whom he therefore of necessity loves, and reverences, and honours, and desires his well-being, with that of the whole Roman Empire, so long as the world shall stand; for it shall last as long. To the Emperor, therefore, we render such homage as is lawful for us and good for him, as the human being who comes next to God, and is what he is by God's decree, and to God alone is inferior.... And so we sacrifice also for the well-being of the Emperor; but to our God and his; but in the way that God has ordained, with a prayer that is pure. For God, the Creator of the universe, has no need of odours or of blood."[35] In another passage Tertullian anticipates the objection that Christians pray for the Emperor, in order to curry favour with the Roman government and thus escape persecution. He says that the heathen have only to look into the Scriptures, which to Christians are the voice of God, and see that to pray for their enemies and to pray for those in authority is a fundamental rule with Christians. And he quotes the passage before us.[36] But he appears to misunderstand the concluding words of the Apostle's injunction,—"that we may lead a tranquil and quiet life in all godliness and gravity." Tertullian understands this as a reason for praying for kings and rulers; because they are the preservers of the public peace, and any disturbance in the empire will necessarily affect the Christians as well as other subjects,—which is giving a rather narrow and selfish motive for this great duty. "That we may lead a tranquil and quiet life in all godliness and gravity," is the object and consequence, not of our praying for kings and rulers in particular, but of our offering prayers and thanksgivings *on behalf of all men.*

When this most pressing obligation is duly discharged, then, and only then, can we hope with tranquil consciences to be able to live Christian lives in retirement from the rivalries and jealousies and squabbles of the world. Only in the attitude of mind which makes us pray and give thanks for our fellow-men is the tranquillity of a godly life possible. The enemies of Christian peace and quietness are anxiety and strife. Are we anxious about the well-being of those near and dear to us, or of those whose interests are bound up with our own? Let us pray for them. Have we grave misgivings respecting the course which events are taking in Church, or in State, or in any of the smaller societies to which we belong? Let us offer supplications and intercessions on behalf of all concerned in them. Prayer offered in faith to the throne of grace will calm our anxiety, because it will assure us that all is in God's hand, and that in His own good time He will bring good out of the evil. Are we at strife with our neighbours, and is this a constant source of disturbance? Let us pray for them. Fervent and frequent prayers for those who are hostile to us will certainly secure this much,—that we ourselves become more wary about giving provocation; and this will go a long way towards bringing the attainment of our desire for the entire cessation of the strife. Is there any one to whom we have taken a strong aversion, whose very presence is a trial to us, whose every gesture and every tone irritates us, and the sight of whose handwriting makes us shiver, because of its disturbing associations? Let us pray for him. Sooner or later dislike must give way to prayer. It is impossible to go on taking a real interest in the welfare of another, and at the same time to go on detesting him. And if our prayers for his welfare are genuine, a real interest in it there must be. Is there any one of whom we are jealous? Of whose popularity, so dangerous to our own, we are envious? Whose success—quite undeserved success, as it seems to us—disgusts and frightens us? Whose mishaps and failures, nay even whose faults and misdeeds, give us pleasure and satisfaction? Let us thank God for the favour which He bestows upon this man. Let us praise our heavenly Father for having in His wisdom and His justice given to another of His children what He denies to us; and let us pray Him to keep this other from abusing His gifts.

Yes, let us never forget that not only prayers but *thanksgivings* are to be offered *for all men*. He who is so good to the whole Church, of which we are members, and to the great human family to which we belong, certainly has claim upon the gratitude of every human being, and especially of every Christian. His bounty is not given by measure or by merit. He maketh His sun to shine upon the evil and the good, and sendeth His rain upon the just and the unjust: and shall we pick and choose as to what we will thank Him for, and what not? The sister who loves her erring or her half-witted brother is grateful to her father for the care which he bestows upon his graceless and his useless son. And shall we not give thanks to our heavenly Father for the benefits which He bestows on the countless multitudes whose interests are so closely interwoven with our own? Benefits bestowed upon any human being are an answer to our prayers, and as such we are bound to give thanks for them. How much more grateful shall we be, when we are able to look on them as benefits bestowed upon those whom we love!

This is the cause of so much of our failure in prayer. We do not couple our prayers with thanksgiving; or at any rate our thanksgivings are far less hearty than our prayers. We give thanks for benefits received by ourselves: we forget to give thanks "for all men." Above all, we forget that the truest gratitude is shown, not in words or feelings, but in conduct. We should send good deeds after good words to heaven. Not that our ingratitude provokes God to withhold His gifts; but that it does render us less capable of receiving them. For the sake of others no less than for ourselves let us remember the Apostle's charge that "thanksgivings be made for all men." We cannot give plenty and prosperity to the nations of the earth. We cannot bestow on them peace and tranquillity. We cannot bring them out of darkness to God's glorious light. We cannot raise them from impurity to holiness. We can only do a little, a very little, towards these great ends. But one thing we can do. We can at least thank Him who has already bestowed some, and is preparing to bestow others, of these blessings. We can praise Him for the end towards which He will have all things work.—"He willeth that *all* men should be saved" (ver. 4), "that God may be all in all."

FOOTNOTES:

[35] *Ad Scapulam*, ii.
[36] *Apol.*, xxxi.

CHAPTER IX
BEHAVIOUR IN CHRISTIAN WORSHIP: MEN'S ATTITUDE OF BODY AND MIND: WOMEN'S ATTIRE AND ORNAMENT

"I desire, therefore, that the men pray in every place, lifting up holy hands, without wrath and disputing. In like manner, that women adorn themselves in modest apparel, with shamefacedness and sobriety; not with braided hair, and gold or pearls or costly raiment; but (which becometh women professing godliness) through good works. Let a woman learn in quietness with all subjection. But I permit not a woman to teach, nor to have dominion over a man, but to be in quietness."—1 Tim. ii. 8–12.

In the preceding verses of this chapter, St. Paul has been insisting on the duty of unselfishness in our devotions. Our prayers and thanksgivings are not to be bounded in their scope by our own personal interests, but are to include the whole human race; and for this obvious and sufficient reason,— that in using such devotions we know that our desires are in harmony with the mind of God, "who willeth that *all* men should be saved, and come to the knowledge of the truth." Having thus laid down the principles which are to guide Christian congregations in the *subject-matter* of their prayers and thanksgivings, he passes on now to give some directions respecting the *behaviour* of men and women, when they meet together for common worship of the one God and the one Mediator between God and man, Christ Jesus.

There is no reasonable doubt (although the point has been disputed) that St. Paul is here speaking of public worship in the congregation; the whole context implies it. Some of the directions would be scarcely intelligible, if we were to suppose that the Apostle is thinking of private devotions, or even of family prayer in Christian households. And we are not to suppose that he is indirectly finding fault with other forms of worship, Jewish or heathen. He is merely laying down certain principles which are to guide Christians, whether at Ephesus or elsewhere, in the conduct of public service. Thus there is no special emphasis on "in every place," as if the meaning were,

"Our ways are not like those of the Jews; for they were not allowed to sacrifice and perform their services anywhere, but assembling from all parts of the world were bound to perform all their worship in the temple. For as Christ commanded us to pray for *all* men, because He died for all men, so it is good to pray *everywhere*."[37] Such an antithesis between Jewish and Christian worship, even if it were true, would not be in place here. Every place is a place of private prayer to both Jew and Christian alike: but not every place is a place of public prayer to the Christian any more than to the Jew.[38] Moreover, the Greek shows plainly that the emphasis is not on "in every place," but on "pray." Wherever there may be a customary "house of prayer," whether in Ephesus or anywhere else, the Apostle desires that prayers should be offered publicly by the men in the congregation. After "pray," the emphasis falls on "the men," public prayer is to be made, and it is to be conducted by the men and not by the women in the congregation.

It is evident from this passage, as from 1 Cor. xiv., that in this primitive Christian worship great freedom was allowed. There is no Bishop, President, or Elder, to whom the right of leading the service or uttering the prayers and thanksgivings is reserved. This duty and privilege is shared by all the males alike. In the recently discovered *Doctrine of the Twelve Apostles* nothing is said as to who is to offer the prayers, of which certain forms are given. It is merely stated that in addition to these forms *extempore* prayer may be offered by "the prophets." And Justin Martyr mentions that a similar privilege was allowed to "the president" of the congregation according to his ability.[39] Thus we seem to trace a gradual increase of strictness, a development of ecclesiastical order, very natural under the circumstances. First, all the men in the congregation are allowed to conduct public worship, as here and in 1 Corinthians. Then, the right of adding to the prescribed forms is restricted to the prophets, as in the *Didache*. Next, this right is reserved to the presiding minister, as in Justin Martyr. And lastly, free prayer is abolished altogether. We need not assume that precisely this development took place in all the Churches; but that something analogous took place in nearly all. Nor need we assume that the development was simultaneous: while one Church was at one stage of the process, another was more advanced, and a third less so. Again, we may conjecture that forms of prayer gradually increased in number, and in extent, and in stringency. But in the directions here given to Timothy we are at the beginning of the development.

"Lifting up holy hands." Here again we need not suspect any polemical purpose. St. Paul is not insinuating that, when Gnostics or heathen lift up their hands in prayer, their hands are not holy. Just as every Christian is ideally a saint, so every hand that is lifted up in prayer is holy. In thus stating the ideal, the Apostle inculcates the realization of it. There is a monstrous incongruity in one who comes red-handed from the commission of a sin, lifting up the very members which witness against him, in order to implore a blessing from the God whom he has outraged. The same idea is expressed in more general terms by St. Peter: "Like as He which called you is holy, be ye yourselves also holy in all manner of living; because it is written, ye shall be holy; for I am holy" (1 Pet. i. 15, 16). In a passage more closely parallel to this, Clement of Rome says, "Let us therefore approach Him in holiness of soul, *lifting up pure and undefiled hands unto Him*, with love towards our gentle and compassionate Father who made us an elect portion unto Himself" (*Cor.* xxix). And Tertullian urges that "a defiled spirit cannot be recognized by the Holy Spirit" (*De Orat.*, xiii). Nowhere else in the New Testament do we read of this attitude of lifting up the hands during prayer. But to this day it is common in the East. Solomon at the dedication of the temple "stood before the altar of the Lord in the presence of all the congregation of Israel, and *spread forth his hands toward heaven*" (1 Kings viii. 22); and the Psalmist repeatedly speaks of "lifting up the hands" in worship (xxviii. 2; lxiii. 4; cxxxiv. 2). Clement of Alexandria seems to have regarded it as the ideal attitude in prayer, as symbolizing the desire of the body to abstract itself from the earth, following the eagerness of the spirit in yearning for heavenly things.[40] Tertullian, on the other hand, suggests that the arms are spread out in prayer in memory of the crucifixion, and directs that they should be extended, but only slightly raised, an attitude which is more in harmony with a humble spirit: and in another place he says that the Christian by his very posture in prayer is ready for every infliction. He asserts that the Jews in his day did *not* raise the hands in prayer, and characteristically gives as a reason that they were stained with the blood of the Prophets and of Christ. With evident reference to this passage, he says that Christian hands must be lifted up pure from falsehood, murder, and all other sins of which the hands can be the instruments.[41] Ancient Christian monuments of the earliest age frequently represent the faithful as standing with raised hands to pray. Eusebius tells us that Constantine had himself represented in this attitude on his coins, "looking upwards, stretching up toward God, like one praying."[42] Of course this does not mean that kneeling was unusual or irregular; there is plenty of evidence to the contrary. But the attitude here commended by St. Paul was very ancient when he wrote, and has continued in some parts of the world ever since. Like so many other things in natural religion and in Judaism, it received a new and intensified meaning when it was adopted among the usages of the Christian Church.

"Without wrath and disputing:" that is, in the spirit of Christian peace and trust. Ill-will and misgiving respecting one another are incompatible with united prayer to our common Father. The atmosphere of controversy is not congenial to devotion. Christ Himself has told us to be reconciled to our brother before presuming to offer our gift on the altar. In a similar spirit St. Paul directs that those who are to conduct public service in the sanctuary must do so without angry feelings or mutual distrust. In the Pastoral Epistles warnings against quarrelsome conduct are frequent; and the experience of every one of us tells us how necessary they are. The bishop is charged to be "no brawler, no striker; but gentle, not contentious." The deacons must not be "double-tongued." Women must not be "slanderers." Young widows have to be on their guard against being "tattlers and busybodies." Timothy is charged to "follow after ... love, patience, meekness," and is reminded that "the Lord's servant must not strive, but be gentle towards all, apt to teach, forbearing, in meekness correcting them that oppose themselves." Titus again is told that a bishop must be "not self-willed, not soon angry," "no brawler, no striker," that the aged women must not be "slanderers," that all men are to be put in mind "to speak evil of no man, not to be contentious, to be gentle, showing all meekness toward all men."[43] There is no need to assume that that age, or that those Churches, had any special need of warnings of this kind. All ages and all Churches need them. To keep one's tongue and one's temper in due order is to all of us one of the most constant and necessary duties of the Christian life; and the neglect cannot fail to be disastrous to the reality and efficacy of our devotions. Those who have ill-will and strife in their hearts cannot unite to much purpose in common thanksgiving and prayer.

And just as the men have to take care that their attitude of body and mind is such as befits the dignity of public worship, in like manner the women also have to take care that their presence in the congregation does not appear incongruous. They must come in seemly attire and with seemly behaviour. Everything which might divert attention from the service to themselves must be avoided. Modesty and simplicity must at all times be the characteristics of a Christian woman's dress and bearing; but at no time is this more necessary than in the public services of the Church. Excessive adornment, out of place at all times, is grievously offensive there. It gives a flat contradiction to the profession of humility which is involved in taking part in common worship, and to that natural sobriety which is a woman's fairest ornament and best protection. Both reverence and self-reverence are injured by it. Moreover, it may easily be a cause of offence to others, by provoking jealousy or admiration of the creature, where all ought to be absorbed in the worship of the Creator.

Here again St. Paul is putting his finger upon dangers and evils which are not peculiar to any age or any Church. He had spoken of the same thing years before, to the women of Corinth, and St. Peter utters similar warnings to Christian women throughout all time.[44] Clement of Alexandria abounds in protests against the extravagance in dress so common in his own day. In one place he says; "Apelles the painter seeing one of his pupils painting a figure thickly with gold colour to represent Helen, said to him; 'My lad, you were unable to paint her beautiful, and so you have made her rich.' Such Helens are the ladies of the present day; not really beautiful, but richly got up. To these the Spirit prophesies by Zephaniah: And their gold shall not be able to deliver them in the day of the Lord's anger."[45] Tertullian is not less emphatic. He says that most Christian women dress like heathen, as if modesty required nothing more than stopping short of actual impurity. "What is the use," he asks, "of showing a decent and Christian simplicity in your face, while you load the rest of your body with the dangling absurdities of pomps and vanities?"[46] Chrysostom also, in commenting on this very passage, asks the congregation at Antioch: "And what then is *modest apparel*? Such as covers them completely and decently, and not with superfluous ornaments; for the one is decent and the other is not. What? Do you approach God to pray with broidered hair and ornaments of gold? Are you come to a ball? to a marriage-feast? to a carnival? There such costly things might have been seasonable: here not one of them is wanted. You are come to pray, to ask pardon for your sins, to plead for your offences, beseeching the Lord, and hoping to render Him propitious to you. Away with such hypocrisy! God is not mocked. This is the attire of actors and dancers, who live upon the stage. Nothing of this kind becomes a modest woman, who should be adorned with shamefastness and sobriety.... And if St. Paul" (he continues) "would remove those things which are merely the marks of wealth, as gold, pearls, and costly array; how much more those things which imply studied adornment, as painting, colouring the eyes, a mincing walk, an affected voice, a languishing look? For he glances at all these things in speaking of modest apparel and shamefastness."

But there is no need to go to Corinth in the first century, or Alexandria and Carthage in the second and third, or Antioch in the fourth, in order to show that the Apostle was giving no unnecessary warning in admonishing Timothy respecting the dress and behaviour of Christian women, especially in the public services of the congregation. In our own age and our own Church we can find abundant illustration. Might not any preacher in any fashionable congregation echo with a good deal of point the questions of Chrysostom? "Have you come to dance or a levée? Have you mistaken this building for a theatre?" And what would be the language of a Chrysostom or a Paul if he were to enter a theatre nowadays and see the attire, I will not say of the actresses, but of the audience? There are some rough epithets, not often heard in polite society, which express in plain language the condition of those women who by their manner of life and conversation have forfeited their characters. Preachers in earlier ages were accustomed to speak very plainly about such things: and what the Apostle and Chrysostom have written in their epistles and homilies does not leave us in much doubt as to what would have been their manner of speaking of them.

But what is urged here is sufficient. "You are Christian women," says St. Paul, "and the profession which you have adopted is reverence towards God (θεοσέβειαν). This profession you have made known to the world. It is necessary, therefore, that those externals of which the world takes cognisance should not give the lie to your profession. And how is unseemly attire, paraded at the very time of public worship, compatible with the reverence which you have professed? Reverence God by reverencing yourselves; by guarding with jealous care the dignity of those bodies with which He has endowed you. Reverence God by coming before Him clothed both in body and soul in fitting attire. Let your bodies be freed from meretricious decoration. Let your souls be adorned with abundance of good works."

FOOTNOTES:

[37] So Chrysostom *in loco*: but this is an exaggeration respecting Jewish limitations.

[38] See Clement of Rome, *Cor.* xli.

[39] *Didache*, x. 7; Just. Mart., *Apol.*, 1. lxvii. Justin probably uses the term "president" ὁ προεστώς in order to be intelligible to heathen readers.

[40] *Strom.*, VII. vii.

[41] *De Orat.*, xiii., xiv., xvii.; *Apol.* xxx.; Comp. *Adv. Jud.*, x.

[42] *Vit. Const.*, IV. xv. 1.

[43] 1 Tim. iii. 3, 8, 11; v. 13; vi. 11; 2 Tim. ii. 24; Tit. i. 7; ii. 3; iii. 2.

[44] 1 Cor. xi. 2–16; 1 Pet. iii. 3, 4.

[45] *Pæd.*, II. xiii.

[46] *De Cult Fem.*, II. i. ix.

CHAPTER X
ORIGIN OF THE CHRISTIAN MINISTRY; VARIOUS CERTAINTIES AND PROBABILITIES DISTINGUISHED

"If a man seeketh the office of a bishop, he desireth a good work. The bishop therefore must be without reproach, the husband of one wife, temperate, sober-minded, orderly, given to hospitality, apt to teach; no brawler, no striker; but gentle, not contentious, no lover of money; one that ruleth well his own house, having his children in subjection with all gravity; (but if a man knoweth not how to rule his own house, how shall he take care of the house of God?) not a novice, lest being puffed up he fall into the condemnation of the devil. Moreover he must have good testimony from them that are without; lest he fall into reproach and the snare of the devil. Deacons in like manner must be grave, not double-tongued, not given to much wine, not greedy of filthy lucre; holding the mystery of the faith in a pure conscience. And let these also first be proved; then let them serve as deacons, if they be blameless."—1 Tim. iii. 1–10.

This passage is one of the most important in the New Testament respecting the Christian ministry; and in the Pastoral Epistles it does not stand alone. Of the two classes of ministers mentioned here, one is again touched upon in the Epistle to Titus (i. 5–9), and the qualifications for this office, which is evidently the superior of the two, are stated in terms not very different from those which are used in the passage before us. Therefore a series of expositions upon the Pastoral Epistles would be culpably incomplete which did not attempt to arrive at some conclusions respecting the question of the primitive Christian ministry; a question which at the present time is being investigated with immense industry and interest, and with some clear and substantial results. The time is probably far distant when the last word will have been said upon the subject; for it is one on which considerable difference of opinion is not only possible but reasonable: and those persons would seem to be least worthy of consideration, who are most confident that they are in possession of the whole truth on the subject. One of the first requisites in the examination of questions of fact is a power of accurately distinguishing what is certain from what is not certain: and the person who is confident that he has attained to certainty, when the evidence in his possession does not at all warrant certainty, is not a trustworthy guide.

It would be impossible in a discussion of moderate length to touch upon all the points which have been raised in connexion with this problem; but some service will have been rendered if a few of the more important features of the question are pointed out and classified under the two heads just indicated, as certain or not certain. In any scientific enquiry, whether historical or experimental, this classification is a useful one, and very often leads to the enlargement of the class of certainties. When the group of certainties has been properly investigated, and when the various items have been placed in their proper relations to one another and to the whole of which they are only constituent parts, the result is likely to be a transfer of other items from the domain of what is only probable or possible to the domain of what is certain.

At the outset it is necessary to place a word of caution as to what is meant, in a question of this kind, by *certainty*. There are no limits to scepticism, as the history of speculative philosophy has abundantly shown. It is possible to question one's own existence, and still more possible to question the irresistible evidence of one's senses or the irresistible conclusions of one's reason. *A fortiori* it is possible to throw doubt upon any historical fact. We can, if we like, classify the assassinations of Julius Cæsar and of Cicero, and the genuineness of the Æneid and of the Epistles to the Corinthians, among things that are not certain. They cannot be demonstrated like a proposition in Euclid or an experiment in chemistry or physics. But a sceptical criticism of this kind makes history impossible; for it demands as a condition of certainty a kind of evidence, and an amount of evidence, which from the nature of the case is unattainable. Juries are directed by the courts to treat evidence as adequate, which they would be willing to recognize as such in matters of very serious moment to themselves. There is a certain amount of evidence which to a person of trained and well-balanced mind makes a thing "practically certain:" *i.e.*, with this amount of evidence before him he would confidently act on the assumption that the thing was true.

In the question before us there are four or five things which may with great reason be treated as practically certain.

1. The solution of the question as to the origin of the Christian ministry, *has no practical bearing upon the lives of Christians*. For us the problem is one of historical interest without moral import. As students of Church

History we are bound to investigate the *origines* of the ministry which has been one of the chief factors in that history: but our loyalty as members of the Church will not be affected by the result of our investigations. Our duty towards the constitution consisting of bishops, priests, and deacons, which existed unchallenged from the close of the second century to the close of the Middle Ages, and which has existed down to the present day in all the three great branches of the Catholic Church, Roman, Oriental, and Anglican, is no way affected by the question whether the constitution of the Church during the century which separates the writings of St. John from the writings of his disciple's disciple, Irenæus, was as a rule episcopal, collegiate, or presbyterian. For a churchman who accepts the episcopal form of government as essential to the well-being of a Church, the enormous prescription which that form has acquired during at least seventeen centuries, is such ample justification, that he can afford to be serene as to the outcome of enquiries respecting the constitution of the various infant Churches from a.d. 85 to a.d. 185. It makes no practical difference either to add, or not to add, to an authority which is already ample. To prove that the episcopal form of government was founded by the Apostles may have been a matter of great practical importance in the middle of the second century. But, before that century had closed, the practical question, *if there ever was one*, had settled itself. God's providence ordained that the universal form of Church government should be the episcopal form and should continue to be such; and for us it adds little to its authority to know that the way in which it became universal was through the instrumentality and influence of Apostles. On the other hand, to prove that episcopacy was established independently of Apostolic influence would detract very little from its accumulated authority.

2. A second point, which may be regarded as certain with regard to this question, is, that *for the period which joins the age of Irenæus to the age of St. John, we have not sufficient evidence to arrive at anything like proof*. The evidence has received important additions during the present century, and still more important additions are by no means impossible; but at present our materials are still inadequate. And the evidence is insufficient in two ways. First, although surprisingly large as compared with what might have been reasonably expected, yet in itself, the literature of this period is fragmentary and scanty. Secondly, the dates of some of the most important witnesses cannot as yet be accurately determined. In many cases to be able to fix the date of a document within twenty or thirty years is quite sufficient: but this is a case in which the difference of twenty years is a really serious difference; and there is fully that amount of uncertainty as to the date of some of the writings which are our principal sources of information; *e.g.*, the *Doctrine*

of the Twelve Apostles, the Epistles of Ignatius, the *Shepherd of Hermas* and the *Clementines*. Here also our position may improve. Further research may enable us to date some of these documents accurately. But, for the present, uncertainty about precise dates and general scantiness of evidence compel us to admit that with regard to many of the points connected with this question nothing that can fairly be called proof is possible respecting the interval which separates the last quarter of the first century from the last quarter of the second.

This feature of the problem is sometimes represented by the useful metaphor that the history of the Church just at this period "passes through a tunnel" or "runs underground." We are in the light of day during most of the time covered by the New Testament; and we are again in the light of day directly we reach the time covered by the abundant writings of Irenæus, Clement of Alexandria, Tertullian, and others. But during the intervening period we are, not indeed in total darkness, but in a passage the obscurity of which is only slightly relieved by an occasional lamp or light-hole. Leaving this tantalizing interval, about which the one thing that is certain is that many certainties are not likely to be found in it, we pass on to look for our two next certainties in the periods which precede and follow it.

3. In the period covered by the New Testament it is certain that the Church had officers who discharged spiritual functions which were not discharged by ordinary Christians; in other words *a distinction was made from the first between clergy and laity*. Of this fact the Pastoral Epistles contain abundant evidence; and further evidence is scattered up and down the New Testament, from the earliest document in the volume to the last. In the First Epistle to the Thessalonians, which is certainly the earliest Christian writing that has come down to us, we find St. Paul beseeching the Church of the Thessalonians "to know them that *labour among you*, and *are over you in the Lord*, and *admonish* you; and to esteem them exceeding highly in love for their work's sake" (v. 12, 13). The three functions here enumerated are evidently functions to be exercised by a few with regard to the many: they are not duties which every one is to discharge towards every one. In the Third Epistle of St. John, which is certainly one of the latest, and perhaps the very latest, of the writings contained in the New Testament, the incident about Diotrephes seems to show that not only ecclesiastical government, but ecclesiastical government by a single official, was already in existence in the Church in which Diotrephes "loved to have the pre-eminence" (9, 10). In between these two we have the exhortation in the Epistle to the Hebrews: "Obey them that *have the rule over you* and submit to them: for they watch in behalf of your *souls*, as they that shall give account" (xiii. 17). And directly we go outside the New Testament and look at the Epistle of

the Church of Rome to the Church of Corinth, commonly called the First Epistle of Clement, we find the same distinction between clergy and laity observed. In this letter, which almost certainly was written during the lifetime of St. John, we read that the Apostles, "preaching everywhere in country and town, appointed their firstfruits, when they had proved them by the Spirit, to be bishops and deacons unto them that should believe. And this they did in no new fashion; for indeed it had been written concerning bishops and deacons from very ancient times; for thus saith the scripture in a certain place, I will appoint their bishops in righteousness, and their deacons in faith"—the last words being an inaccurate quotation of the LXX. of Isa. lx. 17. And a little further on Clement writes: "Our Apostles knew through our Lord Jesus Christ that there would be strife over the name of the bishop's office. For this cause, therefore, having received complete fore-knowledge, they appointed the aforesaid persons, and afterwards they provided a continuance, that if these should fall asleep, other approved men should succeed to their ministration. Those therefore who were appointed by them, or afterward by other men of repute with the consent of the whole Church, and have ministered unblamably to the flock of Christ in lowliness of mind, peacefully and with all modesty, and for long time have borne a good report with all—these men we consider to be unjustly thrust out from their ministration. For it will be no light sin for us, if we thrust out those who have offered the gifts of the bishop's office unblamably and holily. Blessed are those presbyters who have gone before, seeing that their departure was fruitful and ripe, for they have no fear lest any one should remove them from their appointed place. For we see that ye have displaced certain persons, though they were living honourably, from the ministration which they had kept blamelessly" (xlii., xliv.).

Three things come out very clearly from this passage, confirming what has been found in the New Testament. (1) There is a clear distinction made between clergy and laity. (2) This distinction is not a temporary arrangement, but is the basis of a permanent organization. (3) A person who has been duly promoted to the ranks of the clergy as a presbyter or bishop (the two titles being here synonymous, as in the Epistle to Titus) holds that position for life. Unless he is guilty of some serious offence, to depose him is no light sin.

None of these passages, either in the New Testament or in Clement, tell us very clearly the precise nature of the functions which the clergy, as distinct from the laity, were to discharge; yet they indicate that these functions were of a spiritual rather than of a secular character, that they concerned men's souls rather than their bodies, and that they were connected with religious service (λειτουργία). But the one thing which is quite clear is this,—that the

Church had, and was always intended to have, a body of officers distinct from the congregations to which they ministered and over which they ruled.

4. For our fourth certainty we resort to the time when the history of the Church returns once more to the full light of day, in the last quarter of the second century. Then we find two things quite clearly established, which have continued in Christendom from that day to this. We find a *regularly organized clergy*, not only distinctly marked off from the laity, but distinctly *marked off among themselves by well defined gradations of rank*. And, secondly, we find that *each local Church is constitutionally governed by one chief officer*, whose powers are large and seldom resisted, and *who universally receives the title of bishop*. To these two points we may add a third. There is no trace of any belief, or even suspicion, that the constitution of these local Churches had ever been anything else. On the contrary, the evidence (and it is considerable) points to the conclusion that Christians in the latter part of the second century—say a.d. 180 to 200—were fully persuaded that the episcopal form of government had prevailed in the different Churches from the Apostles' time to their own. Just as in the case of the Gospels, Irenæus and his contemporaries not only do not know of either more or less than the four which have come down to us, but cannot conceive of there ever being either more or less than these four: so in the case of Church Government, they not only represent episcopacy as everywhere prevalent in their time, but they have no idea that at any previous time any other form of government prevailed. And although Irenæus, like St. Paul and Clement of Rome, sometimes speaks of bishops under the title of presbyter, yet it is quite clear that there were at that time presbyters who were not bishops and who did not possess episcopal authority. Irenæus himself was such a presbyter, until the martyrdom of Pothinus in the persecution of a.d. 177 created a vacancy in the see of Lyons, which Irenæus was then called upon to fill; and he held the see for upwards of twenty years, from about a.d. 180 to 202. From Irenæus and from his contemporary Dionysius, Bishop of Corinth, we learn not only the fact that episcopacy prevailed everywhere, but, in not a few cases, the name of the existing bishop; and in some cases the names of their predecessors are given up to the times of the Apostles. Thus, in the case of the Church of Rome, Linus the first bishop is connected with "the two most glorious Apostles Peter and Paul": and, in the case of Athens, Dionysius the Areopagite is said to have been appointed first bishop of that Church by the Apostle Paul. This may or may not be correct: but at least it shows that in the time of Irenæus and Dionysius of Corinth episcopacy was not only recognized as the universal form of Church government, but was also believed to have prevailed in the principal Churches from the very earliest times.[47]

5. If we narrow our field and look, not at the whole Church, but at the Churches of Asia Minor and Syria, we may obtain yet another certainty from the obscure period which lies between the age of the Apostles and that of Dionysius and Irenæus. The investigations of Lightfoot, Zahn, and Harnack have placed the genuineness of the short Greek form of the Epistles of Ignatius beyond reasonable dispute. Their exact date cannot as yet be determined. The evidence is strong that Ignatius was martyred in the reign of Trajan: and, if that is accepted, the letters cannot be later than a.d. 117. But even if this evidence be rejected as not conclusive, and the letters be dated ten or twelve years later, their testimony will still be of the utmost importance. They prove that long before a.d. 150 episcopacy was the recognized form of government throughout the Churches of Asia Minor and Syria; and, as Ignatius speaks of "the bishops that are settled *in the farthest parts of the earth* (κατὰ τὰ πέρατα ὁρισθέντες)" they prove that, according to his belief, episcopacy was the recognized form everywhere (*Ephes.* iii.). This evidence is not a little strengthened by the fact that, as all sound critics on both sides are now agreed, the Epistles of Ignatius were evidently not written in order to magnify the episcopal office, or to preach up the episcopal system. The writer's main object is to deprecate schism and all that might tend to schism. And in his opinion the best way to avoid schism is to keep closely united to the bishop. Thus, the magnifying of the episcopal office comes about incidentally; because Ignatius takes for granted that everywhere there is a bishop in each Church, who is the duly appointed ruler of it, loyalty to whom will be a security against all schismatical tendencies.

These four or five points being regarded as established to an extent which may reasonably be called certainty, there remain certain other points about which certainty is not yet possible, some of which admit of a probable solution, while for others there is so little evidence that we have to fall back upon mere conjecture. Among these would be the distinctions of office, or gradations of rank, among the clergy in the first century or century and a half after the Ascension, the precise functions assigned to each office, and the manner of appointment. With regard to these questions three positions may be assumed with a considerable amount of probability.

1. There was a distinction made between itinerant or missionary clergy and stationary or localized clergy. Among the former we find apostles (who are a much larger body than the Twelve), prophets, and evangelists. Among the latter we have two orders, spoken of as bishops and deacons, as here and in the Epistle to the Philippians (i. 1) as well as in the *Doctrine of the Twelve Apostles*, presbyter or elder being sometimes used as synonymous with bishop. This distinction between an itinerant and a stationary ministry appears in the First Epistle to the Corinthians (xii. 28), in the Epistle to

the Ephesians (iv. 11), and perhaps also in the Acts of the Apostles and in the Epistles of St. John. In the *Doctrine of the Twelve Apostles* it is clearly marked.

2. There seems to have been a further distinction between those who did, and those who did not, possess supernatural prophetical gifts. The title of prophet was commonly, but perhaps not exclusively, given to those who possessed this gift: and the *Doctrine of the Twelve Apostles* shows a great respect for prophets. But the distinction naturally died out when these supernatural gifts ceased to be manifested. During the process of extinction serious difficulty arose as to the test of a genuine prophet. Some fanatical persons believed themselves to be prophets, and some dishonest persons pretended to be prophets, when they were not such. The office appears to have been extinct when Ignatius wrote: by prophets he always means the prophets of the Old Testament. Montanism was probably a forlorn attempt to revive this much desired office after the Church as a whole had decided against it. Further discussion of the gift of prophecy in the New Testament will be found in a previous chapter (vi.).

3. The clergy were not elected by the congregation as its delegates or representatives, deputed to perform functions which originally could be discharged by any Christian. They were appointed by the Apostles and their successors or substitutes. Where the congregation selected or recommended candidates, as in the case of the Seven Deacons (Acts vi. 4–6), they did not themselves lay hands on them. The typical act of laying on of hands was always performed by those who were already ministers, whether apostles, prophets, or elders. Whatever else was still open to the laity, this act of ordaining was not. And there is good reason for believing that the celebration of the Eucharist also was from the first reserved to the clergy, and that all ministers, excepting prophets, were expected to use a prescribed form of words in celebrating it.

But, although much still remains untouched, this discussion must draw to a close. In the ideal Church there is no Lord's Day or holy seasons, for all days are the Lord's, and all seasons are holy; there are no places especially dedicated to God's worship, for the whole universe is His temple; there are no persons especially ordained to be His ministers, for all His people are priests and prophets. But in the Church as it exists in a sinful world, the attempt to make all times and all places holy ends in the desecration of all alike; and the theory that all Christians are priests becomes indistinguishable from the theory that none are such. In this matter let us not try to be wiser than God, Whose will may be discerned in His providential guiding of His Church throughout so many centuries. The attempt to reproduce Paradise or to anticipate heaven in a state of society which does not possess the conditions of Paradise or heaven, can end in nothing but disastrous confusion.

In conclusion the following weighty words are gratefully quoted. They come with special force from one who does not himself belong to an Episcopalian Church.

"By our reception or denial of priesthood in the Church, our entire view of what the Church is must be affected and moulded. We shall either accept the idea of a visible and organized body, within which Christ rules by means of a ministry, sacraments, and ordinances to which He has attached a blessing, *the fulness of which we have no right to look for except through the channels He has ordained* (and it ought to be needless to say that this is the Presbyterian idea), or we shall rest satisfied with the thought of the Church as consisting of multitudes of individual souls known to God alone, as invisible, unorganized, with ordinances blessed because of the memories which they awaken, but to which no promise of present grace is tied, with, in short, no thought of a Body of Christ in the world, but only of a spiritual and heavenly principle ruling in the hearts and regulating the lives of men. Conceptions of the Church so widely different from each other cannot fail to affect in the most vital manner the Church's life and relation to those around her. Yet both conceptions are the logical and necessary result of the acceptance or denial of the idea of a divinely appointed and still living priesthood among men."[48]

FOOTNOTES:

[47] See an admirable article on the Christian ministry by Dr. Salmon in the *Expositor* for July, 1887; also the present writer's *Church of the Early Fathers*, pp. 58 ff.; 92 ff.; 2nd ed. Longmans, 1887.

[48] Professor W. Milligan, D.D., on "The Idea of the Priesthood," in the *Expositor* for July, 1888, p. 7.

CHAPTER XI
THE APOSTLE'S RULE RESPECTING SECOND MARRIAGES; ITS MEANING AND PRESENT OBLIGATION

"The husband of one wife."—1 Tim. iii. 2.

The Apostle here states, as one of the first qualifications to be looked for in a person who is to be ordained a bishop, that he must be "husband of one wife." The precise meaning of this phrase will probably never cease to be discussed. But, although it must be admitted that the phrase is capable of bearing several meanings, yet it cannot be fairly contended that the meaning is seriously doubtful. The balance of probability is so largely in favour of one of the meanings, that the remainder may be reasonably set aside as having no valid ground for being supported in competition with it.

Three passages in which the phrase occurs have to be considered together, and these have to be compared with a fourth. (1) There is the passage before us about a bishop, (2) another in ver. 12 about deacons, and (3) another in Tit. i. 6 about elders or presbyters, whom St. Paul afterwards mentions under the title of bishop. In these three passages we have it plainly set forth that Timothy and Titus are to regard it as a necessary qualification in a bishop or elder or presbyter, and also in a deacon, that he should be a "man of one woman" or "husband of one wife" (μιᾶς γυναικὸς ἀνήρ). In the fourth passage (1 Tim. v. 9) he gives as a necessary qualification of one who is to be placed on the roll of church widows, that she must be a "woman of one man" or "wife of one husband" (ἑνὸς ἀνδρὸς γυνή). This fourth passage is of much importance in determining the meaning of the converse expression in the other three passages.

There are four main interpretations of the expression in question.

1. That which the phrase at once suggests to a modern mind,—that the person to be ordained bishop or deacon must have only one wife and not more; that he must not be a *polygamist*. According to this interpretation, therefore, we are to understand the Apostle to mean, that a Jew or barbarian with more wives than one might be admitted to baptism and become a member of the congregation, but ought not to be admitted to the ministry.

This explanation, which at first sight looks simple and plausible, will not bear inspection. It is quite true that polygamy in St. Paul's day still existed among the Jews. Justin Martyr, in the *Dialogue with Trypho*, says to the Jews, "It is better for you to follow God than your senseless and blind teachers, who even to this day allow you each to have four and five wives" (§ 134). But polygamy in the Roman Empire must have been rare. It was forbidden by Roman law, which did not allow a man to have more than one lawful wife at a time, and treated every simultaneous second marriage, not only as null and void, but infamous. Where it was practised it must have been practised secretly. It is probable that, when St. Paul wrote to Timothy and Titus, not a single polygamist had been converted to the Christian faith. Polygamists were exceedingly rare inside the Empire, and the Church had not yet spread beyond it. Indeed, our utter ignorance as to the way in which the primitive Church dealt with polygamists who wished to become Christians, amounts to something like proof that such cases were extremely uncommon. How improbable, therefore, that St. Paul should think it worth while to charge both Timothy and Titus that converted polygamists must not be admitted to the office of bishop, when there is no likelihood that any one of them knew of a single instance of a polygamist who had become a Christian! On these grounds alone this interpretation of the phrase might be safely rejected.

But these grounds do not stand alone. There is the convincing evidence of the converse phrase, "wife of one husband." If men with more than one wife were very rare in the Roman Empire, what are we to think of women with more than one husband? Even among the barbarians outside the Empire, such a thing as a plurality of husbands was regarded as monstrous. It is incredible that St. Paul could have had any such case in his mind, when he mentioned the qualification "wife of one husband." Moreover, as the question before him was one relating to widows, this "wife of one husband" must be a person who at the time had *no* husband. The phrase, therefore, can only mean a woman who after the death of her husband has not married again. Consequently the converse expression, "husband of one wife," cannot have any reference to polygamy.

2. Far more worthy of consideration is the view that what is aimed at in both cases is not polygamy, but *divorce*. Divorce, as we know from abundant evidence, was very frequent both among the Jews and the Romans in the first century of the Christian era. Among the former it provoked the special condemnation of Christ: and one of the many influences which Christianity had upon Roman law was to diminish the facilities for divorce. According to Jewish practice the husband could obtain a divorce for very trivial reasons; and in the time of St. Paul Jewish women sometimes took the initiative. According to Roman practice either husband or wife could obtain a divorce

very easily. Abundant instances are on record, and that in the case of people of high character, such as Cicero. After the divorce either of the parties could marry again; and often enough both of them did so; therefore in the Roman Empire in St. Paul's day there must have been plenty of persons of both sexes who had been divorced once or twice and had married again. There is nothing improbable in the supposition that quite a sufficient number of such persons had been converted to Christianity to make it worth while to legislate respecting them. They might be admitted to baptism; but they must not be admitted to an official position in the Church. A regulation of this kind might be all the more necessary, because in a wealthy capital like Ephesus it would probably be among the upper and more influential classes that divorces would be most frequent; and from precisely these classes, when any of them had become Christians, officials would be likely to be chosen. This explanation, therefore, of the phrases "husband of one wife" and "wife of one husband" cannot be condemned, like the first, as utterly incredible. It has a fair amount of probability: but it remains to be seen whether another explanation (which really includes this one) has not a far greater amount.

3. We may pass over without much discussion the view that the phrases are a vague way of indicating *misconduct of any kind in reference to marriage*. No doubt such misconduct was rife among the heathen, and the Christian Church by no means escaped the taint, as the scandals in the Church of Corinth and the frequent warnings of the Apostles against sins of this kind show. But when St. Paul has to speak of such things he is not afraid to do so in language that cannot be misunderstood. We have seen this already in the first chapter of this Epistle; and the fifth chapters of 1 Corinthians, Galatians, and Ephesians supply other examples. We may safely say that if St. Paul had meant to indicate persons who had entered into illicit unions before or after marriage, he would have used much less ambiguous language than the phrases under discussion.

4. There remains the view, which from the first has been the dominant one, that these passages all refer to *second marriage after the first marriage has been dissolved by death*. A widower who has married a second wife ought not to be admitted to the ministry; a widow who has married a second husband ought not to be placed on the roll of Church widows. This interpretation is reasonable in itself, is in harmony with the context and with what St. Paul says elsewhere about marriage, and is confirmed by the views taken of second marriages in the case of clergy by the early Church.

(*a*) The belief that St. Paul was opposed to the ordination of persons who had contracted a second marriage is reasonable in itself. A second marriage, although perfectly lawful and in some cases advisable, was so far a sign of weakness; and a double family would in many cases be a serious hindrance to work. The Church could not afford to enlist any but its strongest men among its officers; and its officers must not be hampered more than other men with domestic cares. Moreover, the heathen certainly felt a special respect for the *univira*, the woman who did not enter into a second marriage; and there is some reason for believing that second marriages were sometimes thought unfitting in the case of men, *e.g.*, in the case of certain priests. Be that as it may, we may safely conclude that, both by Christians and heathen, persons who had abstained from marrying again would so far be more respected than those who had not abstained.

(*b*) This interpretation is in harmony with the context. In the passage before us the qualification which immediately precedes the expression, "husband of one wife," is "without reproach"; in the Epistle to Titus it is "blameless." In each case the meaning seems to be that there must be nothing in the past or present life of the candidate, which could afterwards with any show of reason be urged against him as inconsistent with his office. He must be above and not below the average of men; and *therefore* he must not have been twice married.

(*c*) This agrees with what St. Paul says elsewhere about marriage. His statements are clear and consistent, and it is a mistake to suppose that there is any want of harmony between what is said in this Epistle and what is said to the Corinthian Church on this subject. The Apostle strongly upholds the lawfulness of marriage for all (1 Cor. vii. 28, 36; 1 Tim. iv. 3). For *those who are equal to it*, whether single or widowed, he considers that their remaining as they are is the more blessed condition (1 Cor. vii. 1, 7, 8, 32, 34, 40; 1 Tim. v. 7). But so few persons are equal to this, that it is prudent for those who desire to marry to do so, and for those who desire to marry again to do so (1 Cor. vii. 2, 9, 39; 1 Tim. v. 14). These being his convictions, is it not reasonable to suppose, that in selecting ministers for the Church he would look for them in the class which had given proof of moral strength by remaining unmarried or by not marrying a second time. In an age of such boundless licentiousness continency won admiration and respect; and a person who had given clear evidence of such self-control would have his moral influence thereby increased. Few things impress barbarous and semi-barbarous people more than to see a man having full control over passions to which they themselves are slaves. In the terrific odds which the infant Church had to encounter, this was a point well worth turning to advantage.

And here we may note St. Paul's wisdom in giving no preference to those who had not married at all over those who had married only once.

Had he done so, he would have played into the hands of those heretics who disparaged wedlock. And perhaps he had seen something of the evils which abounded among the celibate priests of heathenism. It is quite obvious, that, although he in no way discourages celibacy among the clergy, yet he assumes that among them, as among the laity, marriage will be the rule and abstaining the exception; so much so, that he does not think of giving any special directions for the guidance of a celibate bishop or a celibate deacon. [49]

5. Lastly, this interpretation of the phrases in question is strongly confirmed by the views of leading Christians on the subject in the first few centuries, and by the decrees of councils; these being largely influenced by St. Paul's language, and therefore being a guide as to what his words were then supposed to mean.

Hermas, Clement of Alexandria, of course Tertullian, and among later Fathers, Chrysostom, Epiphanius, and Cyril, all write in disparagement of second marriages, not as sin, but as weakness. To marry again is to fall short of the high perfection set before us in the Gospel constitution. Athenagoras goes so far as to call a second marriage "respectable adultery," and to say that one who thus severs himself from his dead wife is an "adulterer in disguise." Respecting the clergy, Origen says plainly, "Neither a bishop, nor a presbyter, nor a deacon, nor a widow, can be twice married." The canons of councils are not less plain, either as to the discouragement of second marriages among the laity, or their incompatibility with what was then required of the clergy. The synods of Ancyra (*Can.* 19), of Neocæsarea (*Can.* 3 and 7), and of Laodicea (*Can.* 1) subjected lay persons who married more than once to a penalty. This penalty seems to have varied in different Churches; but in some cases it involved excommunication for a time. The Council of Nicæa, on the other hand, makes it a condition that members of the Puritan sect of *Cathari* are not to be received into the Church unless they promise in writing to communicate with those who have married a second time (Can. 8). The *Apostolic Constitutions* (vi. 17) and the so-called *Apostolic Canons* (17) absolutely forbid the promotion of one who has married twice, to be a bishop, presbyter, or deacon; and the *Apostolic Constitutions* forbid the marriage of one who is already in Holy Orders. He may marry once before he is ordained: but if he is single at his ordination he must remain so all his life. Of course, if his wife dies, he is not to marry again. Even singers, readers, and door-keepers, although they may marry after they have been admitted to office, yet are in no case to marry a second time or to marry a widow. And the widow of a cleric was not allowed to marry a second time.

All these rigorous views and enactments leave little doubt as to how the early Church understood St. Paul's language: viz., that one who had exhibited the weakness of marrying a second time was not to be admitted to the ministry. From this they drew the inference that one who was already in orders must not be allowed to marry a second time. And from this they drew the further inference that entering into a marriage contract at all was inadmissible for one who was already a bishop, presbyter, or deacon. Marriage was not a bar to ordination, but ordination was a bar to marriage. Married men might become clergy, but the higher orders of clergy might not become married.

A little thought will show that neither of these inferences follows from St. Paul's rule; and we have good reason for doubting whether he would have sanctioned either of them. The Apostle rules that those who have shown want of moral strength in taking a second wife are not to be ordained deacons or presbyters. But he nowhere says or hints that, if they find in themselves a want of moral strength of this kind *after* their ordination, they are to be made to bear a burden to which they are unequal. On the contrary, the general principle, which he so clearly lays down, decides the case: "If they have not continency, let them marry: for it is better to marry than to burn." And if this holds good of clergy who have lost their first wives, it holds good at least as strongly of those who were unmarried at the time of their ordination. Those Churches, therefore, which, like our own, allow the clergy to marry, and even to marry a second time, after ordination, may rightly claim to have the Apostle on their side.

But there are Churches, and among them the Church of England, which disregard the Apostle's directions, in admitting those who have been more than once married to the diaconate, and even to the episcopate. What defence is to be made of an apparent laxity, which seems to amount to lawlessness? The answer is that there is nothing to show that St. Paul is giving rules which are to bind the Church for all time. It is quite possible that his directions are given "by reason of the present distress." We do not consider ourselves bound by the regulation, which has far higher authority than that of a single Apostle, respecting the eating of blood and of things strangled. The first council, at which most of the Apostles were present, forbad the eating of these things. It also forbad the eating of things offered to idols. St. Paul himself led the way in showing that this restriction is not always binding: and the whole Church has come to disregard the other. Why? Because in none of these cases is the act sinful in itself. While the Jewish converts were likely to be scandalized by seeing their fellow-Christians eating blood, it was expedient to forbid it; and while heathen converts were likely to think lightly of idolatry, if they saw their fellow-Christians eating what had been offered in sacrifice to an idol, it was expedient to forbid it. When these dangers ceased the reason for the enactment ceased; and the enactment was rightly disregarded. The same principle applies to the ordination of persons who have been twice married. Nowadays a man is not considered less strong than his fellows, because he has married a second time. To refuse to ordain such a person would be to lose a minister at a time when the need of additional ministers is great; and this loss would be without compensation.

And we have evidence that in the primitive Church the Apostle's rule about digamists was not considered absolute. In one of his Montanist treatises Tertullian taunts the Catholics in having even among their bishops men who had married twice, and who did not blush when the Pastoral Epistles were read;[50] and Hippolytus, in his fierce attack on Callistus, Bishop of Rome, states that under him men who had been twice and thrice married were ordained bishops, priests, and deacons. And we know that a distinction was made in the Greek Church between those who had married twice *as Christians*, and those who had concluded the second marriage before baptism. The latter were not excluded from ordination. And some went so far as to say that if the first marriage took place before baptism, and the second afterwards, the man was to be considered as having been married only once.[51] This freedom in interpreting the Apostle's rule not unnaturally led to its being, in some branches of the Church, disregarded. St. Paul says, "Do not ordain a man who has married more than once." If you may say, "This man, who has married more than once, shall be *accounted* as having married only once;" you may equally well say "The Apostle's rule was a temporary one, and we have the right to judge of its suitableness to our times and to particular circumstances." We may feel confidence that in such a matter it was not St. Paul's wish to deprive Churches throughout all time of their liberty of judgment, and the Church of England is thus justified.

FOOTNOTES:

[49] As the *Dictionary of Christian Antiquities* (vol. i. p. 324) has given its sanction to the view that "St. Paul *required* the presbyter-bishop to have had the experience of marriage and with at least a preference for those who had brought up children (1 Tim. iii. 2, 4), and extended the requirement

even to the deacons of the Church (1 Tim. iii. 11, 12)," it seems to be worth while to repeat the declaration of Ellicott and Huther, that "the strange opinion of Bretschneider, that μιᾶς is here the indefinite article, and that Paul meant that a bishop should be married, hardly needed the elaborate refutation which is accorded to it by Winer, *Grammar of New Testament*, III. 18 (Eng. Tr., p. 146)." Would any Englishman ever say "a bishop must have one wife," when his meaning was "a bishop must have a wife"?

[50] *De Monog.*, xii.

[51] See Döllinger's *Hippolytus and Callistus* (pp. 129–147 Eng. Trans.) for a full discussion of the question.

CHAPTER XII
THE RELATION OF HUMAN CONDUCT TO THE MYSTERY OF GODLINESS

"These things write I unto thee, hoping to come unto thee shortly; but if I tarry long, that thou mayest know how men ought to behave themselves in the house of God, which is the Church of the living God, the pillar and ground of the truth. And without controversy great is the mystery of godliness; He who was manifested in the flesh, justified in the spirit, seen of angels, preached among the nations, believed on in the world, received up in glory"—1 Tim. iii. 14–16.

St. Paul here makes a pause in the Epistle. He has brought to a close some of the principal directions which he has to give respecting the preservation of pure doctrine, the conduct of public worship, and the qualifications for the ministry: and before proceeding to other topics he halts in order to insist upon the importance of these things, by pointing out what is really involved in them. Their importance is one main reason for his writing at all. Although he hopes to be with Timothy again even sooner than might be expected, he nevertheless will not allow matters of this gravity to wait for his return to Ephesus. For, after all, this hope may be frustrated, and it may be a long time before the two friends meet again face to face. The way in which Christians ought to behave themselves in the house of God is not a matter which can wait indefinitely, seeing that this house of God is no lifeless shrine of a lifeless image, which knows nothing and cares nothing about what goes on in its temple; but a congregation of immortal souls and of bodies that are temples of the living God, Who will destroy him who destroys His temple (1 Cor. iii. 17). God's house must have regulations to preserve it from unseeming disorder. The congregation which belongs to the living God must have a constitution to preserve it from faction and anarchy. All the more so, seeing that to it has been assigned a post of great responsibility. Truth in itself is self-evident and self-sustained: it needs no external support or foundation. But truth as it is manifested to the world needs the best support and the firmest basis that can be found for it. And it is the duty and privilege of the Church to supply these. God's household is not only a community which in a solemn and special way belongs to the living God: it is also the "pillar and ground of the truth." These considerations show how vital is the question, In what way ought one to behave oneself in this community?[52]

For the truth, to the support and establishment of which every Christian by his behaviour in the Church is bound to contribute, is indisputably something great and profound. By the admission of all, the mystery of the Christian faith is a deep and weighty one; and the responsibility of helping or hindering its establishment is proportionately deep and weighty. Other things may be matter of dispute, but this not. "Without controversy great is the mystery of godliness."

Why does St. Paul speak of the Truth as "the mystery of godliness"? In order to express both the Divine and the human aspects of the Christian faith. On the Divine side the Gospel is a mystery, a disclosed secret. It is a body of truth originally hidden from man's knowledge, to which man by his own unaided reason and abilities would never be able to find the way. In one word it is a revelation: a communication by God to men of Truth which they could not have discovered for themselves. "Mystery" is one of those words which Christianity has borrowed from paganism, but has consecrated to new uses by gloriously transfiguring its meaning. The heathen mystery was something always kept hidden from the bulk of mankind; a secret to which only a privileged few were admitted. It encouraged, in the very centre of religion itself, selfishness and exclusiveness. The Christian mystery, on the other hand, is something once hidden, but now made known, not to a select few, but to all. The term, therefore, involves a splendid paradox: it is a secret revealed to every one. In St. Paul's own words to the Romans (xvi. 25), "the revelation of the mystery which hath been kept in silence through times eternal, but now is manifested, and by the scriptures of the prophets, according to the commandment of the eternal God, is made known unto all the nations." He rarely uses the word mystery without combining with it some other word signifying to reveal, manifest, or make known.[53]

But the Christian faith is not only a mystery but a "mystery of godliness." It not only tells of the bounty of Almighty God in revealing His eternal counsels to man, but it also tells of man's obligations in consequence of being initiated. It is a mystery, not "of lawlessness" (2 Thess. ii. 7), but "of godliness." Those who accept it "profess godliness"; profess reverence to the God who has made it known to them. It teaches plainly on what principle we are to regulate "how men ought to behave themselves in the household of God." The Gospel is a mystery of piety, a mystery of reverence and of religious life. Holy itself, and proceeding from the Holy One, it bids its recipients be holy, even as He is Holy Who gives it.

"Who was manifested in the flesh, justified in the spirit, seen of angels, preached among the nations, believed on in the world, received up in glory."

After the text about the three Heavenly Witnesses in the First Epistle of St. John, no disputed reading in the New Testament has given rise to more controversy than the passage before us. Let us hope that the day is not far distant when there will be no more disputing about either text. The truth, though still doubted, especially in reference to the passage before us, is not really doubtful. In both cases the reading of the A.V. is indefensible. It is certain that St. John never wrote the words about the "three that bear witness in heaven": and it is certain that St. Paul did not write, "*God* was manifest in the flesh," but "*Who* was manifested in the flesh." The reading "*God* was manifested in the flesh" appears in no Christian writer until late in the fourth century, and in no translation of the Scriptures, earlier than the seventh or eighth century. And it is not found in any of the five great primary MSS., except as a correction made by a later scribe, who knew of the reading "God was manifested," and either preferred it to the other, or at least wished to preserve it as an alternative reading, or as an interpretation. Even so cautious and conservative a commentator as the late Bishop Wordsworth of Lincoln declares that "the preponderance of testimony is overwhelming" against the reading "*God* was manifested in the flesh." In an old Greek MS., it would require only two small strokes to turn "Who" into "God"; and this alteration would be a tempting one, seeing that the masculine "Who" after the neuter "mystery," looks harsh and unnatural.[54]

But here we come upon a highly interesting consideration. The words that follow look like a quotation from some primitive Christian hymn or confession. The rhythmical movement and the parallelism of the six balanced clauses, of which each triplet forms a climax, points to some such fact as this. It is possible that we have here a fragment of one of the very hymns which, as Pliny the Younger tells the Emperor Trajan, the Christians were accustomed to sing antiphonally at daybreak to Christ as a God.[55] Such a passage as this might well be sung from side to side, line by line or triplet by triplet, as choirs still chant the Psalms in our churches.

"Who was manifested in the flesh,
"Justified in the spirit,
"Seen of angels,
"Preached among the nations,
"Believed on in the world,
"Received up in glory."

Let us assume that this very reasonable and attractive conjecture is correct, and that St. Paul is here quoting from some well-known form of words. Then the "Who" with which the quotation begins will refer to something in the preceding lines which are not quoted. How natural, then, that St. Paul should leave the "Who" unchanged, although it does not fit on grammatically to his own sentence. But in any case there is no doubt as to the antecedent of the "Who." "The mystery of godliness" has for its centre and basis the life of a Divine Person; and the great crisis in the long process by which the mystery was revealed was reached when this Divine Person "was manifested in the flesh." That in making this statement or quotation the Apostle has in his mind the Gnostics who "teach a different doctrine" (i. 3), is quite possible, but is by no means certain. The "manifestation" of Christ in the flesh is a favourite topic with him, as with St. John, and is one of the points in which the two Apostles not only teach the same doctrine, but teach it in the same language. The fact that he had used the word "mystery" would be quite enough to make him speak of "manifestation," even if there had been no false teachers who denied or explained away the fact of the Incarnation of the Divine Son. The two words fit into one another exactly. "Mystery," in Christian theology, implies something which once was concealed but has now been made known; "manifest" implies making known what had once been concealed. *An historical appearance of One Who had previously existed, but had been kept from the knowledge of the world,* is what is meant by, "Who was manifested in the flesh."

"Justified in the spirit." Spirit here cannot mean the Holy Spirit, as the A.V. would lead us to suppose. "In spirit" in this clause is in obvious contrast to "in flesh" in the previous clause. And if "flesh" means the material part of Christ's nature, "spirit" means the immaterial part of His nature, and the higher portion of it. His flesh was the sphere of His manifestation: His spirit was the sphere of His justification. Thus much seems to be clear. But what are we to understand by His justification? And how did it take place in His spirit? These are questions to which a great variety of answers have been given; and it would be rash to assert of any one of them that it is so satisfactory as to be conclusive.

Christ's human nature consisted, as ours does, of three elements, body, soul, and spirit. The body is the flesh spoken of in the first clause. The soul (ψυχή), as distinct from the spirit (πνεῦμα), is the seat of the natural affections and desires. It was Christ's soul that was troubled at the thought of impending suffering. "My soul is exceeding sorrowful, even unto death" (Matt. xxvi. 38; Mark xiv. 34). "Now is My soul troubled; and what shall I say? Father, save Me from this hour" (John xii. 27). The spirit is the seat of the religious emotions: it is the highest, innermost part of man's nature; the sanctuary of the temple. It was in His spirit that Christ was affected when the presence of moral evil distressed Him. He was moved with indignation in His spirit when He saw the hypocritical Jews mingling their sentimental lamentations with the heartfelt lamentations of Martha and Mary at the grave of Lazarus (John xi. 33). It was in His spirit also that He was troubled when, as Judas sat at table with Him and possibly next to Him,[56] He said, "Verily, verily, I say unto you, that one of you shall betray Me" (John xiii. 21). This spiritual part of His nature, which was the sphere of His most intense suffering, was also the sphere of His most intense joy and satisfaction. As moral evil distressed His spirit, so moral innocence delighted it. In a way that none of us can measure, Jesus Christ knew the joy of a good conscience. The challenge which He made to the Jews, "Which of you convicteth Me of sin?" was one which He could make to His own conscience. It had nothing against Him and could never accuse Him. He was *justified* when it spake, and clear when it judged (Rom. iii. 4; Ps. li. 4). Perfect Man though He was, and manifested in weak and suffering flesh, He was nevertheless "justified in the spirit."[57]

"Seen of angels." It is impossible to determine the precise occasion to which this refers. Ever since the Incarnation Christ has been visible to the angels; but something more special than the fact of the Incarnation seems to be alluded to here. The wording in the Greek is exactly the same as in "*He appeared to* Cephas; then *to* the twelve; then *He appeared to* above five hundred brethren at once, of whom the greater part remain until now, but some are fallen asleep; then *He appeared to* James; then *to* all the Apostles; last of all, as *to* one born out of due time, *He appeared to* me also" (1 Cor. xv. 5–8). Here, therefore, we might translate "*appeared to* angels." What appearance, or appearances, of the incarnate Word to the angelic host can be intended?

The question cannot be answered with any certainty; but with some confidence we can venture to say what can *not* be intended. "Appeared to angels" can scarcely refer to the angelic appearances which are recorded in connexion with the Nativity, Temptation, Agony, Resurrection, and Ascension of Christ. On those occasions angels appeared to Christ and to others, not He to angels. With still greater confidence we may reject the suggestion that "angels" here means either the Apostles, as the angels or *messengers* of Christ, or evil spirits, as the angels of Satan. It may be doubted whether anything at all parallel to either explanation can be found in Scripture. Moreover, "appeared to evil spirits" is an interpretation which makes the passage more difficult than it was before. The manifestation of Christ to the angelic host either at the Incarnation or at the return to glory is a far more reasonable meaning to assign to the words.

The first three clauses of this primitive hymn may thus be summed up. The mystery of godliness has been revealed to mankind, and revealed in a historical Person, Who, while manifested in human flesh, was in His inmost spirit declared free from all sin. And this manifestation of a perfectly righteous Man was not confined to the human race. The angels also witnessed it and can bear testimony to its reality.

The remaining triplet is more simple: the meaning of each one of its clauses is clear. The same Christ, who was seen of angels, was also preached among the nations of the earth and believed on in the world: yet He Himself was taken up from the earth and received once more in glory. The propagation of the faith in an ascended Christ is here plainly and even enthusiastically stated. To all the nations, to the whole world, this glorified Saviour belongs. All this adds emphasis to the question "how men ought to behave themselves in the house of God" in which such truths are taught and upheld.

It is remarkable how many arrangements of these six clauses are possible, all making excellent sense. We may make them into two triplets of independent lines: or we may couple the two first lines of each triplet together and then make the third lines correspond to one another. In either case each group begins with earth and ends with heaven. Or again, we may make the six lines into three couplets. In the first couplet flesh and spirit are contrasted and combined; in the second, angels and men; in the third, earth and heaven.

Yes, beyond dispute the mystery of godliness is a great one. The revelation of the Eternal Son, which imposes upon those who accept it a holiness of which His sinlessness must be the model, is something awful and profound. But He, Who along with every temptation which He allows "makes also the way of escape," does not impose a pattern for imitation without at the same time granting the grace necessary for struggling towards it. To reach it is impossible—at any rate in this life. But the consciousness that we cannot reach perfection is no excuse for aiming at imperfection. The sinlessness of Christ is immeasurably beyond us here; and it may be that even in eternity the loss caused by our sins in this life will never be entirely cancelled. But to those who have taken up their cross daily and followed their Master, and who have washed their robes and made them white in the blood of the Lamb, will be granted hereafter to stand sinless "before the throne of God and serve Him day and night in His temple." Having followed Christ on earth, they will follow Him still more in heaven. Having shared His sufferings here, they will share His reward there. They too will be "seen of angels" and "received up in glory."

FOOTNOTES:

[52] To take the "pillar and ground of the truth" as meaning Timothy makes sense, but not nearly such good sense: moreover, it is almost certain that if St. Paul had meant this, he would have expressed himself differently. There is no intolerable mixture of metaphors in speaking of Christians first as a house and then as a pillar, any more than in speaking of any one as both a pillar and a basis. In vi. 9 we have the covetous falling into a *snare* and hurtful lusts such as *drown* men.

[53] 1 Cor. ii 1, 7, xv. 51; Eph. i. 9, iii. 3, 9, vi. 19; Col. i. 26, 27, ii. v. 3, comp. Rom. xi. 25, and see Lightfoot on Col. i. 26.

[54] Cf. Col. i. 27, which throws much light on this passage; and also Col. ii. 2. In some MSS. and Versions the "Who" has been changed into "which," in order to make the construction less harsh.

[55] Carmen Christo quasi deo dicere secum invicem (Plin., *Ep.* x. 97).

[56] St. John reclined on our Lord's right; Judas seems to have been on His left. He must have been very close to be able to hear without the others hearing.

[57] Cf. the partly parallel passage 1 Pet. iii. 18: "Put to death in the flesh, but quickened in the spirit." But "flesh" and "spirit" have no preposition in the original Greek in 1 Pet. iii. 18: here each has the ἐν.

CHAPTER XIII
THE COMPARATIVE VALUE OF BODILY EXERCISE AND OF GODLINESS

"Exercise thyself unto godliness: for bodily exercise is profitable for a little; but godliness is profitable for all things, having promise of the life which now is, and of that which is to come"—1 Tim. iv. 7, 8.

It is almost impossible to decide what St. Paul here means by "bodily exercise." Not that either the phrase or the passage in which it occurs is either difficult or obscure. But the phrase may mean either of two things, both of which make excellent sense in themselves, and both of which fit the context.

At the beginning of this chapter the Apostle warns Timothy against apostates who shall "give heed to seducing spirits and doctrines of devils ... forbidding to marry and commanding to abstain from meats." St. Paul has in his mind those moral teachers who made bodily mortifications the road, not to self-discipline, but to self-effacement; and who taught that such things were necessary, not because our bodies are prone to evil, but because they exist at all. To have a body, they held, was a degradation: and such a possession was a curse, a burden, and a shame. Instead of believing, as every Christian must, that a human body is a very sacred thing, to be jealously guarded from all that may harm or pollute it, these philosophers held that it was worse than worthless, fit for nothing but to be trampled upon and abused. That it may be sanctified here and be glorified hereafter,—that it may be the temple of God's Holy Spirit now and be admitted to share the blessedness of Christ's ascended humanity in the world to come,—they could not and would not believe. It must be made to feel its own vileness. It must be checked, and thwarted, and tormented into subjection, until the blessed time should come when death should release the unhappy soul that was linked to it from its loathsome and intolerable companion.

It cannot, of course, for a moment be supposed that St. Paul would admit that "bodily exercise" of this suicidal kind was "profitable" even "for a little." On the contrary, as we have seen already, he condemns the whole system in the very strongest terms. It is a blasphemy against God's goodness and a libel on human nature. But some persons have thought that the Apostle may be alluding to practices which, externally at any rate, had much resemblance to the practices which he so emphatically condemns. He may have in his mind those fasts, and vigils, and other forms of bodily mortification, which within prudent limits and when sanctified by humility and prayer, are a useful, if not a necessary discipline for most of us. And it has been thought that Timothy himself may have been going to unwise lengths in such ascetic practices: for in this very letter we find his affectionate master charging him, "Be no longer a drinker of water, but use a little wine for thy stomach's sake and thine often infirmities."

This then is one possible meaning of the Apostle's words in the passage before us. Discipline of the body by means of a severe rule of life is profitable for something: but it is not everything. It is not even the chief thing, or anything approaching to the chief thing. The chief thing is godliness. To the value of bodily exercise of this kind there are limits, and rather narrow limits: it "is profitable for *a little*." To the value of godliness there are no limits: it is "profitable for *all* things." Mortifications of the body may preserve us from sins of the flesh: but they are no certain protection even against these. They are no protection at all—sometimes they are the very reverse of protection—against sins of self-complacency and spiritual pride. Asceticism may exist without godliness; and godliness may exist without asceticism. Bodily mortifications may be useful; but they may also be harmful to both soul and body. Godliness must always be useful to both; can never be harmful to either.

But it is quite possible to understand the expression "bodily exercise," in the sense in which the phrase is most commonly used in ordinary conversation among ourselves. In the text which we are considering it may mean that exercise of the body which we are accustomed to take, some of us of necessity, because the work by which we earn our daily bread involves a great deal of physical exertion; some of us for health's sake, because our work involves a great deal of sitting still; some of us for pleasure, because bodily exercise of various kinds is delightful to us. This interpretation of the Apostle's statement, like the other interpretation, makes good sense of itself and fits the context. And whereas that was in harmony with the opening words of the chapter, this fits the immediate context.

St. Paul has just said "Exercise thyself unto godliness." In using the expression "Exercise thyself" (γύμναζε σεαυτόν) he was of course borrowing, as he so constantly does borrow, from the language which was used respecting gymnastic contests in the public games. The Christian is an athlete, who must train himself and exercise himself for a lifelong contest.

He has to wrestle and fight with the powers of evil, that he may win a crown of glory that fadeth not away. How natural, then, that the Apostle, having just spoken of spiritual exercise for the attainment of godliness, should go on to glance at bodily exercise, in order to point out the superiority of the one over the other. The figurative would easily suggest the literal sense; and it is therefore quite lawful to take the words "bodily exercise" in their most literal sense. Perhaps we may go further and say, that this is just one of those cases in which, because the literal meaning makes excellent sense, the literal meaning is to be preferred. Let us then take St. Paul's words quite literally and see what meaning they will yield.

"Bodily exercise is profitable for a little." It is by no means a useless thing. In its proper place it has a real value. Taken in moderation it tends to preserve health and increase strength. It may sometimes be the means of gaining for ourselves and for the circle to which we belong praise and distinction. It makes us more capable of aiding ourselves and others in times of physical danger. It may even be the means of enabling us to save life. By taking us out of ourselves and turning our thoughts into new channels, it is an instrument of mental refreshment, and enables us to return to the main business of our lives with increased intellectual vigour. And beyond all this, if kept within bounds, it has a real moral value. It sometimes keeps us out of mischief by giving us innocent instead of harmful recreation. And bodily training and practice, if loyally carried out, involve moral gains of another kind. Dangerous appetites have to be kept in check, personal wishes have to be sacrificed, good temper has to be cultivated, if success is to be secured for ourselves or the side to which we belong. All this is "profitable" in a very real degree. But the limits to all these good results are evident; and they are somewhat narrow. They are confined to this life, and for the most part to the lower side of it; and they are by no means certain. Only indirectly does bodily exercise yield help to the intellectual and spiritual parts of our nature; and as regards both of them it may easily do more harm than good. Like excessive meat and drink, it may brutalize instead of invigorating. Have we not all of us seen men whose extravagant devotion to bodily exercise has extinguished almost all intellectual interests, and apparently all spiritual interests also?

But there are no such drawbacks to the exercise of godliness. "Godliness is profitable for *all* things, having promise" not only "of the life which now is, but of that which is to come." Its value is not confined to the things of this world, although it enriches and glorifies them all. And, unlike bodily exercise, its good results are certain. There is no possibility of excess. We may be unwise in our pursuit of godliness, as in our pursuit of bodily strength and activity; but we cannot have too much exercise in godliness, as we easily can in athletics. Indeed, we cannot with any safety lay aside the one, as we not only can, but must, frequently lay aside the other. And we need to bear this simple truth in mind. Most of us are willing to admit that godliness is an excellent thing for attaining to a peaceful death; but we show little evidence that we are convinced of its being necessary for spending a happy life. We look upon it as a very suitable thing for the weak, the poor, the sickly, the sorrowful, and perhaps also for sentimental persons who have plenty of leisure time at their disposal. We fail to see that there is much need for it, or indeed much room for it, in the lives of busy, capable, energetic, and practical men of the world. In other words, we are not at all convinced of the truth of the Apostle's words, that "Godliness is profitable for *all* things," and we do not act as if they had very much interest for us. They express a truth which is only too likely to be crowded out of sight and out of mind in this bustling age. Let us be as practical as our dispositions lead us and our surroundings require us to be; but let us not forget that godliness is really the most practical of all things. It lays hold on a man's whole nature. It purifies his body, it illumines and sanctifies his intellect; it braces his will. It penetrates into every department of life, whether business or amusement, social intercourse or private meditation. Ask the physicians, ask employers of labour, ask teachers in schools and universities, ask statesmen and philosophers, what their experience teaches them respecting the average merits of the virtuous and the vicious. They will tell you that the godly person has the healthiest body, is the most faithful servant, the most painstaking student, the best citizen, the happiest man. A man who is formed, reformed, and informed by religion will do far more effectual work in the world than the same man without religion. He works with less friction, because his care is cast upon his heavenly Father; and with more confidence, because his trust is placed on One much more sure than himself. Moreover, in the long run he is trusted and respected. Even those who not only abjure religion in themselves, but ridicule it in others, cannot get rid of their own experience. They find that the godly man can be depended upon, where the merely clever man cannot; and they act in accordance with this experience. Nor does the profitableness of godliness end with the possession of blessings so inestimable as these. It holds out rich promises respecting future happiness, and it gives an earnest and guarantee for it. It gives a man the blessing of a good conscience, which is one of our chief foretastes of the blessedness which awaits us in the world to come.

Let us once for all get rid of the common, but false notion that there is anything unpractical, anything weak or unmanly, in the life of holiness to which Christ has called us, and of which He has given us an example: and by the lives which we lead let us prove to others that this vulgar notion *is* a false one. Nothing has done more harm to the cause of Christianity than the misconceptions which the world has formed as to what Christianity is and what it involves. And these misconceptions are largely caused by the unworthy lives which professing Christians lead. And this unworthiness is of two kinds. There is first the utter worldliness, and often the downright wickedness, of many who are not only baptized Christians, but who habitually keep up some of the external marks of an ordinary Christian life, such as going to church, having family prayers, attending religious meetings, and the like. And perhaps the worst form of this is that in which religion is made a trade, and an appearance of godliness is assumed in order to make money out of a reputation for sanctity. Secondly, there is the seriously mistaken way in which many earnest persons set to work in order to attain to true godliness. By their own course of life they lead people to suppose that a religious life, the life of an earnest Christian, is a dismal thing and an unpractical thing. They wear a depressed and joyless look; they not only abstain from, but leave it to be supposed that they condemn, many things which give zest and brightness to life, and which the Gospel does not condemn. In their eagerness to show their conviction as to the transcendent importance of spiritual matters, they exhibit a carelessness and slovenliness in reference to the affairs of this life, which is exceedingly trying to all those who have to work with them. Thus they stand forward before the world as conspicuous evidence that godliness is *not* "profitable for all things." The world is only too ready to take note of evidence which points to a conclusion so in harmony with its own predilections. It is, and has been from the beginning, prejudiced against religion; and its adherents are quick to seize upon, and make the most of, anything which appears to justify these prejudices. "In a world such as this," they say, "so full of care and suffering, we cannot afford to part with anything which gives brightness and refreshment to life. A religion which tells us to abjure all these things, and live perpetually as if we were at the point of death or face to face with the Day of Judgment, may be all very well for monks and nuns, but is no religion for the mass of mankind. Moreover, this is a busy age. Most of us have much to do; and, if we are to live at all, what we have to do must be done quickly and thoroughly. That means that we must give our minds to it; and a religion which tells us that we must not give our minds to our business, but to other things which it says are of far greater importance, is no religion for people who have to make their way in the world and keep themselves and their children from penury. We flatly refuse to accept a gospel which is so manifestly out of harmony with the conditions of average human life." This charge against Christianity is a very old one: we find it taken up and answered in some of the earliest defences of the gospel which have come down to us. The unhappy thing is, not that such charges should be made, but that the lives of Christian men and women should prove that there is at least a *primâ facie* case for bringing such accusations. The early Christians had to confront the charge that they were joyless, useless members of society and unpatriotic citizens. They maintained that, on the contrary, they were the happiest and most contented of men, devoted to the well-being of others, and ready to die for their country. They kept aloof from many things in which the heathen indulged, not because they were pleasures, but because they were sinful. And there were certain services which they could not, without grievous sin, render to the State. In all lawful matters no men were more ready than they were to be loyal and law-abiding citizens. In this, as in any other matter of moral conduct, they were quite willing to be compared with their accusers or any other class of men. On which side were to be found those who were bright and peaceful in their lives, who cherished their kindred, who took care of the stranger, who succoured their enemies, who shrank not from death?

A practical appeal of this kind is found to be in the long run far more telling than exposition and argument. It may be impossible to get men to listen to, or take interest in, statements as to the principles and requirements of the Christian religion. You may fail to convince them that its precepts and demands are neither superstitious nor unreasonable. But you can always show them what a life of godliness really is;—that it is full of joyousness, and that its joys are neither fitful nor uncertain; that it is no foe to what is bright and beautiful, and is neither morose in itself nor apt to frown at lightheartedness in others; that it does not interfere with the most strenuous attention to business and the most capable despatch of it. Men refuse to listen to or to be moved by words; but they cannot help noticing and being influenced by facts which are all round them in their daily lives. So far as man can judge, the number of vicious, mean, and unworthy lives is far in excess of those which are pure and lofty. Each one of us can do something towards throwing the balance the other way. We can prove to all the world that godliness is not an unreality, and does not make those who strive after it unreal; that it is hostile neither to joyousness nor to capable activity; that, on the contrary, it enhances the brightness of all that is really beautiful in life, while it raises to a higher power all natural gifts and abilities; that the Apostle was saying no more than the simple truth when he declared that it is "profitable for all things."

CHAPTER XIV
THE PASTOR'S BEHAVIOUR TOWARDS WOMEN.—THE CHURCH WIDOW

"Honour widows that are widows indeed. But if any widow hath children or grandchildren, let them learn first to shew piety towards their own family, and to requite their parents: for this is acceptable in the sight of God…. Let none be enrolled as a widow under threescore years old, having been the wife of one man, well reported of for good works"—1 Tim. v. 3, 4, 9.

The subject of this fifth chapter is "The Behaviour of the Pastor towards the older and younger men and women in the congregation." Some have thought that it forms the main portion of the letter, to which all the rest is more or less introductory or supplementary. But the structure of the letter cannot easily be brought into harmony with this view. It seems to be much nearer the truth to say that the unpremeditated way in which this subject is introduced, cannot well be explained unless we assume that we are reading a genuine letter, and not a forged treatise. The connexion of the different subjects touched upon is loose and not always very obvious. Points are mentioned in the order in which they occur to the writer's mind without careful arrangement. After the personal exhortations given at the close of Chapter iv., which have a solemnity that might lead one to suppose that the Apostle was about to bring his words to a close, he makes a fresh start and treats of an entirely new subject which has occurred to him.

It is not difficult to guess what has suggested the new subject. The personal exhortations with which the previous section ends contain these words, "Let no man despise thy youth; but be thou an ensample to them that believe, in word, in manner of life, in love, in faith, in purity." Timothy is not to allow the fact that he is younger than many of those over whom he is set to interfere with the proper discharge of his duties. He is to give no one a handle for charging him with want of gravity or propriety. Sobriety of conduct is to counterbalance any apparent lack of experience. But St. Paul remembers that there is another side to that. Although Timothy is to behave in such a way as never to remind his flock of his comparative youthfulness, yet he himself is always to bear in mind that he is still a young man. This is specially to be remembered in dealing with persons of either sex who are older than himself, and in his bearing towards young women. St. Paul begins with the treatment of older men and returns to this point again later on. Between these two passages about men he gives directions for Timothy's guidance respecting the women in his flock, and specially respecting widows. This subject occupies more than half the chapter and is of very great interest, as being our chief source of information respecting the treatment of widows in the early Church. Commentators are by no means unanimous in their interpretation of the details of the passage, but it is believed that the explanation which is now offered is in harmony with the original Greek, consistent with itself, and not contradicted by anything which is known from other sources.

It is quite evident that more than one kind of widow is spoken of: and one of the questions which the passage raises is—How many classes of widows are indicated? We can distinguish four kinds; and it seems probable that the Apostle means to give us four kinds.

1. There is "the widow indeed (ἡ ὄντως χήρα)." Her characteristic is that she is "desolate," *i.e.*, quite alone in the world. She has not only lost her husband, but she has neither children nor any other near relation to minister to her necessities. Her hope is set on God, to Whom her prayers ascend night and day. She is contrasted with two other classes of widow, both of whom are in worldly position better off than she is, for they are not desolate or destitute; yet one of these is far more miserable than the widow indeed, because the manner of life which she adopts is so unworthy of her.

2. There is the widow who "hath children or grandchildren." Natural affection will cause these to take care that their widowed parent does not come to want. If it does not, then they must learn that "to show piety towards their own family and to requite their parents" is a paramount duty, and that the congregation must not be burdened with the maintenance of their mother until they have first done all they can for her. To ignore this plain duty is to deny the first principles of Christianity, which is the Gospel of love and duty, and to fall below the level of the unbelievers, most of whom recognized the duty of providing for helpless parents. Nothing is said of the character of the widow who has children or grandchildren to support her; but, like the widow indeed, she is contrasted with the third class of widow, and therefore we infer that her character is free from reproach.

3. There is the widow who "giveth herself to pleasure." Instead of continuing in prayers and supplications night and day, she continues in frivolity and luxury, or worse. Of her, as of the Church of Sardis, it may be said, "Thou hast a name that thou livest, and thou art dead" (Rev. iii. 1).

4. There is the "enrolled" widow; *i.e.*, one whose name has been entered on the Church rolls as such. She is a "widow indeed" and something more. She is not only a person who needs and deserves the support of the congregation, but has special rights and duties. She holds an office, and has a function to discharge. She is a widow, not merely as having lost her husband, but as having been admitted to the company of those bereaved women whom the Church has entrusted with a definite portion of Church work. This being so, something more must be looked to than the mere fact of her being alone in the world. She must be sixty years of age, must have had only one husband, have had experience in the bringing up of children, and be well known as devoted to good works. If she has these qualifications, she may be enrolled as a Church widow; but it does not follow that because she has them she will be appointed.

The work to which these elderly women had to devote themselves was twofold: (1) Prayer, especially intercession for those in trouble; (2) Works of mercy, especially ministering to the sick, guiding younger Christian women in lives of holiness, and winning over heathen women to the faith. These facts we learn from the frequent regulations respecting widows during the second, third, and fourth, centuries. It was apparently during the second century that the order of widows flourished most.

This primitive order of Church widows must be distinguished from the equally primitive order of deaconesses, and from a later order of widows, which grew up side by side with the earlier order, and continued long after the earlier order had ceased to exist. But it would be contrary to all probability, and to all that we know about Church offices in the Apostolic and sub-Apostolic age, to suppose that the distinctions between different orders of women were as marked in the earliest periods as they afterwards became, or that they were precisely the same in all branches of the Church.

It has been sometimes maintained that the Church widow treated of in the passage before us is identical with the deaconess. The evidence that the two orders were distinct is so strong as almost to amount to demonstration.

1. It is quite possible that this very Epistle supplies enough evidence to make the identification very improbable. If the "women" mentioned in the section about deacons (iii. 11) are deaconesses, then the qualifications for this office are quite different from the qualifications for that of a widow, and are treated of in quite different sections of the letter. But even if deaconesses are not treated of at all in that passage, the limit of age seems quite out of place, if they are identical with the widows.[58] In the case of the widows it was important to enrol for this special Church work none who were likely to wish to marry again. And as their duties consisted in a large measure in

prayer, advanced age was no impediment, but rather the contrary. But the work of the deaconess was for the most part active work, and it would be unreasonable to admit no one to the office until the best part of her working life was quite over.

2. The difference in the work assigned to them points in the same direction. As already stated, the special work of the widow was intercessory prayer and ministering to the sick. The special work of the deaconess was guarding the women's door in the churches, seating the women in the congregation, and attending women at baptisms.[59] Baptism being usually administered by immersion, and adult baptism being very frequent, there was much need of female attendants.

3. At her appointment the deaconess received the imposition of hands, the widow did not. The form of prayer for the ordination of a deaconess is given in the *Apostolical Constitutions* (viii. 19, 20), and is worthy of quotation. "Concerning a deaconess, I Bartholomew make this constitution: O Bishop, thou shalt lay thy hands upon her in the presence of the presbytery and of the deacons and deaconesses, and shalt say; O Eternal God, the Father of our Lord Jesus Christ, the Creator of man and of woman; Who didst replenish with the Spirit Miriam, Deborah, Anna, and Huldah; Who didst not disdain that Thy Only begotten Son should be born of a woman; Who also in the tabernacle of the testimony and in the temple didst ordain women to be *keepers of Thy holy gates;*—look down now also upon this Thy servant, who is to be ordained to the office of a deaconess. Grant her Thy Holy Spirit and *cleanse her from all defilement of flesh and spirit,*[60] that she may worthily discharge the work which is committed to her, to Thy glory and the praise of Thy Christ, with Whom be glory and adoration to Thee and to the Holy Spirit for ever and ever. Amen." Nothing of the kind is found for the appointment of a Church widow.

4. It is quite in harmony with the fact that the deaconesses were ordained, while the widows were not, that the widows are placed under the deaconesses. "The widows ought to be grave, obedient to their bishops, their presbyters, and their deacons; and besides these to the deaconesses, with piety, reverence, and fear."[61]

5. The deaconess might be either an unmarried woman or a widow, and apparently the former was preferred. "Let the deaconess be a pure virgin; or at least a widow who has been but once married."[62] But, although such things did occur, Tertullian protests that it is a monstrous irregularity to admit an unmarried woman to the order of widows.[63] Now, if widows and deaconesses were identical, unmarried "widows" would have been quite common, for unmarried deaconesses were quite common. Yet he

speaks of the one case of a "virgin widow" which had come under his notice as a marvel, and a monstrosity, and a contradiction in terms. It is true that Ignatius in his letter to the Church of Smyrna uses language which has been thought to support the identification: "I salute the households of my brethren with their wives and children, and *the virgins who are called widows*."[64] But it is incredible that at Smyrna *all* the Church widows were unmarried; and it is equally improbable that Ignatius should send a salutation to the unmarried "widows" (if such there were), and ignore the rest. His language, however, may be quite easily explained without any such strange hypothesis. He may mean "I salute those who are called widows, but whom one might really regard as virgins." And in support of this interpretation Bishop Lightfoot quotes Clement of Alexandria, who says that the continent man, like the continent widow, becomes again a virgin; and Tertullian, who speaks of continent widows as being in God's sight maidens (*Deo sunt puellæ*), and as for a second time virgins.[65] But, whatever Ignatius may have meant by "the virgins who are called widows," we may safely conclude that neither in his time, any more than that of St. Paul, were the widows identical with the deaconesses.

The later order of widows, which grew up side by side with the Apostolic order, and in the end supplanted, or at any rate survived, the older order, came into existence about the third century. It consisted of persons who had lost their husbands and made a vow never to marry again. From the middle of the second century or a little later we find a strong feeling against second marriages springing up, and this feeling was very possibly intensified when the Gospel came in contact with the German tribes, among whom the feeling already existed independently of Christianity. In this new order of widows who had taken the vow of continence there was no restriction of age, nor was it necessary that they should be persons in need of the alms of the congregation. In the Apostolic order the fundamental idea seems to have been that destitute widows ought to be supported by the Church, and that in return for this, those of them who were qualified should do some special Church work. In the later order the fundamental idea was that it was a good thing for a widow to remain unmarried, and that a vow to do so would help her to persevere.

In commanding Timothy to "honour widows that are widows indeed" the Apostle states a principle which has had a wide and permanent influence not only on ecclesiastical discipline but upon European legislation. Speaking of the growth of the modern idea of a will, by which a man can regulate the descent of his property inside and outside his family, Sir Henry Maine remarks, that "the exercise of the Testamentary power was seldom allowed to interfere with the right of the widow to a definite share, and of the children to certain fixed proportions, of the devolving inheritance. The shares of the children, as their amount shows, were determined by the authority of Roman law. *The provision for the widow was attributable to the exertions of the Church, which never relaxed its solicitude for the interest of wives surviving their husbands*—winning, perhaps, one of the most arduous of its triumphs when, after exacting for two or three centuries an express promise from the husband at marriage to endow his wife, it at length succeeded in engrafting the principle of Dower on the Customary Law of all Western Europe."[66] This is one of the numerous instances in which the Gospel, by insisting upon the importance of some humane principle, has contributed to the progress and security of the best elements in civilization.

Not only the humanity, but the tact and common sense of the Apostle is conspicuous throughout the whole passage, whether we regard the general directions respecting the bearing of the young pastor towards the different sections of his flock, old and young, male and female, or the special rules respecting widows. The sum and substance of it appears to be that the pastor is to have abundance of zeal and to encourage it in others, but he is to take great care that, neither in himself nor in those whom he has to guide, zeal outruns discretion. Well-deserved rebukes may do far more harm than good, if they are administered without respect to the position of those who need them. And in all his ministrations the spiritual overseer must beware of giving a handle to damaging criticism. He must not let his good be evil spoken of. So also with regard to the widows. No hard and fast rule can be safely laid down. Almost everything depends upon circumstances. On the whole, the case of widows is analogous to that of unmarried women. For those who have strength to forego the married state, *in order to devote more time and energy to the direct service of God*, it is better to remain unmarried, if single, and if widows, not to marry again. But there is no peculiar blessedness in the unmarried state, if the motive for avoiding matrimony is a selfish one, *e.g.*, to avoid domestic cares and duties and have leisure for personal enjoyment. Among younger women the higher motive is less likely to be present, or at any rate to be permanent. They are so likely sooner or later to desire to marry, that it will be wisest not to discourage them to do so. On the contrary, let it be regarded as the normal thing that a young woman should marry, and that a young widow should marry again. It is not the best thing for them, but it is the safest. Although the highest work for Christ can best be done by those who by remaining single have kept their domestic ties at a minimum, yet young women are more likely to do useful work in society, and are less likely to come to harm, if they marry and have children. Of older women this is not true. Age itself is a considerable guarantee: and a woman of sixty, who is willing to give such a pledge, may be encouraged to enter upon a life of perpetual widowhood. But there must be other qualifications as well, if she wishes to be enrolled among those, who not only are entitled by their destitute condition to receive maintenance from the Church, but by reason of their fitness are commissioned to undertake Church work. And these qualifications must be carefully investigated. It would be far better to reject some, who might after all have been useful, than to run the risk of admitting any who would exhibit the scandal of having been supported by the Church and specially devoted to Christian works of mercy, and of having after all returned to society as married women with ordinary pleasures and cares.

One object throughout these directions is the *economy of Christian resources*. The Church accepts the duty which it inculcates of "providing for its own." But it ought not to be burdened with the support of any but those who are really destitute. The near relations of necessitous persons must be taught to leave the Church free to relieve those who have no near relations to support them. Secondly, so far as is possible, those who are relieved by the alms of the congregation must be encouraged to make some return in undertaking Church work that is suitable to them. St. Paul has no idea of pauperizing people. So long as they can, they must maintain themselves. When they have ceased to be able to do this, they must be supported by their children or grandchildren. If they have no one to help them, the Church must undertake their support; but both for their sake as well as for the interests of the community, it must, if possible, make the support granted to be a return for work done rather than mere alms. Widowhood must not be made a plea for being maintained in harmful idleness. But the point which the Apostle insists on most emphatically, stating it in different ways no less than three times in this short section (vv. 4, 8, 16) is this,—that widows as a rule ought to be supported by their own relations; only in exceptional cases, where there are no relations who can help, ought the Church to have to undertake this duty. We have here a warning against the mistake so often made at the present day of *freeing people from their responsibilities* by undertaking for them in mistaken charity the duties which they ought to discharge, and are capable of discharging, themselves.

We may, therefore, sum up the principles laid down thus:—

Discretion and tact are needed in dealing with the different sections of the congregation, and especially in relieving the widows. Care must be taken not to encourage either a rigour not likely to be maintained, or opportunities of idleness certain to lead to mischief. Help is to be generously afforded to the destitute; but the resources of the Church must be jealously guarded. They must not be wasted on the unworthy, or on those who have other means of help. And, so far as possible, the independence of those who are relieved must be protected by employing them in the service of the Church.

In conclusion it may be worth while to point out that this mention of an order of widows is no argument against the Pauline authorship of these Epistles, as if no such thing existed in his time. In Acts vi. 1 the widows appear as a distinct *body* in the Church at Jerusalem. In Acts ix. 39, 41, they appear almost as an *order* in the Church at Joppa. They "show the coats and garments which Dorcas made" in a way which seems to imply that it was their business to distribute such things among the needy. Even if it means no more than that Dorcas made them for the relief of the widows themselves, still the step from a body of widows set apart for the reception of alms to an order of widows set apart for the duty of intercessory prayer and ministering to the sick is not a long one, and may easily have been made in St. Paul's lifetime.

FOOTNOTES:

[58] The Council in Trullo (a.d. 691), the great authority for discipline in the Greek Church, fixed the age of forty for admission to the office of a deaconess and sixty for that of a widow.

[59] In the middle recension of the Ignatian Epistles we read "I salute the keepers of the holy doors, the deaconesses in Christ" (*Ant.* xii.). "Let the deaconesses stand at the entries of the women" (*Apost. Const.* ii. 57, 58). "For we stand in need of a woman, a deaconess, for many necessities, and first in the baptism of women," etc.—(*Ib.* iii. 15.)

[60] 1 Cor. vii. 1.

[61] *Apost. Const.*, iii. 7.

[62] *Apost. Const.*, vi. 17.

[63] *De Virg. Vel.*, ix.

[64] *Smyrn.* xiii.

[65] *Strom.*, vii. 12; *Ad Uxor.*, I. iv.; *De Exh. Cast.*, 1.

[66] *Ancient Law*, p. 224.

CHAPTER XV
THE PASTOR'S RESPONSIBILITIES IN ORDAINING AND JUDGING PRESBYTERS.—THE WORKS THAT GO BEFORE AND THAT FOLLOW US

"Lay hands hastily on no man, neither be partaker of other men's sins: keep thyself pure. Be no longer a drinker of water, but use a little wine for thy stomach's sake and thine often infirmities. Some men's sins are evident, going before unto judgment; and some men also they follow after. In like manner also there are good works that are evident; and such as are otherwise cannot be hid"—1 Tim. v. 22–25.

The section of which these verses form the conclusion, like the preceding section about behaviour towards the different classes of persons in the congregation, supplies us with evidence that we are dealing with a real letter, written to give necessary advice to a real person, and not a theological or controversial treatise, dressed up in the form of a letter, in order to obtain the authority of St. Paul's name for its contents. Here, as before, the thoughts follow one another in an order which is quite natural, but which has little plan or arrangement. An earnest and affectionate friend, with certain points in his mind on which he was anxious to say something, might easily treat of them in this informal way just as they occurred to him, one thing suggesting another. But a forger, bent on getting his own views represented in the document, would not string them together in this loosely connected way: he would disclose more arrangement than we can find here. What forger again, would think of inserting that advice about ceasing to be a water-drinker into a most solemn charge respecting the election and ordination of presbyters? And yet how thoroughly natural it is found to be in this very context when considered as coming from St. Paul to Timothy!

We shall go seriously astray if we start with the conviction that the word "elder" has the same meaning throughout this chapter. When in the first part of it St. Paul says "Rebuke not an elder, but exhort him as a father," it is quite clear that he is speaking simply of elderly men, and not of persons holding the office of an elder: for he goes on at once to speak of the treatment of younger men, and also of older and younger women. But when in the second half of the chapter he says "Let the elders that rule well be counted worthy of double honour," and "Against an elder receive not an accusation, except at the mouth of two or three witnesses," it is equally clear that he is speaking of official persons, and not merely of persons who are advanced in years. The way in which the thoughts suggested one another throughout this portion of the letter is not difficult to trace. "Let no man despise thy youth" suggested advice as to how the young overseer was to behave towards young and old of both sexes. This led to the treatment of widows, and this again to the manner of appointing official widows. Women holding an official position suggests the subject of men holding an official position in the Church. If the treatment of the one class needs wisdom and circumspection, not less does the treatment of the other. And therefore, with even more solemnity than in the previous section about the widows, the Apostle gives his directions on this important subject also. "I charge thee in the sight of God, and Christ Jesus, and the elect angels, that thou observe these things without prejudice, doing nothing by partiality." And then he passes on to the words which form our text.

It has been seriously doubted whether the words "Lay hands hastily on no man" do refer to the ordination of the official elders or presbyters. It is urged that the preceding warnings about the treatment of charges made against presbyters, and of persons who are guilty of habitual sin, point to *disciplinary* functions of some kind rather than to ordination. Accordingly some few commentators in modern times have treated the passage as referring to *the laying on of hands at the readmission of penitents to communion*. But of any such custom in the Apostolic age there is no trace. There is nothing improbable in the hypothesis, imposition of hands being a common symbolical act. But it is a mere hypothesis unsupported by evidence. Eusebius, in speaking of the controversy between Stephen of Rome and Cyprian of Carthage about the re-baptizing of heretics, tells us that the admission of heretics to the Church by imposition of hands with prayer, but without second baptism, was the "old custom." But the admission of heretics is not quite the same as the readmission of penitents: and a custom might be "old" (παλαιὸν ἦθος) in the time of Eusebius, or even of Cyprian, without being Apostolic or coeval with the Apostles. Therefore this statement of Eusebius gives little support to the proposed interpretation of the passage; and we may confidently prefer the explanation of it which has prevailed at any rate since Chrysostom's time, that it refers to ordination.[67] Of the laying on of hands at the appointment of ministers we have sufficient evidence in the New Testament, not only in these Epistles

(1 Tim. iv. 14; 2 Tim. i. 6), but in the Acts (xiii. 3). Moreover this explanation fits the context at least as well as the supposed improvement.

1. The Apostle is speaking of the treatment of presbyters, not of the whole congregation. Imposition of hands at the admission of a heretic or re-admission of a penitent would apply to any person, and not to presbyters in particular. Therefore it is more reasonable to assume that the laying on of hands which accompanied ordination is meant.

2. He has just been warning Timothy against prejudice or partiality in dealing with the elders. While prejudice might lead him to be hasty in condemning an accused presbyter, before he had satisfied himself that the evidence was adequate, partiality might lead him to be hasty in acquitting him. But there is a more serious partiality than this, and it is one of the main causes of such scandals as unworthy presbyters. There is the partiality which leads to a hasty ordination, before sufficient care has been taken to ensure that the qualifications so carefully laid down in chapter iii. are present in the person selected. Prevention is better than cure. Proper precautions taken beforehand will reduce the risk of true charges against an elder to a minimum. Here again the traditional explanation fits the context admirably.

"Neither be partaker of other men's sins." It is usual to understand this warning as referring to the responsibility of those who ordain. If, through haste or carelessness you ordain an unfit person, you must share the guilt of the sins which he afterwards commits as an elder. The principle is a just one, but it may be doubted whether this is St. Paul's meaning. The particular form of negative used seems to be against it. He says "Nor *yet* (μηδέ) be partaker of other men's sins," implying that this is something different from hastiness in ordinary. He seems to be returning to the warnings about partiality to elders who are living in sin. The meaning, therefore, is—"Beware of a haste in ordaining which may lead to the admission of unworthy men to the ministry. And if, in spite of all your care, unworthy ministers come under your notice, beware of an indifference or partiality towards them which will make you a partaker in their sins." This interpretation fits on well to what follows. "Keep *thyself* pure"—with a strong emphasis on the pronoun. "Strictness in enquiring into the antecedents of candidates for ordination and in dealing with ministerial depravity will have a very poor effect, unless your own life is free from reproach." And, if we omit the parenthetical advice about taking wine, the thought is continued thus: "As a rule it is not difficult to arrive at a wise decision respecting the fitness of candidates, or the guilt of accused presbyters. Men's characters both for evil and good are commonly notorious. The vices of the wicked and the virtues of the good outrun any formal judgment about them, and are quite manifest before an enquiry is held. No doubt there are exceptions, and then the consequences of men's lives must be looked to before a just opinion can be formed. But, sooner or later (and generally sooner rather than later) men, and especially ministers, will be known for what they are."

It remains to ascertain the meaning of the curious parenthesis "Be no longer a drinker of water," and its connexion with the rest of the passage.

It was probably suggested to St. Paul by the preceding words, "Beware of making yourself responsible for the sins of others. Keep your own life above suspicion." This charge reminds the Apostle that his beloved disciple has been using ill-advised means to do this very thing. Either in order to mark his abhorrence of the drunkenness, which was one of the most conspicuous vices of the age, or in order to bring his own body more easily into subjection, Timothy had abandoned the use of wine altogether, in spite of his weak health. St. Paul, therefore, with characteristic affection, takes care that his charge is not misunderstood. In urging his representative to be strictly careful of his own conduct, he does not wish to be understood as encouraging him to give up whatever might be abused or made the basis of a slander, nor yet as approving his rigour in giving up the use of wine. On the contrary, he thinks it a mistake; and he takes this opportunity of telling him so, while it is in his mind. Christ's ministers have important duties to perform, and have no right to play tricks with their health. We may here repeat, with renewed confidence, that a touch of this kind would never have occurred to a forger. Hence, in order to account for such natural touches as these, those who maintain that these Epistles are a fabrication now resort to the hypothesis that the forger had some genuine letters of St. Paul and worked parts of them into his own productions. It seems to be far more reasonable to believe that St. Paul wrote the whole of them.

Let us return to the statement with which the Apostle closes this section of his letter. "Some men's sins are evident, going before unto judgment; and some men also they follow after. In like manner also there are good works that are evident; and such as are otherwise cannot be hid."

We have seen already what relation these words have to the context. They refer to the discernment between good and bad candidates for the ministry, and between good and bad ministers, pointing out that in most cases such discernment is not difficult, because men's own conduct acts as a herald to their character, proclaiming it to all the world. The statement, though made with special reference to Timothy's responsibilities towards elders and those who wish to become such, is a general one, and is equally true of all mankind. Conduct in most cases is quite a clear index of character, and there is no need to have a formal investigation in order to ascertain whether a man is leading a wicked life or not. But the words have a still deeper significance—one which is quite foreign to the context, and therefore can hardly have been in St. Paul's mind when he wrote them, but which as being true and of importance, ought not to be passed over.

For a formal investigation into men's conduct before an ecclesiastical or other official, let us substitute the judgment-seat of Christ. Let the question be, not the worthiness of certain persons to be admitted to some office, but their worthiness to be admitted to eternal life. The general statement made by the Apostle remains as true as ever. There are some men who stand, as before God, so also before the world, as open, self-proclaimed sinners. Wherever they go, their sins go before them, flagrant, crying, notorious. And when they are summoned hence, their sins again precede them, waiting for them as accusers and witnesses before the Judge. The whole career of an open and deliberate sinner is the procession of a criminal to his doom.[68] His sins go before, and their consequences follow after, and he moves on in the midst, careless of the one and ignorant of the other. He has laughed at his sins and chased remorse for them away. He has by turns cherished and driven out the remembrance of them; dwelt on them, when to think of them was a pleasant repetition of them; stifled the thought of them, when to think of them might have brought thoughts of penitence; and has behaved towards them as if he could not only bring them into being without guilt, but control them or annihilate them without difficulty. He has not controlled, he has not destroyed, he has not even evaded, one of them. Each of them, when brought into existence, became his master, going on before him to herald his guiltiness, and saddling him with consequences from which he could not escape. And when he went to his own place, it was his sins that had gone before him and prepared the place for him.

"And some men also they follow after." There are cases in which men's sins, though of course not less manifest to the Almighty, are much less manifest to the world, and even to *themselves*, than in the case of flagrant, open sinners. The consequences of their sins are less conspicuous, less easily disentangled from the mass of unexplained misery of which the world is so full. Cause and effect cannot be put together with any precision; for sometimes the one, sometimes the other, sometimes even both, are out of sight. There is no anticipation of the final award to be given at the judgment-seat of Christ. Not until the guilty one is placed before the throne for trial, is it at all known whether the sentence will be unfavourable or not. Even the man himself has lived and died without being at all fully aware what the state of the case is. He has not habitually examined himself, to see whether he has been living in sin or not. He has taken no pains to remember, and repent of, and conquer, those sins of which he has been conscious. The consequences of his sins have seldom come so swiftly as to startle him and convince him of their enormity. When they have at last overtaken him, it has been possible to doubt or to forget that it was his sins which caused them. And consequently he has doubted, and he has forgotten. But for all that, "they follow after." They are never eluded, never shaken off. A cause must have its effect; and a sin must have its punishment, if not in this world, then certainly in the next. "Be sure your sin will find you out"—probably in this life, but at any rate at the day of judgment. As surely as death follows on a pierced heart or on a severed neck, so surely does punishment follow upon sin.

How is it that in the material world we never dream that cause and effect can be separated, and yet easily believe that in the moral world sin may remain for ever unpunished? Our relation to the material universe has been compared to a game of chess. "The chess-board is the world, the pieces are the phenomena of the universe, the rules of the game are what we call the laws of nature. The player on the other side is hidden from us. We know that his play is always fair, just, and patient. But also we know, to our cost, that he never overlooks a mistake, or makes the smallest allowance for ignorance. To the man who plays well, the highest stakes are paid, with that sort of over-flowing generosity with which the strong shows delight in strength. And one who plays ill is checkmated—without haste, but without remorse."[69] We believe this implicitly of the material laws of the universe; that they cannot be evaded, cannot be transgressed with impunity, cannot be obeyed without profit. Moral laws are not one whit less sure. Whether we believe it or not (and it will but be the worse for us if we refuse to believe it), sin, both repented and unrepented, must have its penalty. We might as well fling a stone, or shoot a cannon-ball, or send a balloon into the air, and say "You shall not come down again," as sin, and say "I shall never suffer for it." Repentance does not deprive sin of its natural effect. We greatly err in supposing that, if we repent in time, we escape the penalty. To refuse to repent is a second and a worse sin, which, added to the first sin, increases the penalty incalculably. To repent is to escape this terrible augmentation of the original punishment; but it is no escape from the punishment itself.

But there is a bright side to this inexorable law. If sin must have its own punishment, virtue must have its own reward. The one is as sure as the other; and in the long run the fact of virtue and the reward of virtue will be made clear to all the world, and especially to the virtuous man himself. "The works that are good are evident; and such as are not evident cannot be hid." No saint knows his own holiness; and many a humble seeker after holiness does good deeds without knowing how good they are. Still less are all saints known as such to the world, or all good deeds recognized as good by those who witness them. But, nevertheless, good works as a rule are evident, and, if they are not so, they will become so hereafter. If not in this world, at any rate before Christ's judgment-seat, they will be appraised at their true value. It is as true of the righteous as of the wicked, that "their works do follow them." And, if there is no more terrible fate than to be confronted at the last day by a multitude of unknown and forgotten sins, so there can hardly be any lot more blessed than to be welcomed then by a multitude of unknown and forgotten deeds of love and piety. "Inasmuch as ye did it unto one of these My brethren, even these least, ye did it unto Me." "Come, ye blessed of My Father, inherit the kingdom prepared for you from the foundation of the world."

FOOTNOTES:

[67] Tertullian (*De Bapt.*, xviii.) seems to understand St. Paul to be speaking of the imposition of hands after *Baptism* (Acts viii. 17, xix. 6), which can hardly be correct.

[68] Manning's *Sermons*, vol. iii., p. 74, Burns, 1847.

[69] Huxley's *Lay Sermons*, Essay I. Macmillan.

CHAPTER XVI
THE NATURE OF ROMAN SLAVERY AND THE APOSTLE'S ATTITUDE TOWARDS IT.—A MODERN PARALLEL

"Let as many as are bond-servants under the yoke count their own masters worthy of all honour, that the name of God and the doctrine be not blasphemed. And they that have believing masters, let them not despise them, because they are brethren; but let them serve them the rather, because they that partake of the benefit are believing and beloved. These things teach and exhort."—1 Tim. vi. 1, 2.

There are four passages in which St. Paul deals directly with the relations between slaves and their masters:—in the Epistles to the Ephesians (vi. 5–9), to the Colossians (iii. 22–iv. 1), to Philemon (8–21), and the passage before us. Here he looks at the question from the slave's point of view; in the letter to Philemon from that of the master: in the Epistles to the Colossians and to the Ephesians he addresses both. In all four places his attitude towards this monster abomination is one and the same; and it is a very remarkable one. He nowhere denounces slavery. He does not state that such an intolerable iniquity as man possessing his fellow-man must be done away as speedily as may be. He gives no encouragement to slaves to rebel or to run away. He gives no hint to masters that they ought to let their slaves go free. Nothing of the kind. He not only accepts slavery as a fact; he seems to treat it as a necessary fact, a fact likely to be as permanent as marriage and parentage, poverty and wealth.

This attitude becomes all the more marvellous, when we remember, not only what slavery necessarily is wherever it exists, but what slavery was both by custom and by law among the great slave-owners throughout the Roman Empire. Slavery is at all times degrading to both the parties in that unnatural relationship, however excellent may be the regulations by which it is protected, and however noble may be the characters of both master and slave. It is impossible for one human being to be absolute owner of another's person without both possessor and possessed being morally the worse for it. Violations of nature's laws are never perpetrated with impunity; and when the laws violated are those which are concerned, not with unconscious forces and atoms, but with human souls and characters, the penalties of the violation are none the less sure or severe. But these evils, which are the inevitable consequences of the existence of slavery in any shape whatever, may be increased a hundredfold, if the slavery exists under no regulations, or under bad regulations, or again where both master and slave are, to start with, base and brutalized in character. And all this was the case in the early days of the Roman Empire. Slavery was to a great extent under no check at all, and the laws which did exist for regulating the relationship between owner and slave were for the most part of a character to intensify the evil; while the conditions under which both master and slave were educated were such as to render each of them ready to increase the moral degradation of the other. We are accustomed to regard with well-merited abhorrence and abomination the horrors of modern slavery as practised until recently in America, and as still practised in Egypt, Persia, Turkey, and Arabia. But it may be doubted whether all the horrors of modern slavery are to be compared with the horrors of the slavery of ancient Rome.

From a *political* point of view it may be admitted that the institution of slavery has in past ages played a useful part in the history of mankind. It has mitigated the cruelties of barbaric warfare. It was more merciful to enslave a prisoner than to sacrifice him to the gods, or to torture him to death, or to eat him. And the enslaved prisoner and the warrior who had captured him, at once became mutually useful to one another. The warrior protected his slave from attack, and the slave by his labour left the warrior free to protect him. Thus each did something for the benefit of the other and of the society in which they lived.

But when we look at the institution from a *moral* point of view, it is difficult to avoid the conclusion that its effects have been wholly evil. (1) It has been fatal to one of the most wholesome of human beliefs, *the belief in the dignity of labour*. Labour was irksome, and therefore assigned to the slave, and consequently came to be regarded as degrading. Thus the freeman lost the ennobling discipline of toil; and to the slave toil was not ennobling, because every one treated it as a degradation. (2) It has been disastrous to the personal character of the master. The possession of absolute power is always dangerous to our nature. Greek writers are never tired of insisting upon this in connexion with the rule of despots over citizens. Strangely enough they did not see that the principle remained the same whether the autocrat was ruler of a state or of a household. In either case he almost inevitably became a tyrant, incapable of self-control, and the constant victim of flattery. And in some ways the domestic tyrant was the worse of the two. There was no public opinion to keep him in check, and his tyranny could exercise itself in every detail of daily life. (3) It has been disastrous to the personal character of the slave. Accustomed to be looked upon as an inferior and scarcely human being, always at the beck and call of another, and that for the most menial services, the slave lost all self-respect. His natural weapon was deceit; and his chief, if not his only pleasure, was the gratification of his lowest appetites. The household slave not unfrequently divided his time between pandering to his master's passions and gratifying his own. (4) It has been ruinous to family life. If it did not trouble the relation between husband and wife, it poisoned the atmosphere in which they lived and in which their children were reared. The younger generation inevitably suffered. Even if they did not learn cruelty from their parents, and deceit and sensuality from the slaves, they lost delicacy of feeling by seeing human beings treated like brute beasts, and by being constantly in the society of those whom they were taught to despise. Even Plato, in recommending that slaves should be treated justly and with a view to their moral improvement, says that they must always be punished for their faults, and not reproved like freemen, which only makes them conceited; and one should use no language to them but that of command.[70]

These evils, which are inherent in the very nature of slavery, were intensified a hundredfold by Roman legislation, and by the condition of Roman society in the first century of the Christian era. Slavery, which began by being a mitigation of the barbarities of warfare, ended in becoming an augmentation of them. Although a single campaign would sometimes bring in many thousands of captives who were sold into slavery, yet war did not procure slaves fast enough for the demand, and was supplemented by systematic manhunts. It has been estimated that in the Roman world of St. Paul's day the proportion of slaves to freemen was in the ratio of two, or even three, to one. It was the immense number of the slaves which led to some of the cruel customs and laws respecting them. In the country they often worked, and sometimes slept, in chains. Even in Rome under Augustus the house-porter was sometimes chained. And by a decree of the Senate, if the master was murdered by a slave, all the slaves of the household were put to death. The four hundred slaves of Pedanius Secundus were executed under this enactment in a.d. 61, in which year St. Paul was probably in Rome. Public protest was made; but the Senate decided that the law must take its course. The rabble of slaves could only be kept in check by fear. Again, if the master was accused of a crime, he could surrender his slaves to be tortured in order to prove his innocence.[71]

But it would be a vile task to rehearse all the horrors and abominations to which the cruelty and lust of wealthy Roman men and women subjected their slaves. The bloody sports of the gladiatorial shows and the indecent products of the Roman stage were partly the effect and partly the cause of the frightful character of Roman slavery. The gladiators and the actors were slaves especially trained for these debasing exhibitions; and Roman nobles and Roman ladies, brutalized and polluted by witnessing them, went home to give vent among the slaves of their own households to the passions which the circus and the theatre had roused.

And this was the system which St. Paul left unattacked and undenounced. He never in so many words expresses any authoritative condemnation or personal abhorrence of it. This is all the more remarkable when we remember St. Paul's enthusiastic and sympathetic temperament; and the fact is one more proof of the Divine inspiration of Scripture. That slavery, as he saw it, must often have excited the most intense indignation and distress in his heart we cannot doubt; and yet he was guided not to give his sanction to remedies which would certainly have been violent and possibly ineffectual. To have preached that the Christian master must let his slaves go free, would have been to preach that slaves had a right to freedom; and the slave would understand that to mean that, if freedom was not granted, he might take this right of his by force. Of all wars, a servile war is perhaps the most frightful; and we may be thankful that none of those who first preached the Gospel, gave their sanction to any such movement. The sudden abolition of slavery in the first century would have meant the shipwreck of society. Neither master nor slave was fit for any such change. A long course of education was needed before so radical a reform could be successfully accomplished. It has been pointed out as one of the chief marks of the Divine character of the Gospel, that it never appeals to the spirit of political revolution. It does not denounce abuses; but it insists upon principles which will necessarily lead to their abolition.

This was precisely what St. Paul did in dealing with the gigantic cancer which was draining the forces, economical, political, and moral, of Roman society. He did not tell the slave that he was oppressed and outraged. He did not tell the master that to buy and sell human beings was a violation of the rights of man. But he inspired both of them with sentiments which rendered the permanence of the unrighteous relation between them impossible. To many a Roman it would have seemed nothing less than robbery and revolution to tell him "You have no right to own these persons; you must free your slaves." St. Paul, without attacking the rights of property or existing laws and customs, spoke a far higher word, and one which sooner or later must carry the freedom with it, when he said, "You must *love* your slaves." All the moral abominations which had clustered round slavery,—idleness, deceit, cruelty, and lust,—he denounced unsparingly; but for their own sake, not because of their connexion with this iniquitous institution.

The social arrangements, which allowed and encouraged slavery, he did not denounce. He left it to the principles which he preached gradually to reform them. Slavery cannot continue when the brotherhood of all mankind, and the equality of all men in Christ, have been realized. And long before slavery is abolished, it is made more humane, wherever Christian principles are brought to bear upon it. Even before Christianity in the person of Constantine ascended the imperial throne, it had influenced public opinion in the right direction. Seneca and Plutarch are much more humane in their views of slavery than earlier writers are; and under the Antonines the power of life and death over slaves was transferred from their masters to the magistrates. Constantine went much further, and Justinian further still, in ameliorating the condition of slaves and encouraging emancipation. Thus slowly, but surely, this monstrous evil is being eradicated from society; and it is one of the many beauties of the Gospel in comparison with Islam, that whereas Mahometanism has consecrated slavery and given it a permanent religious sanction, Christianity has steadfastly abolished it. It is among the chief glories of the present century that it has seen the abolition of slavery in the British empire, the emancipation of the serfs in Russia, and the emancipation of the negroes in the United States. And we may safely assert that these tardy removals of a great social evil would never have been accomplished but for the principles which St. Paul preached, at the very time that he was allowing Christian masters to retain their slaves, and bidding Christian slaves to honour and obey their heathen masters.

The Apostle's injunctions to slaves who have Christian masters is worthy of special attention: it indicates one of the evils which would certainly have become serious, had the Apostles set to work to preach emancipation. The slaves being in almost all cases quite unfitted for a life of freedom, wholesale emancipation would have flooded society with crowds of persons quite unable to make a decent use of their newly acquired liberty. The sudden change in their condition would have been too great for their self-control. Indeed we gather from what St. Paul says here, that the acceptance of the principles of Christianity in some cases threw them off their balance. He charges Christian slaves who have Christian masters *not to despise them*. Evidently this was a temptation which he foresaw, even if it was not a fault which he had sometimes observed. To be told that he and his master were brethren, and to find that *his master accepted this view of their relationship*, was more than the poor slave in some instances could bear. He had been educated to believe that he was an inferior order of being, having scarcely anything in common, excepting a human form and passions, with his master. And, whether he accepted this belief or not, he had found himself systematically treated as if it were indisputable. When, therefore, he was assured, as one of the first principles of his new faith, that he was not only human, like his master, but in God's family was his master's equal and brother; above all, when he had a Christian master who not only shared this new faith, but acted upon it and treated him as a brother, then his head was in danger of being turned. The rebound from grovelling fear to terms of equality and affection was too much for him; and the old attitude of cringing terror was exchanged not for respectful loyalty, but for contempt. He began to despise the master who had ceased to make himself terrible. All this shows how dangerous sudden changes of social relationships are; and how warily we need to go to work in order to bring about a reform of those which most plainly need readjustment; and it adds greatly to our admiration of the wisdom of the Apostle and our gratitude to Him Who inspired him with such wisdom, to see that in dealing with this difficult problem he does not allow his sympathies to outrun his judgment, and does not attempt to cure a long-standing evil, which had entwined its roots round the very foundations of society, by any rapid or violent process. All men are by natural right free. Granted. All men are by creation children of God, and by redemption brethren in Christ. Granted. But it is worse than useless to give freedom suddenly to those who from their birth have been deprived of it, and do not yet know what use to make of it; and to give the position of children and brethren all at once to outcasts who cannot understand what such privileges mean.

St. Paul tells the slave that freedom is a thing to be desired; but still more that it is a thing to be deserved. "While you are still under the yoke prove yourselves worthy of it and capable of bearing it. In becoming Christians you have become Christ's freeman. Show that you can enjoy that liberty without abusing it. If it leads you to treat a heathen master with disdain, because he has it not, then you give him an opportunity of blaspheming God and your holy religion; for he can say, 'What a vile creed this must be, which makes servants haughty and disrespectful!' If it leads you to treat a Christian master with contemptuous familiarity, because he recognizes you as a brother whom he must love, then you are turning upside down the obligation which a common faith imposes on you. That he is a fellow-Christian is a reason why you should treat him with more reverence, not less." This is ever the burden of his exhortation to slaves. He bids Timothy to insist upon it. He tells Titus to do the same (ii. 9, 10). Slaves were in special danger of misunderstanding what the liberty of the Gospel meant. It is not for a moment to be supposed that it cancels any existing obligations of a slave to his master. No hint is to be given them that they have a right to demand emancipation, or would be justified in running away. Let them learn to behave as the Lord's freeman. Let their masters learn to behave as the Lord's bond-servants. When these principles have worked themselves out, slavery will have ceased to be.

That day has not yet come, but the progress already made, especially during the present century, leads us to hope that it may be near. But the extinction of slavery will not deprive St. Paul's treatment of it of its practical interest and value. His inspired wisdom in dealing with this problem ought to be our guide in dealing with the scarcely less momentous problems which confront us at the present day. We have social difficulties to deal with, whose magnitude and character make them not unlike that of slavery in the first ages of Christianity. There are the relations between capital and labour, the prodigious inequalities in the distribution of wealth, the degradation which is involved in the crowding of population in the great centres of industry. In attempting to remedy such things, let us, while we catch enthusiasm from St. Paul's sympathetic zeal, not forget his patience and discretion. Monstrous evils are not, like giants in the old romances, to be slain at a blow. They are deeply rooted; and if we attempt to tear them up, we may pull up the foundations of society along with them. We must be content to work slowly and without violence. We have no right to preach revolution and plunder to those who are suffering from undeserved poverty, any more than St. Paul had to preach revolt to the slaves. Drastic remedies of that kind will cause much enmity, and perhaps bloodshed, in the carrying out, and will work no permanent cure in the end. It is incredible that the well-being of mankind can be promoted by stirring up ill-will and hatred between a suffering class and those who seem to have it in their power to relieve them. Charity, we know, never faileth; but neither Scripture nor experience has taught us that violence is a sure road to success. We need more faith in the principles of Christianity and in their power to promote happiness as well as godliness. What is required, is not a sudden redistribution of wealth, or laws to prevent its accumulation, but a proper appreciation of its value. Rich and poor alike have yet to learn what is really worth having in this world. It is not wealth, but happiness. And happiness is to be found neither in gaining, nor in possessing, nor in spending money, but in being useful. To serve others, to spend and be spent for them,—that is the ideal to place before mankind; and just in proportion as it is reached, will the frightful inequalities between class and class, and between man and man, cease to be. It is a lesson that takes much teaching and much learning. Meanwhile it seems a terrible thing to leave whole generations suffering from destitution, just as it was a terrible thing to leave whole generations groaning in slavery. But a general manumission would not have helped matters then; and a general distribution to the indigent would not help matters now. The remedy adopted then was a slow one, but it has been efficacious. The master was not told to emancipate his slave, and the slave was not told to run away from his master; but each was charged to behave to the other, the master in commanding and the slave in obeying, as Christian to Christian in the sight of God. Let us not doubt that the same remedy now, if faithfully applied, will be not less effectual. Do not tell the rich man that he must share his wealth with those who have nothing. Do not tell the poor man that he has a right to a share, and may seize it, if it is not given. But by precept and example show to both alike that the one thing worth living for is to promote the well-being of others. And let the experience of the past convince us that any remedy which involves a violent reconstruction of society is sure to be dangerous and may easily prove futile.

FOOTNOTES:

[70] *Laws*, 777 D.

[71] Tacitus, *Ann.* xiv. 42–45; iii. 14; comp. ii. 30 and iii. 67.

CHAPTER XVII
THE GAIN OF A LOVE OF GODLINESS, AND THE UNGODLINESS OF A LOVE OF GAIN

"Wranglings of men corrupted in mind and bereft of the truth, supposing that godliness is a way of gain. But godliness with contentment is great gain: for we brought nothing into the world, for neither can we carry anything out....

"Charge them that are rich in this present world, that they be not high minded, nor have their hope set on the uncertainty of riches, but on God, Who gives us richly all things to enjoy; that they do good, that they be rich in good works, that they be ready to distribute, willing to communicate; laying up in store for themselves a good foundation against the time to come, that they may lay hold on the life which is life indeed."—1 Tim. vi. 5–7, 17–19.

It is evident that the subject of avarice is much in the Apostle's mind during the writing of the last portion of this Epistle. He comes upon it here in connexion with the teachers of false doctrine, and speaks strongly on the subject. Then he writes what appears to be a solemn conclusion to the letter (vv. 11–16). And then, as if he was oppressed by the danger of large possessions as promoting an avaricious spirit, he charges Timothy to warn the wealthy against the folly and wickedness of selfish hoarding. He, as it were, re-opens his letter in order to add this charge, and then writes a second conclusion. He cannot feel happy until he has driven home this lesson about the right way of making gain, and the right way of laying up treasure. It is such a common heresy, and such a fatal one, to believe that gold is wealth, and that wealth is the chief good.

"Wranglings of men corrupted in mind and bereft of the truth." That is how St. Paul describes the "dissidence of dissent," as it was known to him by grievous experience. There were men who had once been in possession of a sound mind, whereby to recognize and grasp the truth; and they had grasped the truth, and for a time retained it. But they had "given heed to seducing spirits," and had allowed themselves to be robbed of both these treasures,—not only the truth, but the mental power of appreciating the truth. And what had they in the place of what they had lost? Incessant contentions among themselves. Having lost the truth, they had no longer any centre of agreement. Error is manifold and its paths are labyrinthine. When two minds desert the truth, there is no reason why they should remain in harmony any more; and each has a right to believe that his own substitute for the truth is the only one worth considering. As proof that their soundness of mind is gone, and that they are far away from the truth, St. Paul states the fact that they "suppose that godliness is a way of gain."

It is well known that the scholars whose labours during the sixteenth and seventeenth centuries produced at last the Authorized Version, were not masters of the force of the Greek article. Its uses had not yet been analysed in the thorough way in which they have been analysed in the present century. Perhaps the text before us is the most remarkable among the numerous errors which are the result of this imperfect knowledge. It seems so strange that those who perpetrated it were not puzzled by their own mistake, and that their perplexity did not put them right. What kind of people could they have been who "supposed that gain was godliness"? Did such an idea ever before enter into the head of any person? And if it did, could he have retained it? People have devoted their whole souls to gain, and have worshipped it as if it were Divine. But no man ever yet believed, or acted as if he believed, that gain was godliness. To make money-getting a substitute for religion, in allowing it to become the one absorbing occupation of mind and body, is one thing: to believe it to be religion is quite another.

But what St. Paul says of the opinions of these perverted men is exactly the converse of this: not that they supposed "gain to be godliness," but that they supposed "godliness to be a means of gain." They considered godliness, or rather the "form of godliness" which was all that they really possessed, to be a profitable investment. Christianity to them was a "profession" in the mercantile sense, and a profession that paid: and they embarked upon it, just as they would upon any other speculation which offered equally good hopes of being remunerative.

The Apostle takes up this perverted and mean view of religion, and shows that in a higher sense it is perfectly true. Just as Caiaphas, while meaning to express a base and cold-blooded policy of expediency, had given utterance to a profound truth about Christ, so these false teachers had got hold of principles which could be formulated so as to express a profound truth about Christ's religion. There is a very real sense in which godliness (genuine godliness and not the mere externals of it) is even in this world a fruitful source of gain. Honesty, so long as it be not practised merely as a policy, is the best policy. "Righteousness exalteth a nation": it invariably pays in the long run. And so "Godliness with contentment is great gain." They *suppose* that godliness is a good investment:—in quite a different sense from that which they have in their minds, it really *is* so. And the reason of this is manifest.

It has already been shown that "godliness is profitable for all things." It makes a man a better master, a better servant, a better citizen, and both in mind and body a healthier and therefore a stronger man. Above all it makes him a happier man; for it gives him that which is the foundation of all happiness in this life, and the foretaste of happiness in the world to come,—a good conscience. A possession of such value as this cannot be otherwise than great gain: especially if it be united, as it probably will be united, with *contentment*. It is in the nature of the godly man to be content with what God has given him. But godliness and contentment are not identical; and therefore, in order to make his meaning quite clear, the Apostle says not merely "godliness," but "godliness with contentment." Either of these qualities far exceeds in value the profitable investment which the false teachers saw in the profession of godliness. They found that it *paid*; that it had a tendency to advance their worldly interests. But after all even mere worldly wealth does not consist in the abundance of the things which a man possesses. That man is well off, who has as much as he wants; and that man is rich, who has more than he wants. Wealth cannot be measured by any absolute standard. We cannot name an income to rise above which is riches, and to fall below which is poverty. Nor is it enough to take into account the unavoidable calls which are made upon the man's purse, in order to know whether he is well off or not: we must also know something of his *desires*. When all legitimate claims have been discharged, is he satisfied with what remains for his own use? Is he *contented*? If he is, then he is indeed well-to-do. If he is not, then the chief element of wealth is still lacking to him.

The Apostle goes on to enforce the truth of the statement that even in this world godliness with contentment is a most valuable possession, far superior to a large income; and to urge that, even from the point of view of earthly prosperity and happiness, those people make a fatal mistake who devote themselves to the accumulation of wealth, without placing any check upon their growing and tormenting desires, and without knowing how to make a good use of the wealth which they are accumulating. With a view to enforce all this he repeats two well-known and indisputable propositions: "We brought nothing into the world" and "We can carry nothing out." As to the words which connect these two propositions in the original Greek, there seems to be some primitive error which we cannot now correct with any certainty. We are not sure whether one proposition is given as a reason for accepting the other, and, if so, which is premise and which is conclusion.

But this is of no moment. Each statement singly has been abundantly proved by the experience of mankind, and no one would be likely to dispute either. One of the earliest books in human literature has them as its opening moral. "Naked came I out of my mother's womb, and naked shall I return thither," are Job's words in the day of his utter ruin; and they have been assented to by millions of hearts ever since.

"We brought nothing into the world." What right then have we to be discontented with what has since been given to us? "We can take nothing out." What folly, therefore, to spend all our time in amassing wealth, which at the time of our departure we shall be obliged to leave behind us! *There* is the case against avarice in a nutshell. Never contented. Never knowing what it is to rest and be thankful. Always nervously anxious about the preservation of what has been gained, and laboriously toiling in order to augment it. What a contrast to the godly man, who has found true independence in a trustful dependence upon the God Whom he serves! Godliness with contentment is indeed great gain.

There is perhaps no more striking example of the incorrigible perversity of human nature than the fact that, in spite of all experience to the contrary, generation after generation continues to look upon mere wealth as the thing best worth striving after. Century after century we find men telling us, often with much emphasis and bitterness, that great possessions are an imposture, that they promise happiness and never give it. And yet those very men continue to devote their whole energies to the retention and increase of their possessions: or, if they do not, they hardly ever succeed in convincing others that happiness is not to be found in such things. If they could succeed, there would be far more contented, and therefore far more happy people in the world than can be found at present. It is chiefly the desire for greater temporal advantages than we have at present that makes us discontented. We should be a long way on the road to contentment, if we could thoroughly convince ourselves that what are commonly called temporal advantages—such as large possessions, rank, power, honours, and the like—are on the whole *not* advantages; that they more often detract from this world's joys than augment them, while they are always a serious danger, and sometimes a grievous impediment, in reference to the joys of the world to come.

What man of wealth and position does not feel day by day the worries and anxieties and obligations, which his riches and rank impose upon him. Does he not often wish that he could retire to some cottage and there live quietly on a few hundreds a year, and sometimes even seriously think of doing it? But at other times he fancies that his unrest and disquiet is owing to his not having enough. If he could only have some thousands a year added to his present income, then he would cease to be anxious about the future; he could afford to lose some and still have sufficient. If he could only attain to a higher position in society, then he would feel secure from detraction or serious downfall; he would be able to treat with unconcerned neglect the criticisms which are now such a source of annoyance to him. And in most cases this latter view prevails. What determines his conduct is not the well-grounded suspicion that he already has more than is good for him; that it is his abundance which is destroying his peace of mind; but the baseless conviction that an increase of the gifts of this world will win for him the happiness that he has failed to secure. The experience of the past rarely destroys this fallacy. He knows that his enjoyment of life has not increased with his fortune. Perhaps he can see clearly that he was a happier man when he possessed much less. But, nevertheless, he still cherishes the belief that with a few things more he would be contented, and for those few things more he continues to slave. There is no man in this world that has not found out over and over again that success, even the most complete success, in the attainment of any worldly desire, however innocent or laudable, does not bring the permanent satisfaction which was anticipated. Sooner or later the feeling of satiety, and therefore of disappointment, must set in. And of all the countless thousands who have had this experience, how few there are that have been able to draw the right conclusion, and to act upon it!

And when we take into account the difficulties and dangers which a large increase in the things of this world places in the way of our advance towards moral and spiritual perfection, we have a still stronger case against the fallacy that increase of wealth brings an increase in well-being. The care of the things which we possess takes up thought and time, which could be far more happily employed on nobler objects; and it leads us gradually into the practical conviction that these nobler objects, which have so continually to be neglected in order to make room for other cares, are really of less importance. It is impossible to go on ignoring the claims which intellectual and spiritual exercises have upon our attention without becoming less alive to those claims. We become, not contented, but self-sufficient in the worst sense. We acquiesce in the low and narrow aims which a devotion to worldly advancement has imposed upon us. We habitually act as if there were no other life but this one; and consequently we cease to take much interest in the other life beyond the grave; while even as regards the things of this world our interests become confined to those objects which can gratify our absorbing desire for financial prosperity.

Nor does the mischief done to our best moral and spiritual interests end here; especially if we are what the world calls successful. The man who steadily devotes himself to the advancement of his worldly position, and who succeeds in a very marked way in raising himself, is likely to acquire in the process a kind of brutal self-confidence, very detrimental to his character. He started with nothing, and he now has a fortune. He was once a shop-boy, and he is now a country gentleman. And he has done it all by his own shrewdness, energy, and perseverance. The result is that he makes no account of Providence, and very little of the far greater merits of less conspicuously successful men. A contempt for men and things that would have given him a higher view of this life, and some idea of a better life, is the penalty which he pays for his disastrous prosperity.

But his case is one of the most hopeless, whose desire for worldly advantages has settled down into a mere love of money. The worldly man, whose leading ambition is to rise to a more prominent place in society, to outshine his neighbours in the appointments of his house and in the splendour of his entertainments, to be of importance on all public occasions, and the like, is morally in a far less desperate condition than the miser. There is no vice more deadening to every noble and tender feeling than avarice. It is capable of extinguishing all mercy, all pity, all natural affection. It can make the claims of the suffering and sorrowful, even when they are combined with those of an old friend, or a wife, or a child, fall on deaf ears. It can banish from the heart not only all love, but all shame and self-respect. What does the miser care for the execrations of outraged society, so long as he can keep his gold? There is no heartless or mean act, and very often no deed of fraud or violence, from which he will shrink in order to augment or preserve his hoards. Assuredly the Apostle is right when he calls the love of money a "root of all kinds of evil." There is no iniquity to which it does not form one of the nearest roads. Every criminal who wants an accomplice can have the avaricious man as his helper, if he only bids high enough.

And note that, unlike almost every other vice, it never loses its hold: its deadly grip is never for an instant relaxed. The selfish man can at a crisis become self-sacrificing, at any rate for a time. The sensualist has his moments when his nobler nature gets the better of his passions, and he spares those whom he thought to make his victims. The drunkard can sometimes be lured by affection or innocent enjoyments to forego the gratification of his craving. And there are times when even pride, that watchful and subtle foe, sleeps at its post and suffers humble thoughts to enter. But the demon avarice never slumbers, and is never off its guard. When it has once taken full possession of a man's heart, neither love, nor pity, nor shame, can ever surprise it into an act of generosity. We all of us have our impulses; and, however little we may act upon them, we are conscious that some of our impulses are generous. Some of the worst of us could lay claim to as much as that. But the miser's nature is poisoned at its very source. Even his impulses are tainted. Sights and sounds which make other hardened sinners at least wish to help, if only to relieve their own distress at such pitiful things, make him instinctively tighten his purse-strings. Gold is his god; and there is no god who exacts from his worshippers such undivided and unceasing devotion. Family, friends, country, comfort, health, and honour must all be sacrificed at its shrine. Certainly the lust for gold is one of those "foolish and hurtful lusts, such as drown men in destruction and perdition."

In wealthy Ephesus, with its abundant commerce, the desire to be rich was a common passion; and St. Paul feared—perhaps he knew—that in the Church in Ephesus the mischief was present and increasing. Hence this earnest reiteration of strong warnings against it. Hence the reopening of the letter in order to tell Timothy to charge the rich not to be self-confident and arrogant, not to trust in the wealth which may fail them, but in the God Who cannot do so; and to remind them that the only way to make riches secure is to give them to God and to His work. The wealthy heathen in Ephesus were accustomed to deposit their treasures with "the great goddess Diana," whose temple was both a sanctuary and a bank. Let Christian merchants deposit theirs with God by being "rich in good works;" so that, when He called them to Himself, they might receive their own with usury, and "lay hold on the life which is life indeed."

THE EPISTLE TO TITUS

CHAPTER XVIII
THE EPISTLE TO TITUS.—HIS LIFE AND CHARACTER

"Paul, a servant of God, and an apostle of Jesus Christ ... to Titus, my true child after a common faith: Grace and peace from God the Father, and Christ Jesus our Saviour"—Titus i. 1, 4.

The title "Pastoral Epistle" is as appropriate to the Epistle to Titus as to the First Epistle to Timothy. Although there is a good deal in the letter that is personal rather than pastoral, yet the pastoral element is the main one. The bulk of the letter is taken up with questions of Church doctrine and government, the treatment of the faithful members of the congregation and of the unruly and erring. The letter is addressed to Titus, not as a private individual, but as the delegate of the Apostle holding office in Crete. Hence, as in the First Epistle to Timothy, St. Paul styles himself an Apostle: and the official character of this letter is still further marked by the long and solemn superscription. It is evidently intended to be read by other persons besides the minister to whom it is addressed.

The question of the authenticity of the Epistle to Titus, has already been in a great measure discussed in the first of these expositions. It was pointed out there that the external evidence for the genuineness in all three cases is very strong, beginning almost certainly with Clement of Rome, Ignatius, and Polycarp, becoming clear and certain in Irenæus, and being abundant in Clement of Alexandria and Tertullian. Of the very few people who rejected them, Tatian seems to have been almost alone in making a distinction between them. He accepted the Epistle to Titus, while rejecting the two to Timothy. We may rejoice that Tatian, Marcion, and others raised the question. It cannot be said that the Churches accepted this Epistle without consideration. Those who possessed evidence now no longer extant were convinced, in spite of the objections urged, that in this letter and its two companions we have genuine writings of St. Paul.

With regard to modern objections, it may be freely admitted that there is no room in St. Paul's life, as given in the Acts, for the journey to Crete, and the winter at Nicopolis required by the Epistle to Titus. But there is plenty of room for both of these *outside* the Acts, viz., between the first and second imprisonment of the Apostle. And, as we have already seen good reason for believing in the case of 1 Timothy, the condition of the Church indicated in this letter is such as was already in existence in St. Paul's time; and the language used in treating of it resembles that of the Apostle in a way which helps us to believe that we are reading his own words and not those of a skilful imitator. For this imitator must have been a strange person; very skilful in some things, very eccentric in others. Why does he give St. Paul and Titus a work in Crete of which there is no mention in the Acts? Why does he make the Apostle ask Titus to meet him in Nicopolis, a place never named in connexion with St. Paul? Why bracket a well-known person, like Apollos, with an utterly unknown person, such as Zenas? It is not easy to believe in this imitator.

Yet another point of resemblance should be noted. Here, as in 1 Timothy, there is no careful arrangement of the material. The subjects are not put together in a studied order, as in a treatise with a distinct theological or controversial purpose. They follow one another in a natural manner, just as they occur to the writer. Persons with their hearts and heads full of things which they wish to say to a friend, do not sit down with an analysis before them to secure an orderly arrangement of what they wish to write. They start with one of the main topics, and then the treatment of this suggests something else: and they are not distressed if they repeat themselves, or if they have to return to a subject which has been touched upon before and then dropped. This is just the kind of writing which meets us once more in the letter to Titus. It is thoroughly natural. It is not easy to believe that a forger in the second century could have thrown himself with such simplicity into the attitude which the letter pre-supposes.

It is not possible to determine whether this letter was written before or after the First to Timothy. But it was certainly written before the Second to Timothy. Therefore, while one has no sufficient reason for taking it before the one, one has excellent reason for taking it before the other. The precise year and the precise place in which it was written, we must be content to leave unsettled. It may be doubted whether either the one or the other would throw much light on the contents of the letter. These are determined by what the Apostle remembers and expects concerning affairs in Crete, and not by his own surroundings. It is the official position of Titus in Crete which is chiefly before his mind.

Titus, as we learn from the opening words of the letter, was, like Timothy, converted to Christianity by St. Paul. The Apostle calls him "his true child after a common faith." As regards his antecedents he was a marked contrast to Timothy. Whereas Timothy had been brought up as a Jew under the care of his Jewish mother Eunice, and had been circumcised by St. Paul's desire, Titus was wholly a Gentile, and "was not compelled to be circumcised," as St. Paul states in the passage in which he tells the Galatians (ii. 1—3) that he took Titus with him to Jerusalem on the occasion when he and Barnabas went thither seventeen years after St. Paul's conversion. Paul and Barnabas went up to Jerusalem on that occasion to protect Gentile converts from the Judaizers, who wanted to make all such converts submit to circumcision. Titus and others went with them as representatives of the Gentile converts, and in their persons a formal protest was made against this imposition. It is quite possible that Titus was with St. Paul when he wrote to the Galatians; and if so this mention of him becomes all the more natural. We may fancy the Apostle saying to Titus, as he wrote the letter, "I shall remind them of your case, which is very much to the point." Whether Titus was personally known to the Galatian Church is not certain; but he is spoken of as one of whom they have at any rate heard.

Titus was almost certainly one of those who carried the First Epistle to the Corinthian Church, *i.e.*, the first of the two that have come down to us; and St. Paul awaited his report of the reception which the letter had met with at Corinth with the utmost anxiety. And he was quite certainly one of those who were entrusted with the Second Epistle to the Corinthians. St. Paul wrote the first letter at Ephesus about Easter, probably in the year 57. He left Ephesus about Pentecost, and went to Troas, where he hoped to meet Titus with news from Corinth. After waiting in vain he went on to Macedonia in grievous anxiety; and there Titus met him. He at once began the second letter, which apparently was written piece-meal during the journey; and when it was completed he sent Titus back to Corinth with it.

That Titus should twice have been sent as the messenger and representative of St. Paul to a Church in which difficulties of the gravest kind had arisen, gives us a clear indication of the Apostle's estimate of his character. He must have been a person of firmness, discretion, and tact. There was the monstrous case of incest, the disputes between the rival factions, contentions in public worship and even at the Eucharist, litigation before the heathen, and wild ideas about the resurrection, not to mention other matters which were difficult enough, although of a less burning character. And in all these questions it was the vain, fitful, vivacious, and sensitive Corinthians who had to be managed and induced to take the Apostle's words (which sometimes were very sharp and severe) patiently. Nor was this all. Besides the difficulties in the Church of Corinth there was the collection for the poor Christians in Judæa, about which St. Paul was deeply interested, and which had not been progressing in Corinth as he wished. St. Paul was doubly anxious that it should be a success; first, because it proved to the Jewish converts that his interest in them was substantial, in spite of his opposition to some of their views; secondly, because it served to counteract the tendency to part asunder, which was manifesting itself between the Jewish and Gentile Christians. And in carrying out St. Paul's instructions about these matters Titus evidently had to suffer a good deal of opposition; and hence the Apostle writes a strong commendation of him, coupling him with himself in his mission and zeal. "Whether any inquire about Titus, he is my partner and my fellow-worker to you-ward." "Thanks be to God, which putteth the same earnest care for you into the heart of Titus. For indeed he accepted our exhortation; but being himself very earnest, he went forth unto you of his own accord." With great delicacy the Apostle takes care that, in making it clear to the Corinthians that Titus has his full authority for what he does, no slight is cast upon Titus's own zeal and interest in the Corinthians. "He is my representative; but he comes of his own free will out of love to you. His visit to you is his own doing; but he has my entire sanction. He is neither a mechanical delegate, nor an unauthorized volunteer."

A curtain falls on the career of this valued help-mate of the great Apostle, from the time when he carried the second letter to Corinth to the time when the letter to himself was written. The interval was probably some eight or ten years, about which we know only one thing, that during it, and probably in the second half of it, the Apostle and Titus had been together in Crete, and Titus had been left behind to consolidate the Church there. The Acts tell us nothing. Probably Titus is not mentioned in the book at all. The reading "Titus Justus" in xviii. 7, is possibly correct, but it is far from certain: and even if it were certain, we should still remain in doubt whether Titus and Titus Justus are the same person. And the attempts which have been made to identify Titus with other persons in the Acts, such as Silvanus or Timothy, are scarcely worth considering. Nor has the conjecture that Titus is the author of the Acts (as Krenkel, Jacobsen, and recently Hooykaas in the *Bible for Young People* have suggested) very much to recommend it. The hypothesis has two facts to support it: (1) the silence of the Acts respecting Titus, and (2) the fact that the writer must have been a companion of St. Paul. But these two facts are equally favourable to the tradition that St. Luke was the author, a tradition for which the evidence is both very early and very abundant. Why should such a tradition yield to a mere conjecture?

One thing, however, we may accept as certain:—that the time when St. Paul was being carried a prisoner to Rome in an Alexandrian corn-ship which touched at Crete, was *not* the time when the Church in Crete was founded. What opportunity would a prisoner have of doing any such work during so short a stay? Cretans were among those who heard the Apostles at Pentecost preaching in their own tongue the wonderful works of God. Some of these may have returned home and formed the first beginnings of a Christian congregation: and among imperfect converts of this kind we might expect to find the errors of which St. Paul treats in this Epistle. But we can hardly suppose that there was much of Christian organization until St. Paul and Titus came to the island after the Apostle's first Roman imprisonment. And the necessity of having some one with a calm head and a firm hand on the spot, forced the Apostle to leave his companion behind him. The man who had been so successful in aiding him respecting the difficulties at Corinth was just the man to be entrusted with a somewhat similar but rather more permanent post in Crete. The Cretans were less civilized, but in their own way scarcely less immoral, than the Corinthians; and in both cases the national failings caused serious trouble in the Church. In both cases ecclesiastical authority has to be firmly upheld against those who question and oppose it. In both cases social turbulence has to be kept in check. In both cases there is a tendency to wild theological and philosophical speculations, and (on the part of some) to a bigoted maintenance of Jewish ordinances and superstitions. Against all these Titus will have to contend with decision, and if need be with severity.

The letter, in which directions are given for the carrying out of all this, is evidence of the great confidence which the Apostle reposed in him. One of those who had worked also in Corinth, is either already with him in Crete, or may soon be expected,—Apollos, and with him Zenas. So that the Corinthian experience is doubly represented. Other helpers are coming, viz., Artemas and Tychicus; and, when they arrive, Titus will be free to rejoin the Apostle, and is to lose no time in doing so at Nicopolis.

One commission Titus has in Crete which very naturally was not given to him at Corinth. He is to perfect the organization of the Christian Church in the island by appointing elders in every city. And it is this charge among others which connects this letter so closely with the first to Timothy, which very likely was written about the same time.

Whether Titus was set free from his heavy charge in Crete in time to join St. Paul at Nicopolis, we have no means of knowing. At the time when the second letter to Timothy was written, Titus had gone to Dalmatia; but we are left in doubt as to whether he had gone thither by St. Paul's desire, or (like Demas in going to Thessalonica) against it. Nor does it appear whether

Titus had gone to Dalmatia from Nicopolis, which is not far distant, or had followed the Apostle from Nicopolis to Rome, and thence gone to Illyria. With the journey to Dalmatia our knowledge of him ends. Tradition takes him back to Crete as permanent bishop; and in the Middle Ages the Cretans seem to have regarded him as their patron saint.

The impression left upon our mind by the Acts is that St. Luke knew Timothy and did not know Titus: and hence frequently mentions the one and says nothing about the other. The impression left upon our mind by the mention of both in Paul's Epistles, and by the letters addressed to each, is that Titus, though less tenderly beloved by the Apostle, was the stronger man of the two. St. Paul seems to be less anxious about the conduct of Titus and about the way in which others will treat him. The directions as to his personal behaviour are much slighter than in the case of Timothy. He seems to credit him with less sensitiveness and more decision and tact; perhaps also with less liability to be carried away by fanatical views and practices than the other.

Titus shares with Timothy the glory of having given up everything in order to throw in his lot with St. Paul, and of being one of his most trusted and efficient helpers. What that meant the Epistles of St. Paul tell us:— ceaseless toil and anxiety, much shame and reproach, and not a little peril to life itself. He also shares with Timothy the glory of being willing, when the cause required such sacrifice, to separate from the master to whom he had surrendered himself, and to work on by himself in isolation and difficulty. The latter was possibly the more trying sacrifice of the two. To give up all his earthly prospects and all the sweetness of home life, in order to work for the spread of the Gospel side by side with St. Paul, was no doubt a sacrifice that must have cost those who made it a great deal. But it had its attractive side. Quite independently of the beauty and majesty of the cause itself, there was the delight of being associated with a leader so able, so sagacious, so invigorating, and so affectionate as the Apostle who "became all things to all men that he might by all means save some." Hard work became light, and difficulties became smooth, under the inspiring sympathy of such a colleague. But it was quite another thing to have given up everything for the sake of such companionship and support, or at least in the full expectation of enjoying it, and then to have to undergo the hard work and confront the difficulties without it. The new dispensation in this respect repeats the old. Elisha leaves his home and his inheritance to follow Elijah, and then Elijah is taken from him. Timothy and Titus leave their homes and possessions to follow St. Paul, and then St. Paul sends them away from him. And to this arrangement they consented, Timothy (as we know) with tears, Titus (we may be sure) with much regret. And what it cost the loving Apostle thus to part with them and to pain them we see from the tone of affectionate longing which pervades these letters.

The example set by both master and disciples is one which Christians, and especially Christian ministers, must from time to time need. Christ sent forth both the Twelve and the Seventy "two and two"; and what is true of mankind generally is true also of the ministry—"It is not good for man to be alone." But cases often arise in which not more than one man can be spared for each post; and then those who have been all in all to one another, in sympathy and counsel and co-operation, have to part. And it is one of the greatest sacrifices that can be required of them. Paul and Timothy and Titus were willing to make this sacrifice; and it is one which Christ's servants throughout all ages are called upon at times to make. Many men are willing to face, especially in a good cause, what is repulsive to them, if they have the company of others in the trial, especially if they have the presence and support of those whose presence is in itself a refreshment, and their support a redoubling of strength. But to enter upon a long and trying task with the full expectation of such advantages, and then to be called upon to surrender them,—this is, indeed, a trial which might well make the weak-hearted turn back. But their devotion to their Lord's work, and their confidence in His sustaining power, enabled the Apostle and his two chief disciples to make the venture; and the marvellous success of the Church in the age which immediately succeeded them, shows how their sacrifice was blessed. And we may be sure that even in this world they had their reward. "Verily I say unto you, There is no man that hath left house, or brethren, or sisters, or mother, or father, or children, or lands, for My sake, and for the Gospel's sake, but he shall receive a hundredfold now in this time, houses, and brethren, and sisters, and mothers, and children, and lands, *with persecutions*; and in the world to come *eternal life*."

CHAPTER XIX
THE CHURCH IN CRETE AND ITS ORGANIZATION.—THE APOSTLE'S DIRECTIONS FOR APPOINTING ELDERS

> "For this cause left I thee in Crete, that thou shouldest set in order the things that were wanting, and appoint elders in every city, as I gave thee charge; if any man is blameless, the husband of one wife, having children that believe, who are not accused of riot or unruly. For the bishop must be blameless, as God's steward."—Titus i. 5–7.

This passage tells us a great deal about the circumstances which led to the writing of the letter. They have been touched upon in the previous chapter, but may be treated more comprehensively here.

It is quite evident: (1) that the Gospel had been established in Crete for a considerable time when St. Paul wrote this to his delegate, Titus; (2) that during the Apostle's stay in the island he had been unable to complete the work which he had in view with regard to the full establishment of the Church there; and (3) that one of the chief things which remained undone, and which St. Paul had been compelled to leave to Titus to accomplish, was a properly organized ministry. There was a large and scattered flock; but for the most part it was without shepherds.

It is quite possible that the Gospel of Christ was at least known, if not by any one believed, in Crete before St. Paul visited the islands. Cretans were among those who heard the miraculous preaching of the Apostles on the day of Pentecost; and some of these may have returned to their country, if not converts to Christianity, at any rate full of what they had seen and heard of "the mighty works of God," as shown forth in the words spoken on that day, and in their consequences. Certainly there were many Jews in the island; and these, though often the bitterest opponents of the Gospel, were nevertheless the readiest and best converts, when they did not oppose; for they already knew and worshipped the true God, and they were acquainted with the prophecies respecting the Messiah. We may therefore conclude that the way was already prepared for the preaching of Christ, even if He as yet had no worshippers in Crete, before St. Paul began to teach there.

There are three things which tend to show that Christianity had been spreading in Crete for at least some years when the Apostle wrote this letter to Titus. First, the latter is charged to "appoint elders *in every city*," or "city by city," as we might render the original expression (κατὰ πόλιν). This implies that among the multitude of cities, for which Crete even in Homer's day had been famous, not a few had a Christian congregation in need of supervision; and it is not improbable that the congregation in some cases was a large one. For the interpretation is certainly an untenable one which forces into the Apostle's words a restriction which they do not contain, that each city is to have just one presbyter and no more. St. Paul tells Titus to take care that no city is left without a presbyter. Each Christian community is to have its proper ministry; it is not to be left to its own guidance. But how many elders each congregation is to have, is a point to be decided by Titus according to the principles laid down for him by St. Paul. For we must not limit the "as I gave thee charge" to the mere fact of appointing elders. The Apostle had told him, not merely that elders must be appointed, but that they must be appointed in a particular way, and according to a prescribed system. The passage, therefore, tells us that there were a good many cities in which there were Christian congregations, and leaves us quite free to believe that some of these congregations were large enough to require several elders to minister to them and govern them. Secondly, the kind of person to be selected as overseer seems to imply that Christianity has been established for a considerable time among the Cretans. The "elder" or "bishop" (for in this passage, at any rate, the two names indicate one and the same officer) is to be the father of a family, with children who are believers and orderly persons.

The injunction implies that there are cases in which the father is a good Christian, but he has not succeeded in making his children good Christians. Either they have not become believers at all; or, although nominal Christians, they do not conduct themselves as such. They are profligate, riotous, and disobedient. This implies that the children are old enough to think for themselves and reject the Gospel in spite of their parent's conversion; or that they are old enough to rebel against its authority. And one does not use such strong words as "profligacy" or "riotous living" of quite young children. The prodigal son, of whom the same expression is used, was no mere child. Cases of this kind, therefore, in which the father had been converted to Christianity, but had been unable to make the influences of Christianity tell upon his own children, were common enough to make it worth St. Paul's while to give injunctions about them. And this implies a condition of things in which Christianity was no newly planted religion. The injunctions are intelligible enough. Such fathers are not to be selected by Titus as elders.

A man who has so conspicuously failed in bringing his own household into harmony with the Gospel, is not the man to be promoted to rule the household of the Church. Even if his failure is his misfortune rather than his fault, the condition of his own family cannot fail to be a grave impediment to his usefulness as an overseer of the congregation.[72] Thirdly, there is the fact that heresies already exist among the Cretan Christians. Titus, like Timothy, has to contend with teaching of a seriously erroneous kind. From this also we infer that the faith has long since been introduced into the island. The misbeliefs of the newly converted would be spoken of in far gentler terms. They are errors of ignorance, which will disappear as fuller instruction in the truth is received. They are not erroneous doctrines held and propagated in opposition to the truth. These latter require time for their development. From all these considerations, therefore, we conclude that St. Paul is writing to Titus as his delegate in a country in which the Gospel is no new thing. We are not to suppose that the Apostle left Titus in charge of Christians who had been converted a very short time before to the faith.

The incompleteness of the Apostle's own work in the island is spoken of in plain terms. Even in Churches in which he was able to remain for two or three years, he was obliged to leave very much unfinished; and we need not be surprised that such was the case in Crete, where he can hardly have stayed so long. It was this incompleteness in all his work, a defect quite unavoidable in work of such magnitude, that weighed so heavily upon the Apostle's mind. It was "that which pressed upon him daily,—anxiety for all the Churches." There was so much that had never been done at all; so much that required to be secured and established; so much that already needed correction. And while he was attending to the wants of one Church, another not less important, not less dear to him, was equally in need of his help and guidance. And here was the comfort of having such disciples as, Timothy and Titus, who, like true friends, could be indeed a "second self" to him. They could be carrying on his work in places where he himself could not be. And thus there was no small consolation for the sorrow of parting from them and the loss of their helpful presence. They could be still more helpful elsewhere. "For this cause left I thee in Crete, that thou shouldest set in order the things that were wanting."

There were many things that were wanting in Crete; but one of the chief things which pressed upon the Apostle's mind was the lack of a properly organized ministry, without which everything must soon fall into confusion and decay. Hence, as soon as he has concluded his salutation, the fulness and solemnity of which is one of the many evidences of the genuineness of the letter, he at once repeats to Titus the charge which he had previously given to him by word of mouth respecting this pressing need. A due supply of elders or overseers is of the first importance for "setting in order" those things which at present are in so unsatisfactory a state.

There are several points of interest in connexion with St. Paul's directions to Titus respecting this need and the best way of meeting it.

First. It is Titus himself who is to appoint these elders throughout the cities in which congregations exist. It is not the congregations that are to elect the overseers, subject to the approval of the Apostle's delegate; still less that he is to ordain any one whom they may elect. The full responsibility of each appointment rests with him. Anything like popular election of the ministers is not only not suggested, it is by implication entirely excluded. But, secondly, in making each appointment Titus is to consider the congregation. He is to look carefully to the reputation which the man of his choice bears among his fellow-Christians:—"if any man is *blameless* ... having children who are not *accused* of riot.... For the bishop must be *blameless*." A man in whom the congregation have no confidence, because of the bad repute which attaches to himself or his family, is not to be appointed. In this way the congregation have an indirect veto; for the man to whom they cannot give a good character may not be taken to be set over them. Thirdly, the appointment of Church officers is regarded as imperative: it is on no account to be omitted. And it is not merely an arrangement that is as a rule desirable: it is to be universal. Titus is to "appoint elders in every city." He is to go through the congregations "city by city," and take care that each has its elder or body of elders. Fourthly, as the name itself indicates, these elders are to be taken from the older men among the believers. As a rule they are to be heads of families, who have had experience of life in its manifold relations, and especially who have had experience of ruling a Christian household. That will be some guarantee for their capacity for ruling a Christian congregation. Lastly, it must be remembered that they are not merely delegates, either of Titus, or of the congregation. The essence of their authority is not that they are the representatives of the body of Christian men and women over whom they are placed. It has a far higher origin. They are "God's stewards." It is His household that they direct and administer, and it is from Him that their powers are derived. They are His ministers, solemnly appointed to act in His Name. It is on His behalf that they have to speak, as His agents and ambassadors, labouring to advance the interests of His kingdom. They are "stewards of His mysteries," bringing out of what is committed to them "things new and old." As God's agents they have a work to do among their fellow-men, through themselves, for Him. As God's ambassadors they have a message to deliver, good tidings to proclaim, ever the same, and yet ever new. As "God's stewards" they have treasures to guard with reverent care, treasures to augment by diligent cultivation, treasures to distribute with prudent liberality. There is the flock, sorely needing, but it may be not greatly craving, God's spiritual gifts. The longing has to be awakened: the longing, when awakened, has to be cherished and directed: the gifts which will satisfy it have to be dispensed. There is a demand; and there is a supply; a human demand and a Divine supply. It is the business of God's stewards to see that the one meets the other.

"God's steward" is the key to all that follows respecting the qualities to be looked for in an elder or overseer of the Church: and, as the order of the words in the Greek shows, the emphasis is on "God's" rather than on "steward." The point accentuated is, not that in the Church as in his own home he has a household to administer, but that the household to which he has to minister is God's. That being so, he "as God's steward" must prove himself worthy of the Commission which he holds: "not self-willed, not soon angry, no brawler, no striker, not greedy of filthy lucre; but given to hospitality, a lover of good, sober-minded, just, holy, temperate; holding to the faithful word which is according to the teaching, that he may be able both to exhort in the sound doctrine, and to convict the gainsayers."

Such men, wherever he can find them,—and "*if* any man is blameless" is not meant to hint that among Cretans it may be impossible to find such,— Titus is to "*appoint*" as elders in every city. In the A.V. the phrase runs "*ordain* elders in every city." As we have seen already (Chap. V.), there are several passages in which the Revisers have changed "ordain" into "appoint." Thus in Mark iii. 14, "He ordained twelve" becomes "He appointed twelve." In John xv. 16, "I have chosen you and ordained you" becomes, "I chose you and appointed you." In 1 Tim. ii. 7, "Whereunto I am ordained a preacher, and an apostle" becomes "whereunto I was appointed a preacher and an apostle." In Heb. v. 1, and viii. 3, "Every high priest is ordained" becomes "every high priest is appointed." In these passages three different Greek words (ποιέω, τίθημι, καθίστημι) are used in the original; but not one of them has the special ecclesiastical meaning which we so frequently associate with the word "ordain"; not one of them implies, as "ordain" in such context almost of necessity implies, a *rite* of ordination, a special ceremonial, such as the laying on of hands. When in English we say, "He ordained twelve," "I am ordained an apostle," "Every high priest is ordained," the mind almost inevitably thinks of ordination in the common sense of the word; and this is foisting upon the language of the New Testament a meaning which the words there used do not rightly bear. They all three of them refer to the *appointment* to the office, and not to rite or ceremony by which the person appointed is admitted to the office. The Revisers, therefore, have done wisely in banishing from all such texts a word which to English readers cannot fail to suggest ideas which are not contained at all in the original

Greek. If we ask in what way Titus admitted the men whom he selected to serve as presbyters to their office, the answer is scarcely a doubtful one. Almost certainly he would admit them, as Timothy himself was admitted, and as he is instructed to admit others, by the laying on of hands. But this is neither expressed nor implied in the injunction to "*appoint* elders in every city." The appointment is one thing, the ordination another; and even in cases in which we are sure that the appointment involved ordination, we are not justified in saying "ordain" where the Greek says "appoint." The Greek words used in the passages quoted might equally well be used of the appointment of a magistrate or a steward. And as we should avoid speaking of *ordaining* a magistrate or a steward, we ought to avoid using "ordain" to translate words which would be thoroughly in place in such a connexion. The Greek words for "ordain" and "ordination," in the sense of imposition of hands in order to admit to an ecclesiastical office (χειροθετεῖ, χειροθεσία), do not occur in the New Testament at all.

It is worthy of note that there is not a trace here, any more than there is in the similar passage in 1 Timothy, of the parallel between the threefold ministry in the Old Testament and a threefold ministry in the Christian Church, high-priest, priests, and Levites being compared with bishop, presbyters, and deacons. This parallel was a favourite one and it was made early. The fact therefore that we do not find it in any of these Epistles, nor even any material out of which it could be constructed, confirms us in the belief that these letters belong to the first century and not to the second.

In giving this injunction to Titus, St. Paul assumes that his disciple and delegate is as free as he himself is from all feelings of jealousy, or envy. "Art thou jealous for my sake? would God that all the Lord's people were prophets," is the spirit in which these instructions are given, and no doubt were accepted. There is no grasping after power in the great Apostle of the Gentiles; no desire to keep everything in his own hands, that he might have the credit of all that was done. So long as Christ is rightly preached, so long as the Lord's work is faithfully done, he cares not who wins the glory. He is more than willing that Timothy and Titus should share in his work and its reward; and he without hesitation applies to them to admit others in like manner to share with them in their work and its reward. This generous willingness to admit others to co-operate is not always found, especially in men of strong character and great energy and decision. They will admit subordinates as a necessary evil to work out details, because they cannot themselves afford time for all these. But they object to anything like colleagues. Whatever of any serious importance is done must be in their own hands and must be recognized as their work. There is nothing of this spirit in St. Paul. He could rejoice when some "preached Christ even of envy and strife," "not sincerely, thinking to raise up affliction for him in his bonds." He rejoiced, not because of their evil temper, but because that at any rate Christ was preached. How much more, therefore, did he rejoice when Christ was preached "of good will" by disciples devoted to himself and his Master. They all had the same end in view; not their own glory, but the glory of God.

And this is the end which all Christian ministers have to keep in view, and which they too often exchange for ends that are far lower, and far removed (it may be) from the cause with which we choose to identify them. And as time goes on, and we look less and less with a single eye at the will of God, and have less and less of the single purpose of seeking His glory, our aims become narrower and our ends more selfish. At first it is the triumph of a system, then it is the advancement of a party. Then it becomes the propagation of our own views, and the extension of our own influence. Until at last we find ourselves working, no longer for God's glory, but simply for our own. While professing to work in His Name and for His honour, we have steadily substituted our own wills for His.

But it is only by forgetting ourselves that we find ourselves; only by losing our life that we find it. "God's steward" must be ready to sink every personal interest in the interests of the great Employer. He has nothing of his own. He deals with his Master's goods, and must deal with them in his Master's way. He who labours in this spirit will one day be rewarded by the Divine voice of welcome: "Well done, good and faithful servant: thou hast been faithful over a few things; I will set thee over many things; enter thou into the joy of thy Lord."

FOOTNOTES:

[72] It is worth while here to repeat the caution that the Apostle's language by no means implies that the "elder" or "bishop" *must* be a married man with children. But it implies that he will generally be such; and in appointing him, the character of his family must be carefully considered.

CHAPTER XX
CHRISTIANITY AND UNCHRISTIAN LITERATURE

"One of themselves, a prophet of their own, said, Cretans are always liars, evil beasts, idle gluttons. This testimony is true. For which cause reprove them sharply, that they may be sound in the faith."—Titus i. 12, 13.

The hexameter verse which St. Paul here cites from the Cretan poet Epimenides is one of three quotations from profane literature which are made by St. Paul. Of the other two, one occurs in 1 Cor. xv. 33, "Evil communications corrupt good manners"; and the other in the Apostle's speech on the Areopagus at Athens, as recorded in the Acts (xvii. 28): "For we are also his offspring." They cannot be relied upon as sufficient to prove that St. Paul was well read in classical literature, any more than the quoting of a hackneyed line from Shakespeare, from Byron, and from Tennyson, would prove that an English writer was well acquainted with English literature. It may have been the case that St. Paul knew a great deal of Greek classical literature, but these three quotations, from Epimenides, from some Greek tragedian, and from Cleanthes or Aratus, do not at all prove the point. In all three cases the source of the quotation is not certain. In the one before us the Apostle no doubt tells us that he is quoting a Cretan "prophet," and therefore quotes the line as coming from Epimenides. But a man may know that "Friends, Romans, countrymen, lend me your ears" is Shakespeare, without having read a single play. And we are quite uncertain whether St. Paul had even seen the poem of Epimenides on Oracles in which the line which he here quotes occurs. The iambic which he quotes in the letter to the Corinthians, although originally in some Greek play (perhaps of Euripides or Menander), had passed into a proverb, and proves even less than the line from Epimenides that St. Paul knew the work in which it occurred. The half-line which is given in his speech at Athens, stating the Divine parentage of mankind, may have come from a variety of sources: but it is not improbable that the Apostle had read it in the *Phænomena* of Aratus, in which it occurs in the form in which it is reproduced in the Acts. This astronomical poem was popular in St. Paul's day, and he was the more likely to have come across it, as Aratus is said to have been a native of Tarsus, or at any rate of Cilicia. But even when we have admitted that the Apostle had read the *Phænomena* of Aratus or Cleanthes' Hymn to Zeus, we have not made much way towards proving that he was well read in Greek literature. Indeed the contrary has been argued from the fact that, according to the reading of the best authorities, the iambic line in the Corinthians is quoted in such a way as to spoil the scanning; which would seem to show that St. Paul was not familiar with the iambic metre.[73] If that was the case, he can scarcely have read even a single Greek play.

But the question is not one of great importance, although doubtless of some interest. We do not need this evidence to prove that the Apostle was a person, not only of great energy and ability, but of culture. There are passages in his writings, such as chapters xiii. and xv. in 1 Corinthians, which are equal for beauty and eloquence to anything in literature. Even among inspired writers few have known better than St. Paul how to clothe lofty thoughts in noble language. And of his general acquaintance with the moral philosophy of his age, especially of the Stoic school, which was very influential in the neighbourhood of Tarsus, there can be no doubt. Just as St. John laid the thoughts and language of Alexandrian philosophy under contribution, and gave them fuller force and meaning to express the dogmatic truths of the Gospel, so St. Paul laid the thoughts and language of Stoicism under contribution, and transfigured them to express the moral teaching of the Gospel. Cleanthes or Aratus, from one or both of whom one of the three quotations comes (and St. Paul seems to know both sources, for he says "as *certain* even of your own *poets* have said"), were both of them Stoics: and the speech in which the quotation occurs, short as it is in the Acts, abounds in parallels to the teaching of St. Paul's Stoic contemporary Seneca. If St. Paul tells us that "the God that made the world and all things therein ... dwelleth not in temples made with hands," Seneca teaches that "temples must not be built to God of stones piled on high: He must be consecrated in the heart of man." While St. Paul reminds us that God "is not far from each one of us," Seneca says "God is near thee: He is with thee; He is within." Again, St. Paul warns his hearers that "we ought not to think that the Godhead is like unto gold, or silver, or stone, graven by art and device of man"; and Seneca declares "Thou shalt not form Him of silver and gold: a true likeness of God cannot be moulded of this material."[74]

But the quotations are of other interest than their bearing upon the question as to the Greek elements in the education and teaching of St. Paul. They have a bearing also on the question of Christian use of profane authors, and on the duty of self-culture in general.

The leading teachers of the early Church differed widely in their estimate of the value of heathen literature, and especially of heathen philosophy. On the whole, with some considerable exceptions, the Greek Fathers valued it highly, as containing precious elements of truth, which were partly the result of direct inspiration, partly echoes of the Old Testament. The Latin Fathers, on the other hand, for the most part treated all pagan teaching with suspicion and contempt. It was in no sense useful. It was utterly false, and simply stood in the way of the truth. It was rubbish, which must be swept on one side in order to make room for the Gospel. Tertullian thinks that heathen philosophers are "blockheads when they knock at the doors of truth," and that "they have contributed nothing whatever that a Christian can accept." Arnobius and Lactantius write in a similar strain of contemptuous disapproval. Tertullian thinks it out of the question that a right-minded Christian should teach in pagan schools. But even he shrinks from telling Christian parents that they must allow their children to remain uneducated rather than send them to such schools. The policy of permitting Christian children to attend heathen schools, while forbidding Christian adults from teaching in them, appears singularly unreasonable. Every Christian teacher in a school rendered that school less objectionable for Christian children. But Tertullian urges that one who teaches pagan literature seems to give his sanction to it: one who merely learns it does nothing of the kind. The young must be educated: adults need not become school-masters. One can plead necessity in the one case; not in the other (*De Idol.*, x). But the necessity of sending a child to a pagan school, because otherwise it could not be properly educated, did not settle the question whether it was prudent, or even right, for a Christian in afterlife to study pagan literature; and it required the thought and experience of several centuries to arrive at anything like a consensus of opinion and practice on the subject. But during the first four or five centuries the more liberal view, even in the West, on the whole prevailed. From Irenæus, Tatian, and Hermias, among Greek writers, and from various Latin Fathers, disapproving opinions proceeded. But the influence of Clement of Alexandria and Origen in the East, and of Augustine and Jerome in the West, was too strong for such opinions. Clement puts it on the broad ground that all wisdom is a Divine gift; and maintains that the philosophy of the Greeks, limited and particular as it is, contains the rudiments of that really perfect knowledge, which is beyond this world." Origen, in rebutting the reproach of Celsus, that the Gospel repelled the educated and gave a welcome only to the ignorant, quotes the Epistle to Titus, pointing out that "Paul, in describing what kind of man the bishop ought to be, lays down as a qualification that he must be a teacher, saying that he ought to be able to convince the gainsayers, that by the wisdom which is in him he may stop the mouths of foolish talkers and deceivers." The Gospel gives a welcome to the learned and unlearned alike: to the learned, that they may become teachers; to the unlearned, not because it prefers such, but because it wishes to instruct them. And he points out that in enumerating the gifts of the Spirit St. Paul places wisdom and knowledge before faith, gifts of healing, and miracles (1 Cor. xii. 8–10). But Origen does not point out that St. Paul himself makes use of heathen literature; although immediately before dealing with the accusation of Celsus, that Christians hate culture and promote ignorance, he quotes from Callimachus half of the saying of Epimenides, "Cretans are alway liars" (*Con. Cels.*, III. xliii). What Origen's own practice was we learn from the *Panegyric* of his enthusiastic pupil, Gregory Thaumaturgus (xiii.).

With the exception of atheistic philosophy, which was not worth the risk, Origen encouraged his scholars to study everything; and he gave them a regular course of dialectics, physics, and moral philosophy, as a preparation for theology. Augustine, who ascribes his first conversion from a vicious life to the *Hortensius* of Cicero (*Conf., III.* iv. I), was not likely to take an extreme line in condemning classical literature, from which he himself frequently quotes. Of Cicero's *Hortensius* he says, "This book in truth changed my affections, and turned my prayers to Thyself, O Lord, and made me have other hopes and desires." He quotes, among other classical authors, not only Virgil, Livy, Lucan, Sallust, Horace, Pliny and Quintillian, but Terence, Persius, and Juvenal, and of the last from those Satires which are sometimes omitted by editors on account of their grossness. In his treatise *On Christian Doctrine* (*II.* xl.), he contends that we must not shrink from making use of all that is good and true in heathen writings and institutions. We must "spoil the Egyptians." The writings of his instructor Ambrose show that he also was well acquainted with the best Latin classics. In Jerome we have what may be called an essay on the subject. Ruffinus had suggested to Magnus, a Roman rhetorician, that he should ask Jerome why he filled his writings with so many allusions and quotations taken from pagan literature, and Jerome in reply, after quoting the opening verses of the Book of Proverbs, refers him to the example of St. Paul in the Epistles to Titus and the Corinthians, and in the speech in the Acts. Then he points to Cyprian, Origen, Eusebius, and Apollinaris: "read them, and you will find that in comparison with them we have little skill (in quotation)." Besides these he appeals to the examples, among Greek writers, of Quadratus, Justin Martyr, Dionysius, Clement of Alexandria, Basil, Gregory Nazianzen, etc.; and among Latins, Tertullian, Minucius Felix, Arnobius, Hilary, and Juvencus. And he points out that quotations from profane authors occur in nearly all the works of these writers, and not merely in those which are addressed to heathen. But while Jerome defends the study of classical authors as a necessary part of education, he severely condemns those clergy who amused themselves with such writers as Plautus (of whom he himself had been very fond), Terence, and Catullus, when they ought to have been studying the Scriptures. Later in life his views appear to have become more rigid; and we find him rejoicing that the works of Plato and Aristotle are becoming neglected.

It was the short reign of Julian, commonly called "the Apostate" (a.d. 361–363), which had brought the question very much to the front. His policy and legislation probably influenced Augustine and Jerome in taking a more liberal line in the matter, in spite of Latin dislike of Greek philosophy and their own ascetic tendencies. Julian, jealous of the growing influence of Christian teachers, tried to prevent them from lecturing on classical authors. From this he hoped to gain two advantages. (1) Secular education would to a large extent be taken out of Christian hands. (2) The Christian teachers themselves would become less well educated, and less able to contend with heathen controversialists. He sarcastically pointed out the inconvenience of a teacher expounding Homer and denouncing Homer's gods: Christians had better confine themselves to "expounding Matthew and Luke in the Churches of the Galileans," and leave the interpretation of the masterpieces of antiquity to others. And he seems not to have contented himself with cynical advice, but to have passed a law that no Christian was to teach in the public schools. This law was at once cancelled by his successor Valentinian; but it provoked a strong feeling of resentment, and stirred up Christians to recognize and hold fast the advantages of a classical education.

But while the influence of the first three of the four great Latin Fathers was in favour of a wise use of the products of pagan genius, the influence of the last of the four was disastrously in the opposite direction.

In the period between Jerome and Gregory the Great two facts had had a calamitous effect upon the cause of liberal education. (1) The inroads of the barbarians almost destroyed the imperial schools in Gaul and Italy. (2) The miserable controversies about Origen produced an uneasy suspicion that secular study was prejudical to orthodoxy. It is perhaps to this latter influence that we may attribute two ecclesiastical canons of unknown date and origin. In the *Apostolical Constitutions* (I. vi.) we read, "Abstain from all heathen books. For what hast thou to do with such foreign discourses, or laws, or false prophets, which subvert the faith of the unstable? For what defect dost thou find in the law of God, that thou shouldest have recourse to those heathenish fables?" etc., etc. Again in a collection of canons, which is sometimes assigned to a synod at Carthage a.d. 398, the 16th canon in the collection runs thus: "A bishop shall read no heathen books, and heretical books only when necessary." The Carthaginian synod of 398 is a fiction, and some of the canons in the collection deal with controversies of a much later date: but we need not doubt that all the canons were enacted in some

Church or other in the course of the first six centuries. The spirit of this one is very much in harmony with the known tendencies of the sixth century; and we find Gregory the Great (a.d. 544–604) making precisely the same regulation. He forbad bishops to study heathen literature, and in one of his letters (*Epp.*, ix. 48) he rebukes Desiderius, Bishop of Vienne, for giving his clergy instruction in grammar, which involved the reading of the heathen poets. "The praises of Christ do not admit of being joined in the same mouth with the praises of Jupiter; and it is a grave and execrable thing for bishops to sing what even for a religious layman is unbecoming." The story that he purposely burnt the Palatine library is not traced earlier than the twelfth century, and is probably untrue; but it indicates the traditional belief respecting his attitude towards classical literature. And it is certainly true that he was twice in Constantinople, and on the second occasion remained there three years (a.d. 579–582), and yet never learnt Greek. In his time, as we learn both from himself and his contemporary, Gregory of Tours, the belief was very prevalent that the end of the world was at hand; and it was argued that mankind had more serious things to attend to than the study of pagan literature—or indeed any literature that was not connected with the Scriptures or the Church. Henceforward, in the words of Gregory of Tours, "the study of literature perished": and, although there were some bright spots at Jarrow and elsewhere, yet on the whole the chief services which Christianity rendered to classical learning during the next few centuries, were the preservation of classical authors in the libraries of monasteries and the preservation of the classical languages in the liturgies of the Church.

The question will perhaps never cease to be argued, although it is hardly probable that so extreme a view as that of Gregory the Great will ever again become prevalent. Let us take a statement of the question from the utterances of one who will not be suspected of want of capacity or of experience in the matter, or of want of sympathy with stern and serious views respecting education and life.

"Some one will say to me perhaps," wrote John Henry Newman in 1859, "our youth shall not be corrupted. We will dispense with all general or national literature whatever, if it be so exceptional; we will have a Christian Literature of our own, as pure, as true as the Jewish." "You cannot have it.... From the nature of the case, if Literature is to be made a study of human nature, you cannot have a Christian Literature. It is a contradiction in terms to attempt a sinless Literature of sinful man. You may gather together something very great and high, something higher than any literature ever was; and when you have done so, you will find that it is not Literature at all. You will simply have left the delineation of man, as such, and have substituted for it, as far as you have had anything to substitute, that of man, as he is or might be, under certain special advantages. Give up the study of man, as such, if so it must be; but say you do so. Do not say you are studying him, his history, his mind and his heart, when you are studying something else. Man is a being of genius, passion, intellect, conscience, power. He exercises his great gifts in various ways, in great deeds, in great thoughts, in heroic acts, in hateful crimes.... Literature records them all to the life....

"We should be shrinking from a plain duty, did we leave out Literature from Education. For why do we educate except to prepare for the world? Why do we cultivate the intellect of the many beyond the first elements of knowledge, except ... to fit men of the world for the world? We cannot possibly keep them from plunging into the world, with all its ways and principles and maxims, when their time comes; but we can prepare them against what is inevitable; and it is not the way to learn to swim in troubled waters, never to have gone into them. Proscribe (I do not say particular authors, particular works, particular passages) but Secular Literature as such: cut out from your class books all broad manifestations of the natural man; and those manifestations are waiting, for your pupil's benefit, at the very doors of your lecture room in living and breathing substance. They will meet him there in all the charm of novelty, and all the fascination of genius or of amiableness. To-day a pupil, to-morrow a member of the great world: to-day confined to the Lives of the Saints, to-morrow thrown upon Babel;—thrown on Babel, without the honest indulgence of wit and humour and imagination ever permitted to him, without any fastidiousness of taste wrought into him, without any rule given him for discriminating 'the precious from the vile,' beauty from sin, the truth from the sophistry of nature, what is innocent from what is poison."[75]

Many Christians are apt to forget that all truth is of God; and that every one who in an earnest spirit endeavours to ascertain and to teach what is true in any department of human knowledge, is doing God's work. The Spirit, we are promised by Christ Himself, "shall lead you *into all the Truth,*" and "the Truth shall make you free." Our business is to see that nothing claims the name of truth unlawfully. It is not our business to prohibit anything that can make good its claim to be accounted true.

Those who enjoy large opportunities of study, and especially those who have the responsibility not only of learning but of teaching, must beware of setting their own narrow limits to the domain of what is useful and true. It has a far wider range than the wants which we feel in ourselves or which we can trace in others. Even the whole experience of mankind would not suffice to give the measure of it. We dishonour rather than reverence the Bible, when we attempt to confine ourselves and others to the study of it. Much of its secret and inexhaustible store of treasure will remain undiscovered by us, until our hearts are warmed, our intellects quickened, and our experience enlarged, by the masterpieces of human genius. "To the pure all things are pure." In the first century, in which the perils of heathenism to Christianity were tenfold what they are at present, St. Paul in plain terms told his converts that if they liked to accept the invitations of their heathen friends and acquaintances, they need not scruple to do so (1 Cor. x. 27); and by his own example, he shows them that they may enjoy and use what is beautiful and true in heathen literature. Let us beware of narrowing the liberty wisely allowed by him. Each one of us can readily find out what is dangerous for *himself*. There is plenty that is not dangerous: let him freely enjoy that. But the limits that are wise for ourselves are not to bind others. Their liberty is not to be circumscribed by our conscience. "The earth is the Lord's and the fulness thereof."

FOOTNOTES:

[73] χρηστὰ ὁμιλίαι instead of χρησθ' ὁμιλίαι.

[74] Lightfoot on "Seneca and St. Paul," in *Philippians*, pp. 288, 300.

[75] J. H. Newman, *The Scope and Nature of University Education*, pp. 336–342. The whole discourse, "The Church and Liberal Education," is an eloquent and noble vindication of the claims of literature.

CHAPTER XXI
THE MEANING AND VALUE OF SOBERMINDEDNESS.—THE USE AND ABUSE OF RELIGIOUS EMOTION

> "But speak thou the things which befit the sound doctrine: that aged men be temperate, grave, soberminded, sound in faith, in love, in patience, that aged women likewise be reverent in demeanour, not slanderers nor enslaved to much wine, teachers of that which is good; that they may train the young women to love their husbands, to love their children, to be soberminded, chaste, workers at home, kind, being in subjection to their own husbands, that the word of God be not blasphemed: the younger men likewise exhort to be soberminded."—Titus ii. 1–6.

In marked contrast to the seducing teachers who are described in the concluding verses of the first chapter, Titus is charged to teach that which is right. "But speak *thou* the things which befit the sound doctrine." What *they* taught was to the last degree unwholesome, full of senseless frivolities and baseless distinctions respecting meats and drinks, times and seasons. Such things were fatal alike to sound and robust faith and to all moral earnestness. Belief was frittered away in a credulous attention to "Jewish fables," and character was depraved by a weak punctiliousness about fanciful details. As in the Pharisees, whom Jesus Christ denounced, scrupulosity about trifles led to neglect of "the weightier matters of the law." But in these "vain talkers and deceivers," whom Titus had to oppose, the trifles by which they distracted their hearers from matters of the highest importance were not even the minor duties enjoined by the Law or the Gospel: they were mere "commandments of men." In opposition to calamitous teaching of this kind, Titus is to insist upon what is healthy and sound.

All classes are to be attended to, and the exhortations specially needed are to be given to each: to the older men and older women, the younger women and the younger men, to whom Titus is to show himself an example: and finally to slaves, for salvation is offered to all men, and is for no privileged class.

It will be observed that the sound teaching which Titus is charged to give to the different sections of his flock relates almost exclusively to *conduct*. There is scarcely a hint in the whole of this chapter that can be supposed to have reference to errors of *doctrine*. In quite a general way the old men are to be exhorted to be "sound in *faith*" as well as in love and patience: but otherwise all the instruction to be given to old and young, male and female, bond and free, relates to conduct in thought, word, and deed.[76]

Nor is there any hint that the "vain talkers and deceivers" contradicted (otherwise than by an unholy life) the moral precepts which the Apostle here tells his delegate to communicate abundantly to his flock. We are not to suppose that these mischievous teachers taught people that there was no harm in intemperance, or slander, or unchastity, or theft. The mischief which they did consisted in their telling people to devote their attention to things that were morally unprofitable, while no care was taken to secure attention to those things, the observance of which was vital. On the contrary, the emphasis laid upon silly superstitions led people to suppose that, when these had been attended to, all duties had been fulfilled; and a careless, godless life was the result. Thus whole households were subverted by men who made religion a trade. This disastrous state of things is to be remedied by pointing out and insisting upon the observances which are of real importance for the spiritual life. The fatal lowering of moral tone, which the morbid and fanciful teaching of these seducers produced, is to be counteracted by the bracing effects of wholesome moral teaching.

No one can read through the indications which the Apostle gives of what he means by "wholesome teaching," without perceiving the key-note which rings through it all;—*sobriety* or *sobermindedness*. The aged men are to be taught to be "temperate, grave, *soberminded*." The aged women to be "reverent in demeanour," "that they may *school* the young women ... to be *soberminded*." The younger men are to be "exhorted to be *soberminded*." And in giving the reason for all this he points out God's purpose in His revelation to mankind; "to the intent that, denying ungodliness and worldly lusts, we should live *soberly*."

Now, what is the precise meaning of this sobriety or sobermindedness, on which St. Paul insists so strongly as a duty to be impressed upon men and women both old and young?

The words used in the original Greek (σώφρων, σωφρονίζειν, σωφρονεῖν) signify, according to their derivation,[77] "of *sound* mind," "to make of sound mind," and "to be of sound mind;" and the quality which they indicate is that *mens sana* or healthiness of mental constitution which shows itself in discreet and prudent conduct, and especially in *self-control*. This latter meaning is specially predominant in Attic writers.

Thus Plato defines it as "a kind of order and a controlling of certain pleasures and desires, as is shown by the saying that a man is 'master of himself' ... an expression which seems to mean that in the man's soul there are two elements, a better and a worse, and when the better controls the worse, then he is said to be master of himself" (*Rep.*, IV. p. 431). Similarly, Aristotle tells us that the lowest bodily pleasures are the sphere in which this virtue of self-control is specially displayed; that is, those bodily pleasures which the other animals share with man, and which are consequently shown to be slavish and bestial, viz., the pleasures of touch and taste (*Eth. N.*, III. x. 4, 9; *Rhet.*, I. ix. 9). And throughout the best Attic writers the vices to which self-control is opposed are those which imply immoderate indulgence in sensual pleasures. It is a virtue which has a very prominent place in heathen moral philosophy. It is one of the most obvious of virtues. It is manifest that in order to be a virtuous man at all one must at least have control over one's lowest appetites. And to a heathen it is one of the most impressive of virtues. All of us have experience of the difficulty of regulating our passions; and to those who know nothing of Christian teaching or of the grace of God the difficulty is increased tenfold. Hence to the savage the ascetic seems to be almost superhuman; and even in the cultivated pagan abstinence from bodily pleasure and steadfast resistance of sensual temptation excite wonder and admiration. The beautiful panegyric of Socrates put into the mouth of Alcibiades in the *Symposium* of Plato illustrates this feeling: and Euripides styles such virtue as the "noblest gift of the gods."

But when this virtue becomes illuminated by the Gospel its meaning is intensified. The "sobermindedness" or "sobriety" of the New Testament is something more than the "self-control" or "temperance" of Plato and Aristotle. Its sphere is not confined to the lowest sensual enjoyments. Self-mastery with regard to such things is still included; but other things are included also. It is that power over ourselves which keeps under control, not only bodily impulses, but spiritual impulses also. There is a spiritual frenzy analogous to physical madness, and there are spiritual self-indulgences analogous to bodily intemperance. For these things also self-mastery is needed.

St. Paul in writing to the Corinthians sums up his own life under the two conditions of being out of his mind and in his right mind. His opponents at Corinth, like Festus (Acts xxvi. 24), accused him of being mad. He is quite ready to admit that at times he has been in a condition which, if they like, they may call madness. But that is no affair of theirs. Of his sanity and sobriety at other times there can be no question; and his conduct during these times of sobriety is of importance to them. "For whether we went out of our mind" (ἐξέστημεν), "it was for God, or are in our right mind" (σωφρονοῦμεν, "are of sober mind," R.V.), "it is for you" (2 Cor. v. 13). The Apostle "went out of his mind," as his enemies chose to say, at his conversion on the road to Damascus, when a special revelation of Jesus Christ was granted to him: and to this phase of his existence belonged his visions (Acts xvi. 9; xxvii. 23), ecstasies and revelations (2 Cor. xii. 1–7), and his "speaking with tongues" (1 Cor. xiv. 18). And he was "in his right mind" in all the great tact, and sagacity, and self-denial, which he exhibited for the well-being of his converts.

It was absolutely necessary that the latter condition of mind should be the predominant one, and should control the other; that the ecstasy should be exceptional and the sobermindedness habitual, and that the sobermindedness should not be turned into self-exaltation by the remembrance of the ecstasy. There was so much danger of this evil in St. Paul's case, owing to "the exceeding greatness of the revelations" granted to him, that the special discipline of the "stake for the flesh" was given to him to counteract the temptation; for it was in the flesh, that is the sinful principle of his nature, that the tendency to pride himself on his extraordinary spiritual experiences was found.

St. Paul's case was, no doubt, highly exceptional; but in degree, rather than in kind. Very many of his converts had similar, although less sublime, and perhaps less frequent, experiences. Spiritual gifts of a supernatural kind had been bestowed in great abundance upon many of the members of the Church of Corinth (1 Cor. xii. 7–10), and were the occasion of some of the grievous disorders which were found there, because they were not always accompanied by sobriety, but were allowed to become incitements to licence and spiritual pride. Few things show more plainly the necessity for self-control and sobermindedness, when men are under the influence of strong religious emotion, than the state of things existing among the Corinthian converts, as indicated in St. Paul's two letters to them. They had been guilty of two errors. First, they had formed an exaggerated estimate of some of the gifts bestowed upon them, especially of the mysterious power of speaking with tongues. And, secondly, they had supposed that persons so highly gifted as themselves were above, not only ordinary precautions, but ordinary principles. Instead of seeing that such special privileges required them to be specially on their guard, they considered that they stood in no need of vigilance, and might safely disregard custom, and common decency, and even principles of morality. Previous to their conversion they had been idolaters, and therefore had had no experience of spiritual gifts and manifestations. Consequently, when the experience came, they were thrown off their balance, and knew neither how to estimate these gifts, nor how to prevent "what should have been to their wealth, becoming to them an occasion of falling."

It might be thought that the conditions of the Christian life of St. Paul and of his converts were too unlike our own to yield any clear lesson in this respect. We have not been converted to Christianity from either Judaism or paganism; and we have received no special revelations or extraordinary spiritual gifts. But this is not so. Our religious life, like theirs, has its two different phases; its times of excitement, and its times of freedom from excitement. We no longer work miracles, or speak with tongues; but we have our exceptional moments of impassioned feelings, and high-strung aspirations, and sublime thoughts; and we are just as liable as the Corinthians were to plume ourselves upon them, to rest in them, and to think that, because we have them, all must necessarily be well with us. We cannot too often remind ourselves that such things are not religion, and are not even the material out of which religion is made. They are the scaffolding and appliances, rather than the formed edifice or the unformed stones and timber. They supply helps and motive power. They are intended to carry us over difficulties and drudgery; and hence are more common in the earlier stages of a Christian's career than in the time of maturity, and at crises when the career has been interrupted, than when it is progressing with steadfast regularity. Conversion to Christianity in the case of a pagan, and the realization of what Christianity really means in the case of a nominal Christian, involve pain and depression: and the attempt to turn again and repent after grievous sin involves pain and depression. Strong religious emotion helps us to get the better of these, and may, if we use it aright, give us an impetus in the right direction. But, from the very nature of things, it cannot continue, and it is not desirable that it should. It will soon run its course, and we shall be left to go on our way with our ordinary resources. And our duty then is twofold;—first, not to repine at its withdrawal; "the Lord gave, and the Lord hath taken away, blessed be the Name of the Lord": and, secondly, to take care that it does not evaporate in empty self-complacency, but is translated into action. Impassioned feeling, that leads on to conduct, strengthens character; impassioned feeling, that ends with itself, weakens it. If religious excitement is not to do us more harm than good, by leaving us more insensible to spiritual influences than we were before, it must be accompanied by the sobriety which refuses to be exalted by such an experience, and which, in making use of it, controls it. And, moreover, these warm feelings and enthusiastic aspirations after what is good must lead on to calm and steadfast performance of what is good. One act of real self-denial, one genuine sacrifice of pleasure to duty, is worth hours of religious emotion and thousands of pious thoughts.

But sobermindedness will not only keep us from being pleased with ourselves for our impassioned feelings about spiritual things, and help us to turn them to good account; it will also preserve us from what is even worse than allowing them to pass away without result, viz., talking about them. To feel warmly and to do nothing is to *waste* motive power: it leads to hardening of the heart against good influences in the future. To feel warmly and talk about it is to *abuse* motive power: it leads to puffing up of the heart in spiritual pride and to blinding the inward eye with self-complacency. And this is the fatal mistake which is made by some religious teachers at the present day. Strong feelings are excited in those whom they wish to lead from a life of sin to a life of holiness. Sorrow for the past and a desire for better things are aroused, and the sinner is thrown into a condition of violent distress and expectation. And then, instead of being gently led on to work out his salvation in fear and trembling, the penitent is encouraged to seek excitement again and again, and to attempt to produce it in others, by constant rehearsing of his own religious experiences. What should have been a secret between himself and his Saviour, or at most shared only with some wise adviser, is thrown out publicly to the whole world, to the degradation both of what is told and of the character of him who tells it.

The error of mistaking religious feeling for holiness, and good thoughts for good conduct, is a very common one; and it is confined to neither sex, and to no period of life. Men as well as women, and the old as well as the young, need to be on their guard against it. And therefore the Apostle urges Titus to exhort all alike to be soberminded. There are times when to be agitated about religion, and have warm feelings either of sorrow or joy, is natural and right. When one is first roused to desire a life of holiness; when one is conscience-stricken at having fallen into some grievous sin; when one is bowed down under the weight of some great private or public calamity, or elated by the vivid appreciation of some great private or public blessing. At all such seasons it is reasonable and proper that we should experience strong religious emotion. Not to do so would be a sign of insensibility and deadness of heart. But do not let us suppose that the presence of such feelings mark us out as specially religious or spiritually gifted people. They do nothing of the kind. They merely prove that we are not utterly dead to spiritual influences. Whether we are the better or the worse for such feelings, depends upon the use that we make of them. And do not let us expect that these emotions will be permanent, which will certainly not be the case, or that they will frequently return, which will probably not be the case. Above all, let us not be discouraged if they become more and more rare, as time goes on. They *ought* to become more rare; for they are sure to become less frequent as we advance in holiness. In the steady growth and natural development of the spiritual life there is not much need of them or room for them. They have done their work when they have carried us over the breakers, which troubled our early efforts, into the less excited waters of consistent obedience. And to be able to progress without them is a surer token of God's grace than to have them. To continue steadfast in our obedience, without the luxury of warm feelings and impassioned devotion, is more pleasing in His sight than all the intense longings to be freed from sin, and all the passionate supplications for increased holiness that we have ever felt and offered. The test of fellowship with God is not warmth of devotion but holiness of life. "Hereby know we that we know Him, if we *keep His commandments.*"

FOOTNOTES:

[76] This makes one again inclined to regret that the Revisers here and elsewhere have left "doctrine" as the translation of διδασκαλία, while they have in most cases substituted "teaching" for "doctrine" as the translation of διδαχή. It would hardly be possible to confine either English word to either Greek word as its invariable rendering: but where both English words are admissible, it seems better to keep "teaching" (which is close to "teacher") for διδασκαλία (which is close to διδάσκαλος) and reserve "doctrine" for διδαχή (see p. 47).

[77] From σῶς, "safe and sound," and φρήν, "mind." The associations of the word are seen in Aristotle's erroneous derivation (*Eth. N.*, VI. v. 5); Ἔνθεν καὶ τὴν σωφροσύνην τούτῳ προσαγορεύομεν τῷ ὀνόματι, ὡς σώζουσαν τὴν φρόνησιν.

CHAPTER XXII
THE MORAL CONDITION OF SLAVES.—THEIR ADORNMENT OF THE DOCTRINE OF GOD

"Exhort servants to be in subjection to their own masters, and to be well-pleasing to them in all things; not gainsaying; not purloining, but showing all good fidelity; that they may adorn the doctrine of God our Saviour in all things."—Titus ii. 9, 10.

Something has already been said in a previous discourse (on 1 Tim. vi. 1, 2) respecting the institution of slavery in the Roman Empire in the first age of Christianity. It was not only unchristian but inhuman; and it was so widespread that the slaves outnumbered the freemen. Nevertheless the Apostles and their successors taught neither to the slaves that they ought to resist a dominion which was immoral both in effect and in origin, nor to the masters that as Christians they were bound to set their servants free.[78] Christianity did indeed labour for the abolition of slavery, but by quite other methods. It taught masters and slaves alike that all men have a common Divine parentage and a common Divine redemption, and consequently are equally bound to show brotherly love and equally endowed with spiritual freedom. It showed that the slave and his master are alike children of God, and as such free; and alike servants of Jesus Christ, and as such bondmen,—bondmen in that service which is the only true freedom. And thus very slowly, but surely, Christianity disintegrated and dispersed those unwholesome conditions and false ideas, which made slavery to be everywhere possible, and to seem to most men to be necessary. And wherever these conditions and ideas were swept away, slavery gradually died out or was formally abolished.[79]

As the number of slaves in the first century was so enormous, it was only in accordance with human probability that many of the first converts to Christianity belonged to this class; all the more so, as Christianity, like most great movements, began with the lower orders and thence spread upwards. Among the better class of slaves, that is those who were not so degraded as to be insensible of their own degradation, the Gospel spread freely. It offered them just what they needed, and the lack of which had turned their life into one great despair. It gave them something to hope for and something to live for. Their condition in the world was both socially and morally deplorable. Socially they had no rights beyond what their lord chose to allow them. They were ranked with the brutes, and were in a worse condition than any brutes, for they were capable of wrongs and sufferings of which the brutes are incapable or insensible. And St. Chrysostom in commenting on this passage points out how inevitable it was that the moral character of slaves should as a rule be bad. They have no motive for trying to be good, and very little opportunity of learning what is right. Every one, slaves included, admits that as a race they are passionate, intractable, and indisposed to virtue, not because God has made them so, but from bad education and the neglect of their masters. The masters care nothing about their slaves' morals, except so far as their vices are likely to interfere with their masters' pleasures or interests. Hence the slaves, having no one to care for them, naturally sink into an abyss of wickedness. Their chief aim is to avoid, not crime, but being found out. For if free men, able to select their own society, and with many other advantages of education and home life, find it difficult to avoid the contact and contaminating influence of the vicious, what can one expect from those who have none of these advantages, and have no possibility of escape from degrading surroundings? They are never taught to respect themselves; they have no experience of persons who do respect themselves; and they never receive any respect from either their superiors or their fellows. How can virtue or self-respect be learnt in such a school? "For all these reasons it is a difficult and surprising thing that there should ever be a good slave." And yet this is the class which St. Paul singles out as being able in a peculiar way to "*adorn* the doctrine of God our Saviour in *all* things."

"To *adorn* the doctrine of God." How is the doctrine of God to be adorned? And how are slaves capable of adorning it?

"The doctrine of God" is that which He teaches, which He has revealed for our instruction. It is His revelation of Himself. He is the author of it, the giver of it, and the subject of it. He is also its end or purpose. It is granted in order that men may know Him, and love Him, and be brought home to Him. All these facts are a guarantee to us of its importance and its security. It comes from One Who is infinitely great and infinitely true. And yet it is capable of being adorned by those to whom it is given.

There is nothing paradoxical in this. It is precisely those things which in themselves are good and beautiful that we consider capable of adornment and worthy of it. To add ornament to an object that is intrinsically vile or hideous, does but augment the existing bad qualities by adding to them a glaring incongruity. Baseness, which might otherwise have escaped notice, becomes conspicuous and grotesque. No person of good taste and good sense would waste and degrade ornament by bestowing it upon an unworthy object. The very fact, therefore, that adornment is attempted proves that those who make the attempt consider the object to be adorned an object worthy of honour and capable of receiving it. Thus adornment is a form of homage: it is the tribute which the discerning pay to beauty.

But adornment has its relations not only to those who bestow, but to those also who receive it. It is a reflexion of the mind of the giver; but it has also an influence on the recipient. And, first, it makes that which is adorned more conspicuous and better known. A picture in a frame is more likely to be looked at than one that is unframed. An ornamented building attracts more attention than a plain one. A king in his royal robes is more easily recognized as such than one in ordinary clothing. Adornment, therefore, is an advertisement of merit: it makes the adorned object more readily perceived and more widely appreciated. And, secondly, if it is well chosen and well bestowed, it augments the merit of that which it adorns. That which was fair before is made still fairer by suitable ornament. The beautiful painting is still more beautiful in a worthy frame. Noble ornament increases the dignity of a noble structure. And a person of royal presence becomes still more regal when royally arrayed. Adornment, therefore, is not only an advertisement of beauty, it is also a real enhancement of it.

All these particulars hold good with regard to the adornment of the doctrine of God. By trying to adorn it and make it more beautiful and more attractive, we show our respect for it; we pay our tribute of homage and admiration. We show to all the world that we think it estimable, and worthy of attention and honour. And by so doing we make the doctrine of God better known: we bring it under the notice of others who might otherwise have overlooked it: we force it upon their attention. Thus, without consciously intending to be anything of the kind, we become evangelists: we proclaim to those among whom we live that we have received a Gospel that satisfies us. Moreover, the doctrine which we thus adorn becomes really more beautiful in consequence. Teaching which nobody admires, which nobody accepts— teaching which teaches nobody, is a poor thing. It may be true, it may have great capabilities; but for the present it is as useless as a book in the hands of an illiterate savage, and as valueless as treasures lying at the bottom of the sea. Our acceptance of the doctrine of God, and our efforts to adorn it, bring out its inherent life and develop its natural value, and every additional person who joins us in doing this is an augmentation of its powers. It is within our power not only to honour and make better known, but also to enhance, the beauty of the doctrine of God.

But slaves,—and such slaves as were found throughout the Roman Empire in St. Paul's day,—what have they to do with the adornment of the doctrine of God? Why is this duty of making the Gospel more beautiful specially mentioned in connexion with them? That the aristocracy of the Empire, its magistrates, its senators, its commanders,—supposing that any of them could be induced to embrace the faith of Jesus Christ,—should be charged to adorn the doctrines which they had accepted, would be intelligible. Their acceptance of it would be a tribute to its dignity. Their loyalty to it would be a proclamation of its merits. Their accession to its ranks would be a real augmentation of its powers of attraction. But almost the reverse of all this would seem to be the truth in the case of slaves. Their tastes were so low, their moral judgment so debased, that for a religion to have found a welcome among slaves would hardly be a recommendation of it to respectable people. And what opportunities had slaves, regarded as they were as the very outcasts of society, of making the Gospel better known or more attractive?

So many a person, and especially many a slave, might have argued in St. Paul's hearing; and not altogether without reason and support from experience. The fact that Christianity was a religion acceptable to slaves and the associates of slaves was from very early times one of the objections made against it by the heathen, and one of the circumstances which prejudiced men of culture and refinement against it. It was one of the many bitter reproaches that Celsus brought against Christianity, that it laid itself out to catch slaves, women, and children, in short the immoral, the unintellectual, and the ignorant classes. And we need not suppose that this was merely a spiteful taunt: it represented a deep-seated and not altogether unreasonable prejudice. Seeing how many religions there were at that time which owed much of their success to the fact that they pandered to the vices, while they presumed upon the folly and ignorance of mankind, it was not an unjustifiable presumption that a new faith which won many adherents in the most degraded and vicious class of society, was itself a degrading and corrupting superstition.

Yet St. Paul knew what he was about when he urged Titus to commit the "adorning of the doctrine of God" in a special manner to slaves: and experience has proved the soundness of his judgment. If the mere fact that many slaves accepted the faith could not do a great deal to recommend the power and beauty of the Gospel, the Christian lives, which they thenceforward led, could. It was a strong argument *à fortiori*. The worse the unconverted sinner, the more marvellous his thorough conversion. There must be something in a religion which out of such unpromising material as slaves could make obedient, gentle, honest, sober, and chaste men and women. As Chrysostom puts it, when it was seen that Christianity, by giving a settled principle of sufficient power to counterbalance the pleasures of sin, was able to impose a restraint upon a class so self-willed, and render them singularly well-behaved, then their masters, however unreasonable they might be, were likely to form a high opinion of the doctrines which accomplished this. So that it is neither by chance, nor without reason, that the Apostle singles out this class of men: since, the more wicked they are, the more admirable is the power of that preaching which reforms them. And St. Chrysostom goes on to point out that the way in which slaves are to endeavour to adorn the doctrine of God is by cultivating precisely those virtues which contribute most to their masters' comfort and interest,—submissiveness, gentleness, meekness, honesty, truthfulness, and a faithful discharge of all duties. What a testimony conduct of this kind would be to the power and beauty of the Gospel; and a testimony all the more powerful in the eyes of those masters who became conscious that these despised Christian slaves were living better lives than their owners! The passionate man, who found his slave always gentle and submissive; the inhuman and ferocious man, who found his slave always meek and respectful; the fraudulent man of business, who noticed that his slave never pilfered or told lies; the sensualist, who observed that his slave was never intemperate and always shocked at immodesty;—all these, even if they were not induced to become converts to the new faith, or even to take much trouble to understand it, would at least at times feel something of respect, if not of awe and reverence, for a creed which produced such results. Where did their slaves learn these lofty principles? Whence did they derive the power to live up to them?

The cases in which masters and mistresses were converted through the conduct of their own slaves were probably by no means rare. It was by the gradual influence of numerous Christian lives, rather than by organized missionary effort, that the Gospel spread during the first ages of the Church; and nowhere would this gradual influence make itself more strongly and permanently felt than in the family and household. Some slaves then, like some domestic servants now, stood in very close relations with their masters and mistresses; and the opportunities of "adorning the doctrine of God" would in such cases be frequent and great. Origen implies that it was no uncommon thing for families to be converted through the instrumentality of the slaves (Migne, *Series Græca*, xi. 476, 483). One of the grievous moral defects of that most immoral age was the low view taken of the position of women in society. Even married women were treated with but scant respect. And as the marriage-tie was very commonly regarded as an irksome restraint, the condition of most women, even among the free-born, was degraded in the extreme. They were scarcely ever looked upon as the social equals and the necessary complement of the other sex; and, when not required to minister to the comforts and pleasures of the men, were often left to the society of slaves. Untold evil was the natural result; but, as Christianity spread, much good came out of the evil. Christian slaves sometimes made use of this state of things to interest their mistresses in the teaching of the Gospel; and when the mistress was converted, other conversions in the household became much more probable. Another grievous blot on the domestic life of the time was the want of parental affection. Fathers had scarcely any sense of responsibility towards their children, especially as regards their moral training. Their education generally was left almost entirely to slaves, from whom they learnt some accomplishments and many vices. They too often became adepts in wickedness before they had ceased to be children. But here again through the instrumentality of the Gospel good was brought out of this evil also. When the slaves, who had the care and the training of the children, were Christians, the morals of the children were carefully guarded; and in many cases the children, when they came to years of discretion, embraced Christianity.

Nor were these the only ways in which the most degraded and despised class in the society of that age were able to "adorn the doctrine of God." Slaves were not only an ornament to the faith by their lives; they adorned it also by their deaths. Not a few slaves won the martyr's crown. Those who have read that most precious relic of early Christian literature, the letter of the Churches of Lyons and Vienne to the Churches of Asia Minor and Phrygia, will not need to be reminded of the martyrdom of the slave Blandina with her mistress in the terrible persecution in Gaul under Marcus Aurelius in the year 177. Eusebius has preserved the greater portion of the letter at the beginning of the fifth book of his Ecclesiastical History. Let all who can do so read it, if not in the original Greek, at least in a translation. It is an authentic and priceless account of Christian fortitude.

What slaves could do then we all of us can do now. We can prove to all for whom and with whom we work that we really do believe and endeavour to live up to the faith that we profess. By the lives we lead we can show to all who know anything of us that we are loyal to Christ. By avoiding offence in word or in deed, and by welcoming opportunities of doing good to others, we can make His principles better known. And by doing all this brightly and cheerfully, without ostentation or affectation or moroseness, we can make His principles attractive. Thus we also can "adorn the doctrine of God in all things."

"In all things." That all-embracing addition to the Apostolic injunction must not be lost sight of. There is no duty so humble, no occupation so trifling, that it cannot be made into an opportunity for adorning our religion. "Whether ye eat, or drink, or *whatsoever ye do*, do all to the glory of God" (1 Cor. x. 31).

FOOTNOTES:

[78] The stories told in Bollandus of Roman converts under Trajan and Diocletian, who at their baptism manumitted their slaves, are not very credible. Such things, if they happened at all, were very exceptional.

[79] Pagan inscriptions carefully distinguish between freemen and slaves; Christian inscriptions seldom or never. There seems to be no well-ascertained instance in the Roman catacombs. *Dict. of Christ Ant.*, Vol. ii. p. 1904.

CHAPTER XXIII
HOPE AS A MOTIVE POWER.—THE PRESENT HOPES OF CHRISTIANS

"For the grace of God hath appeared, bringing salvation to all men, instructing us, to the intent that, denying ungodliness and worldly lusts, we should live soberly and righteously and godly in this present world; looking for the blessed hope and appearing of the glory of our great God and Saviour Jesus Christ; who gave Himself for us, that He might redeem us from all iniquity, and purify unto Himself a people for His own possession, zealous of good works. These things speak and exhort and reprove with all authority. Let no man despise thee."—Titus ii. 11–15.

There are not many passages in the Pastoral Epistles which treat so plainly as this does of doctrine. As a rule St. Paul assumes that his delegates, Timothy and Titus, are well instructed (as he knew they were) in the details of the Christian faith, and he does not stay even to remind them of what he had frequently taught to them and to others in their presence. The purpose of the Epistles is to give practical rather than doctrinal instruction; to teach Timothy and Titus how to shape their own conduct, and what kind of conduct they are chiefly to insist upon in the different classes of Christians committed to their charge. Here, however, and in the next chapter, we have marked exceptions to this method. Yet even here the exception is more apparent than real; for the doctrinal statements are introduced, not as truths to be recognized and believed (it is taken for granted that they *are* recognized and believed), but as the basis of the practical exhortations which have just been given. It is because these great truths have been revealed, because life is so real and so important, and because eternity is so certain, that Titus is to exert all his influence to produce the best kind of conduct in his flock, whether men or women, old or young, bond or free.

The passage before us might almost serve as a summary of St. Paul's teaching. In it he once more insists upon the inseparable connexion between creed and character, doctrine and life, and intimates the close relations between the past, the present, and the future, in the Christian scheme of salvation. There are certain facts in the past, which must be believed; and there is a kind of life in the present, which must be lived; and there are things in store for us in the future, which must be looked for. Thus the three great virtues of faith, charity, and hope are inculcated. Two Epiphanies or appearances of Jesus Christ in this world are stated as the two great limits of the Christian dispensation. There is the Epiphany of grace, when the Christ appeared in humility, bringing salvation and instruction to all men; and there is the Epiphany of glory, when He will appear again in power, that He may claim as His own possession the people whom He has redeemed. And between these two there is the Christian life with its "blessed hope," the hope of the Lord's return in glory to complete the kingdom which His first Advent began.

Most of us make far too little of this "blessed hope." It is of incalculable value; first, as a test of our own sincerity and reality; and secondly, as a source of strength to carry us over the difficulties and disappointments which beset our daily course.

There is perhaps no more certain test of a Christian's earnestness than the question whether he does, or does not, look forward with hope and longing for Christ's return. Some men have seriously persuaded themselves that there is no such thing either to hope for or to dread. Others prefer not to think about it; they know that doubts have been entertained on the subject, and as the topic is not a pleasant one to them, they dismiss it as much as possible from their minds, with the wish that the doubts about there being any return of Christ to judgment may be well-founded; for their own lives are such that they have every reason to desire that there may be no judgment. Others again, who on the whole are trying to lead Christian lives, nevertheless so far share the feelings of the godless, in that the thought of Christ's return (of the certainty of which they are fully persuaded) inspires them with fear rather than with joy. This is especially the case with those who are kept in the right way much more by the fear of hell than by the love of God, or even the hope of heaven. They believe and tremble. They believe in God's truth and justice much more than in His love and mercy. He is to them a Master and Lord to be obeyed and feared, much more than a God and Father to be adored and loved. Consequently their work is half-hearted, and their life servile, as must always be the case with those whose chief motive is fear of punishment. Hence they share the terrors of the wicked, while they lose their share of the joys of the righteous. They are too much afraid to find any real pleasure either in sin or in good works. To have sinned fills them with terror at the thought of inevitable punishment; and to have done what is right fills them with no joy, because they have so little love and so little hope.

Those who find from experience that the thought of Christ's return in glory is one on which they seldom dwell, even if it be not positively unwelcome, may be sure that there is something defective in their life. Either they are conscious of shortcomings which they make little or no attempt to correct, the recollection of which becomes intolerable when confronted with the thought of the day of judgment (and this shows that there is a great lack of earnestness in their religious life); or they are being content with low motives for avoiding iniquity and striving after righteousness, and thus are losing a real source of strength to help them in their efforts. No doubt there are persons over whom high motives have little influence, and can have but little influence, because they are as yet unable to appreciate them. But no one in watching over either his own soul or the souls of others can afford to be content with such a state of things. Childish things must be put away, when they cease to be appropriate. As the character develops under the influence of lower motives, higher motives begin at times to make themselves felt; and these must gradually be substituted for the others. And when they do make themselves felt, high motives are much more powerful than low ones; which is a further reason for appealing to them rather than to the others. Not only is a man, who is capable of being moved both by the fear of hell and by the love of God, more influenced by the love than by the fear; but love has more power over his will than fear has over the will of one who cannot be influenced by love.

All this tends to show how much is lost by those who make no effort to cultivate in their minds a feeling of joy at the thought of "the appearing of the glory of our great God and Saviour Jesus Christ." They lose a great source of strength by neglecting to cultivate what would be a powerful motive to help them on the right way. Nor does the loss end here. With it they lose much of the interest which they would otherwise take in all that helps to "accomplish the number of God's elect and to hasten His kingdom." Christians pray daily, and perhaps many times daily, "Thy kingdom come." But how few realize what they are praying for! How few really long that their prayer may be speedily granted! How few take a keen and untiring interest in all that promotes the coming of the kingdom! And thus again motive power is lost; for if we had but the eyes to see, and the heart to appreciate, all that is going on round about us, we should feel that we live, as compared with our forefathers, in very encouraging times.

We are often enough told that Christianity in general, and the Church of England in particular, is at the present time passing through a great crisis; that this is an age of peculiar dangers and difficulties; that we live in times of unblushing vice and uncompromising scepticism; and that the immensity of our social, commercial, and political corruption is only the natural outcome of the immensity of our irreligion and unbelief. These things may be true; and there is no earnest Christian who has not at times been perplexed and saddened by them. But, thank God, there are other things which are equally true, and which ought to be equally recognized and remembered. If the present is an age of peculiar dangers and boundless irreligion, it is also an age of peculiar encouragements and boundless hope.

There are Christians who love to look back to some period in the history of the Church, which they have come to regard as a sort of golden age; an age in which communities of saintly men and women were ministered to by a still more saintly clergy, and in which the Church went beautifully on its way, not altogether free from persecutions, which were perhaps necessary for its perfection, but untroubled by doubts, or dissensions, or heresies, and unstained by worldliness, apostasy, or sloth. So far as the experience of the present writer has carried him, no such golden age can be found in the actual history of the Church.

It is not to be found in the New Testament, either before or after Pentecost.

We do not find it, where we might have expected to find it, in the period when Christ was still present in the flesh as the Ruler and Instructor of His Church. That period is marked by the ignorance and unbelief of the Apostles, by their quarrels, their ambition for the first places in an earthly kingdom, their intolerant spirit, by the flight of all of them in the hour of Christ's danger, by the denials of St. Peter, by the treachery and suicide of Judas. Nor do we find it, where again we might have expected to find it, in the age immediately succeeding the completion of Christ's work, when the Apostles, newly anointed with the Spirit, were still alive to direct and foster the Church which He had founded. That period also is marred by many disfiguring marks. Apostles can still be timeserving, can still quarrel among themselves; and they also experience what it is to be forsaken and opposed by their own disciples. Their converts, as soon as the Apostle who established them in the faith is withdrawn, and sometimes even while he is still with them, become guilty of the gravest errors in conduct and belief. Witness the monstrous disorders in the Church of Corinth, the fickleness of the Galatian converts, the unchristian asceticism of the Colossian heretics, the studied immorality of those of Ephesus. The Church which was presided over by St. Timothy was the Church of Alexander, Hymenæus, and Philetus, who removed the very corner-stone of the faith by denying the Resurrection; and the Churches which were presided over by St. John contained the Nicolaitans, condemned as hateful by Jesus Christ, and Diotrephes, who repudiated the Apostle and excommunicated those who received the Apostle's messengers. And there is much more of the same sort, as the Pastoral Epistles show us, proving that what comes to us at first as a sad surprise is of still sadder frequency, and that the Apostolic age had defects and stains at at least as serious as those which deface our own.

The failure to find any golden age in either of these two divisions of the period covered by the New Testament ought to put us on our guard against expecting to find it in any subsequent period. And it would not be difficult to take each of the epochs in the history of the Church which have been selected as specially bright and perfect, and show that in every case, directly we pass through the hazy glow, which the imagination of later writers has thrown around such periods, and get down to solid facts, then, either the brightness and perfection are found to be illusory, or they are counter-balanced by many dark spots and disorders. The age of the martyrs is the age of the lapsed; the ages of faith are the ages of fraud; and the ages of great success are the ages of great corruption. In the first centuries increase of numbers was marked by increase of heresies and schisms; in the middle ages, increase of power by increase of pride. A fair comparison of the period in which our own lot has been cast with any previous period in the history of the Church will never lead to any just feeling of discouragement. Indeed it may reasonably be contended that at no era since Christianity was first founded have its prospects been so bright as at the present time.

Let us look at the contest between the Gospel and heathenism,—that great contest which has been going on since "the grace of God appeared bringing salvation to all men," and which is to continue until "the appearing of the glory of our great God and Saviour." Was there ever a time when missions were more numerous or better organized, and when missionaries were as a rule better instructed, better equipped, or more devoted? And although it is impossible to form a correct estimate on such a subject, because some of the most important data are beyond our reach, yet it may be doubted whether there ever was a time when missions achieved more solid success. The enormous growth of the colonial and missionary episcopate during the last hundred years is at any rate one great fact which represents and guarantees a great deal. Until 1787 there was not a single episcopal see of the Anglican communion in any of the colonies or settlements of the British Empire; still less was there a single missionary bishop. And now, as the Lambeth Conferences remind us, these colonial and missionary bishops are not far short of a hundred, and are always increasing.[80]

Or let us look at the relations between the great Churches into which Christendom is unhappily divided. Was there ever a period at which there was less bitterness, or more earnest and wide-spread desire for the restoration of unity? And the increased desire for reunion comes hand in hand with an increase of the conditions which would render reunion possible. Two things are absolutely indispensable for a successful attempt in this direction. First, a large measure of culture and learning, especially among the clergy of the divided Churches; and secondly, intelligent religious zeal. Ignorant controversialists cannot distinguish between important and unimportant differences, and thus aggravate rather than smooth difficulties. And without religious earnestness the attempt to heal differences ends in indifferentism. Both these indispensable elements are increasing, at any rate in the Anglican and in the Eastern Churches: and thus reunion, which "must be possible, because it is a duty," is becoming not only a desire but a hope.

Let us look again at our own Church; at its abundant machinery for every kind of beneficent object; at the beautiful work which is being done in a quiet and simple way by numbers of Christian men and women in thousands of parishes; at the increase in services, in confirmations, in communions; at the princely offerings of many of the wealthy laity; at the humble offerings—equally princely in God's sight—of many of the poor. Can we point to a time when party feeling (bad as it still is) was less rancorous, when parishes were better worked, when the clergy were better educated or more self-sacrificing, when the people were more responsive to what is being done for them?

The very possibility of seriously raising such questions as these is in itself a reason for taking courage, even if we cannot answer all of them in the way that would please us most. There are at any rate good grounds for hoping that much is being done for the advancement of Christ's dominion, and that the prayer "Thy kingdom come" is being answered day by day. If we could but convince ourselves more thoroughly of the truth of all this, we should work more hopefully and more earnestly. More hopefully, because we should be working with a consciousness of being successful and making progress, with a conviction that we are on the winning side. And more earnestly, not merely because hope makes work more earnest and thorough, but also because we should have an increased sense of responsibility: we should fear lest through any sloth or negligence on our part such bright prospects should be marred. The expectation of defeat makes some men strive all the more heroically; but most men it paralyses. In our Christian warfare we certainly need hope to carry us onward to victory.

"The appearing of the glory of our great God and Saviour Jesus Christ." Among the foolish charges which have been brought against the Revisers is that of favouring Arian tendencies by blurring those texts which teach the Divinity of Jesus Christ. The present passage would be a sufficient answer to such a charge. In the A.V. we have "the glorious appearing of the great God, and our Saviour Jesus Christ," where both the wording and the comma make it clear that "the great God" means the Father and not our Saviour.

The Revisers, by omitting the comma, for which there is no authority in the original, and by placing the "our" before both substantives, have given their authority to the view that St. Paul means both "great God" and "Saviour" to apply to Jesus Christ. It is not any Epiphany of the Father which is in his mind, but the "Epiphany of the glory of our great God and Saviour Jesus Christ."

The wording of the Greek is such that absolute certainty is not attainable; but the context, the collocation of the words, the use of the word "Epiphany," and the omission of the article before "Saviour" (ἐπιφάνειαν τῆς δόξης τοῦ μεγάλου Θεοῦ καὶ σωτῆρος ἡμῶν Ἰ. Χ.), all seem to favour the Revisers' rendering. And, if it be adopted, we have here one of the plainest and most direct statements of the Divinity of Christ to be found in Scripture. As such it was employed in the Arian controversy, although Ambrose seems to have understood the passage as referring to the Father and Christ, and not to Christ alone. The force of what follows is enhanced, if the Revisers' rendering, which is the *strictly grammatical* rendering, is maintained. It is as being "our great God" that He gave Himself for us, that He might "redeem us from all iniquity;" and it was because He was God as well as man, that what was uttered as a bitter taunt was really a glorious truth;—"He saved others; Himself He *cannot* save." It was morally impossible that the Divine Son should turn back from making us "a people for His own possession." Let us strengthen ourselves in the hope that our efforts to fulfil this gracious purpose are never thrown away.

FOOTNOTES:

[80] Including the English and American bishops, invitations to two hundred and nine prelates were issued for the Lambeth Conference in 1888.

CHAPTER XXIV
THE DUTY OF OBEDIENCE TO AUTHORITY, WITH ITS LIMITS; THE DUTY OF COURTESY WITHOUT LIMITS

"Put them in mind to be in subjection to rulers, to authorities, to be obedient, to be ready unto every good work, to speak evil of no man, not to be contentious, to be gentle, showing all meekness toward all men. For we also were aforetime foolish, disobedient, deceived, serving divers lusts and pleasures, living in malice and envy, hateful, hating one another"—Titus iii. 1–3.

St. Paul, having in the previous chapter sketched the special duties which Titus is to inculcate upon different classes of Christians,—aged men and aged women, young women, young men, and slaves,—now passes on to point out what must be impressed upon all Christians alike, especially as regards their conduct towards those who are in authority and who are not Christians.

Here he is on delicate ground. The Cretans are said to have been a turbulent race, or rather a group of turbulent races; neither peaceable among themselves, nor very patient of foreign dominion: and the Roman rule had been established there for less than a century and a half. Previous to their conquest by Metellus in b.c. 67, they had been accustomed to democratic forms of government, and therefore would be likely to feel the change to the Roman yoke all the more acutely. As our own experiences in a neighbouring island have taught us, people who have been allowed to misgovern themselves, and to fight among themselves, for many generations, do not readily give a welcome to a power which deprives them of these liberties, even when it offers in exchange for them the solid but prosaic advantages of peace and security. Besides this, there was in Crete a strong mixture of Jews, whose rebellious propensities seemed to be unquenchable. Nor was this all. Within the Church itself the spirit of anarchy had displayed itself: partly because, as in the Churches of Corinth and Galatia, the characteristic faults of the people still continued to show themselves after the acceptance of Christianity; partly because, as everywhere in the Churches of that age, the contests between Jewish and Gentile converts were always producing disorder. This appears in the first chapter of our Epistle, in which the Apostle states that "there are many unruly men, ... specially they of the circumcision," and in which he finds it necessary to make it a qualification for the office of bishop or overseer, that the persons appointed should be such as "are not accused of riot or are unruly." Besides which, as we learn from numerous sources in the New Testament, there was in various quarters a tendency to gross misconceptions respecting Christian liberty. Through Gnostic and other antinomian influences there was a disposition in many minds to translate liberty into license, and to suppose that the Christian was above the distinctions of the moral law, which for him had no meaning. Lastly, there were probably some earnest Christians, who, without going to any of these disastrous extremes, or sympathizing with the factious and seditious spirit of their fellow-countrymen, nevertheless had serious doubts as to whether Christians were under any obligation to obey a pagan magistrate, and perhaps were inclined to believe that it was their duty to disobey him.

For all these reasons St. Paul must have known that he was charging Titus to give instructions, which would be very unwelcome to a large number of Cretan converts, when he told him to "put them in mind to be in subjection to rulers and authorities, and to be obedient." But it was the very fact that the instructions would be unwelcome to many, that made it so necessary that they should be given. Both for the internal well-being of the Church, and for the maintenance of right relations with the State, it was imperative that the principle of obedience to authority, whether ecclesiastical or civil, should be upheld. There must be peace, and there must be liberty: but there could be neither the one nor the other without a respect for law and for those who have to administer it.

The Apostle does not here argue the case. He lays down certain positions as indisputable. The loyal Christian must submit himself to those who are placed over him; he must render obedience to existing authorities. There is one obvious limit to this which he indicates by a single word to be noticed hereafter, but with that one qualification the duty of obedience is imperative and absolute. Jew and Gentile Christian alike must obey the laws, not only of the Church, as administered by its overseers, but also of the State, as administered by the magistrates, even though the State be a heathen power and the magistrate an idolater. The reason why St. Paul does not argue the matter is obvious. He is not writing to those who are likely to dispute or disobey these injunctions, but to one who has to see that they are obeyed. His object is not to prove the excellence of the rules which he lays down, but to advise Titus as to what rules are to be most insisted upon. Titus was well aware of the principles upon which these rules were based and of the arguments by which the Apostle was accustomed to defend them. He does not need information on that point. What the Apostle thinks may be necessary for his guidance is a clear intimation of those practical lessons of which the Cretans needed most to be reminded. It was quite possible that Titus might have taken the view that the question about obedience to existing authorities was a burning one, and that it would be better for the present to say as little about it as possible. To object, therefore, that these directions in the second and third chapters of this Epistle are unworthy of St. Paul, and consequently not written by him, because they contain nothing which might serve as a sufficient refutation of the adversaries, is to beat the air without effect. They contain nothing calculated to serve as a refutation of the adversaries, because the Apostle writes with no intention of refuting opponents, but in order to give practical instructions to his delegate.

But although the Apostle does not here argue the case, we are not left in ignorance as to the principles upon which he based the rules here laid down so emphatically. The thirteenth chapter of the Epistle to the Romans is quite clear on that point. "There is no power but of God; and the powers that be are ordained of God. Therefore he that resisteth the power, withstandeth the ordinance of God." That is the kernel of the whole matter. The fact that a few rule over the many is not to be traced to a worldwide usurpation of the rights of the simple and the weak by the selfishness of the crafty and the strong. That theory may explain the terrorism of a bully, or of a band of brigands, or of a secret society; it is no explanation of the universal relations between governors and the governed. Nor is it the result of a primeval "social compact," in which the weak voluntarily surrendered some of their rights in order to have the advantage of the protection of the strong: that theory is pure fiction, and finds no support either in the facts of man's nature, or in the relics of primitive society, or in the records of the past. The one explanation which is at once both adequate and true, is, that all authority is of Divine origin. This was the declaration of the Forerunner, when his disciples complained to him of the influence which Jesus exercised over those who came in contact with His teaching: "A man can receive nothing, except it have been given him from heaven" (John iii. 27). This was the declaration of the Christ, when the Roman Procurator pointed out to Him that he had power of life and death over Him: "Thou wouldest have no power against Me, except it were given thee from above" (John xix. 11). The power of the Redeemer over the minds of men and the power of a heathen governor over the bodies of men have one and the same source,—Almighty God. Christ declared His innocence and asserted His claims; but He made no protest against being tried by a pagan official, who represented the power that had deprived the Jewish nation of its liberties, because he also represented the principle of law and order, and as such was the representative of God Himself.

St Paul, therefore, is doing no more than restating what the Lord had already taught both by word and example. Christians must show submission to rulers and constituted authorities, and must yield ready obedience to magistrates, even when they are heathen. As heathen they were no doubt rebels against God, however little they might be aware of the fact. But as magistrates they were His delegates, however little they were aware of the fact. The Christian is aware of both facts; and he must not suppose that the one cancels the other. The magistrate still remains God's delegate, however inconsistent his own life may be with such a position. Therefore it is not only allowable for Christians to obey him; they must make it a matter of conscience to do so: and the history of the Church throughout the eras of persecution shows how greatly such teaching was needed. Whatever may have been the case when St. Paul wrote the Epistle to the Romans, we may safely maintain that persecution had already taken place when he wrote these instructions to Titus. Not that he seems to have a persecuting power in his mind, when he enjoins simple obedience to existing authority; but he writes with full knowledge of the extreme cases that might occur. A moralist who could insist upon the duty of submission to rulers, when a Nero had been on the throne for twelve or fourteen years, was certainly not one who could be ignorant of what his principles involved. Nor could it be said that the evils of Nero's insolent despotism were counteracted by the excellence of his subordinates. The infamous Tigellinus was Prætorian Prefect and the Emperor's chief adviser. Helius, who acted as governor of Italy during the Emperor's absence in Greece, was in character a second Nero. And Gessius Florus, one of Pilate's successors as Procurator of Judæa, was so shameless in his enormities, that the Jews regretted the departure of his predecessor Albinus, although he also had mercilessly oppressed them. But all these facts, together with many more of the same kind, and some also of an opposite character, were beside the question. Christians were not to concern themselves with discussing whether rulers governed well or ill, or whether their private lives were good or bad. The one fact which concerned them was that the rulers were there to administer the law, and as such must be respected and obeyed. The conscience of Christians and the experiences of politicians, whether rulers or ruled, throughout all the subsequent ages have ratified the wisdom of St. Paul's injunctions; and not only their wisdom but their profound morality. Renan says with truth, but with a great deal less than the whole truth, that "Paul had too much tact to be a preacher of sedition: he wished that the name of Christian should stand well, and that a Christian should be a man of order, on good terms with the police, and of good repute in the eyes of the pagans" (*St. Paul*, p. 477). The criticism which resolves a profound moral principle into a mere question of tact is worthy of the critic who makes it. Certainly St. Paul was far-sighted enough to see that frequent collisions between Christians and the recognized administrators of the law would be no good thing for Christianity: but it was not because he believed obedience to be the best policy that he charged Titus to insist upon it.

It is of the very essence of a ruler that he is "not a terror to the good work, but to the evil: ... for he is a minister of God to thee for good, ... an avenger for wrath to him that doeth evil." It is quite possible that the law which he administers is unjust, or that he administers it in such a way as to make it work injustice, so that good deeds are punished and evil deeds are rewarded. But nowhere is good punished *as* good, or evil rewarded *as* evil. When Naboth was judicially murdered to gratify Jezebel, it was on the assumption that he was a blasphemer and a rebel; and when Jesus of Nazareth was condemned to death by the Sanhedrin and by the Procurator, it was on the assumption that he was guilty of similar crimes. So also with all the monstrous and iniquitous laws which have been made against Christianity and Christians. The persecuting edict "cast out their name as *evil*."

It was because men believed, or professed to believe, that Christians were grievous offenders or dangerous citizens, that they brought them before the magistrates. And the same holds good of the religious persecutions of which Christians have been guilty against other Christians. Nowhere can we point to a case in which a person has been condemned for having been virtuous, or for having failed to commit a crime. Many have been condemned for what was really meritorious, or for refusing to do what was really wicked; but in all such cases the meritorious conduct and the wicked conduct were held to be of exactly the opposite character by the representatives of the law. Legally constituted authority, therefore, is always by profession, and generally in fact also, a terror to the evil and a supporter of the good. It is charged with the all-important duty of upholding right and punishing wrong in human conduct, *a duty which it never disowns*. For even when through blindness or perversity it upholds what is wrong or punishes what is right, it professes to be doing the opposite. Therefore to rebel against it is to rebel against the principle of moral government; it is a revolt against that principle which reflects and represents, and that by His ordinance, the moral government of Almighty God.

St. Paul assumes that rulers aim at what is just and right. The Christian is "to be ready unto every good work": and, although the words are no doubt intended to have a general meaning as well, yet the context suggests that their primary meaning in this place is that Christians are always, not only to be obedient to rulers and magistrates, but to be ready to support and assist them in any good work: the presumption being that what the authorities direct is good. But, without perhaps having this object in view, the Apostle here indirectly intimates the limits to a Christian's obedience and support. They are to be given to further "every *good* work": they cannot of course be given to further what is evil. What then must a Christian do when lawful authority requires him to do what he knows to be wrong? Is he to rebel? to stir up a revolt against those who make this demand? No, he is still "to be in subjection to rulers": that is, he must disobey and *quietly take the consequences.* He owes it to his conscience to refuse to do what it condemns: but he also owes it to the representative of Divine law and order to abstain from shaking its authority. It has the power to give commands and the right to punish disobedience, and he has no right to refuse both obedience and punishment. To disobey and submissively take the consequences of disobedience is his plain duty in so painful a case. In this way, and in this way *only*, will loyalty to conscience and loyalty to authority both alike be preserved. In this way, and in this way *best* (as history has again and again shown), is the reformation of unjust laws effected. The moral sense of society is far more impressed by the man who disobeys for conscience' sake and unresistingly goes to prison or mounts the scaffold for his disobedience, than by him who violently resists all attempts to punish him and stirs up rebellion against the authority which he cannot conscientiously obey. Rebellion may succeed in redressing injustice, but at a cost which is likely to be more grievous than the injustice which it redresses. Conscientious disobedience, accompanied by loyal submission to the penalty of disobedience, is sure to succeed in reforming unjust laws, and that without any cost to counterbalance the good thus gained.

Having thus trenchantly determined the duty of believers towards rulers and magistrates, St. Paul passes on to sketch their proper attitude towards other members of society. And just as in speaking of conduct towards authorities he evidently has in his mind the fact that most authorities are unbelievers, so in speaking of conduct in society he evidently is thinking of a state of society in which many of its members are unbelievers. What kind of conduct will Titus have to insist upon as befitting a Christian? "To speak evil of no man, not to be contentious, to be gentle, showing all meekness towards all men."

It would be difficult to point to a precept which is more habitually violated by Christians at the present day, and therefore more worthy of being constantly brought to the front and urged upon their consideration. There are plenty of precepts both of the Old and of the New Testament, which are habitually violated by the godless and irreligious, by those who, while bearing the name of Christian, scarcely make even a pretence of endeavouring to live Christian lives. But here we have a group of precepts, which a large number, not only of those who profess to live soberly and righteously, but of those who do indeed in other respects live as Christians should, consent to forget or ignore. "To speak evil of no man; not to be contentious; to be gentle, showing all meekness towards all men." Let us consider calmly what such words as these really mean; and then let us consider what we constantly meet with in the controversial writing, and still more in the controversial speaking, of the present day. Consider the tone of our party newspapers, and especially of our religious newspapers, on the burning questions of the hour and on the men who take a leading part in them. Read what a High Church paper says of a Low Church Bishop, or what a Low Church paper says of a High Church Bishop, and measure it by the injunction "to speak evil of no man." Or again, read what some of the organs of Dissent allow themselves to say respecting the clergy of the Established Church, or what some Church Defence orators have allowed themselves to say respecting Liberationists, and measure it by the injunctions "not to be contentious, to be gentle, showing all meekness towards all men." It is sometimes necessary to speak out and call attention to real or suspected evils; although not nearly so frequently as we like to think. But it is never necessary to throw mud and deal in personal abuse.

Moreover, it is very unbecoming to do so. It is doubly unbecoming, as St. Paul reminds us. First, such conduct is utterly un-Christian. Secondly, it is very much out of place in those who before now have been guilty of quite as grave faults as those for which we now abuse others. We are just the persons who ought to remember, because we know from personal experience, how much the grace of God can effect. If we have by His mercy been brought out of the sins which we now condemn in other people, what may we not hope for in their case, provided we do not disgust them with virtue by our acrimonious and uncharitable fault-finding? Abuse is the wrong weapon to use against unrighteous conduct, just as rebellion is the wrong weapon to use against unrighteous laws.

CHAPTER XXV
THE CO-OPERATION OF THE DIVINE PERSONS IN EFFECTING THE NEW BIRTH.—THE LAVER OF REGENERATION

> "But when the kindness of God our Saviour, and His love toward man, appeared, not by works done in righteousness, which we did ourselves, but according to His mercy He saved us, through the washing of regeneration and renewing of the Holy Ghost, which He poured out upon us richly, through Jesus Christ our Saviour; that, being justified by His grace, we might be made heirs according to the hope of eternal life."—Titus iii. 4–7.

For the second time in this short letter we have one of those statements of doctrine which are not common among the practical instructions which form the main portion of the Pastoral Epistles. The other doctrinal statement was noticed in a previous discourse on chap. ii. 11–14. It is worth while to compare the two. Though similar, they are not identical in import, and they are introduced for quite different purposes. In the earlier passage, in order to show why different classes of Christians should be taught to exhibit the virtues which specially befit them, the Apostle states the purpose of Christ's work of redemption, a purpose which all Christians are bound to help in realizing, stimulated by what has been done for them in the past and by the hope which lies before them in the future. In the passage which we have now to consider, St. Paul contrasts with the manifold wickedness of unbelievers the undeserved mercies of God towards them, in order to show what gratitude those who have been brought out of their unbelief ought to feel for this unearned blessing, a gratitude which they ought to exhibit in gentle forbearance and goodwill towards those who are still in the darkness of unbelief as well as to others.

The passage before us forms the main part of the Second Lesson for the evening of Christmas Day in both the old and the new lectionaries. Its appropriateness in setting forth so explicitly the Divine bounty in the work of regeneration is manifest. But it would have been equally appropriate as a lesson for Trinity Sunday, for the part which each Person of the Blessed

Trinity takes in the work of regeneration is plainly indicated. The passage is in this respect strikingly parallel to what St. Peter had written in the opening of his Epistle: "According to the foreknowledge of God the Father, in sanctification of the Spirit, unto obedience and sprinkling of the blood of Jesus Christ" (1 Pet. i. 2). The goodness and love of God the Father towards mankind is the source of man's redemption. From all eternity He saw man's fall; and from all eternity He devised the means of man's recovery. He appointed His Son to be our representative; and He accepted Him on our behalf. In this way the Father is "our Saviour," by giving and accepting One Who could save us. The Father "saved us ... through Jesus Christ our Saviour." Thus the Father and the Son co-operate to effect man's salvation, and each in a very real and proper sense is called "our Saviour." But it is not in man's own power to accept the salvation thus wrought for him and offered to him. For power to do this he needs Divine assistance; which, however, is abundantly granted to him. By means of the outward laver of baptism the inward regeneration and renewal by the Spirit is granted to him through the merits of Christ; and then the work of his salvation on the Divine side is complete. Through the infinite mercy of the Blessed Trinity, and not through his own merits, the baptized Christian is in a state of salvation, and is become an heir of eternal life. It remains to be seen whether the Christian, thus richly endowed, will continue in this blessed state, and go on, by the daily renewal of the Holy Spirit, from grace to grace; or will through his own weakness and wilfulness, fall away. But, so far as God's share in the transaction is concerned, his salvation is secured; so that, as the Church of England affirms in the note added to the service for the Public Baptism of Infants: "It is certain by God's Word, that children which are baptized, dying before they commit actual sin, are undoubtedly saved." And the several parts which the Persons of the Blessed Trinity take in the work of salvation are clearly indicated in one of the prayers before the baptismal act, as in the present passage by St. Paul. Prayer is offered to the "heavenly Father," that He will "give His Holy Spirit to this Infant, that he may be born again, and be made an heir of everlasting salvation; through our Lord Jesus Christ." Thus, as at the baptism of the Christ, so also at that of every Christian, the presence and co-operation of Father, Son, and Holy Spirit is indicated.

It is the Apostle's object in this condensed doctrinal statement to emphasize the fact that it was "not by works in righteousness which *we ourselves* did," but by the work of the Blessed Trinity, that we were placed in a state of salvation. He does not stop to make the qualifications, which, however true and necessary, do not alter this fact. In the case of adults, who are converted to Christianity,—and it is of such that he is thinking,—it is necessary that they should be duly prepared for baptism by repentance and faith. And in the case of all (whether adults, or infants, who live to become responsible for their actions), it is necessary that they should appropriate and use the graces bestowed upon them; in other words, that they should grow in holiness. All this is true; but it does not affect the position. For although man's co-operation is indispensable—for God saves no man against his will—yet without God's assistance man cannot either repent or believe before baptism, nor can he continue in holiness after baptism. This passage expressly denies that we effect our own salvation, or that God effected it in return for our merits. But it gives no encouragement to the belief that we have nothing to do with "working out our own salvation," but have merely to sit still and accept what has been done for us.

That "the washing of regeneration," or (as the margin of the R.V. more exactly has it) "the *laver* of regeneration,"[81] signifies the Christian rite of baptism, ought to be regarded as beyond dispute. This is certainly one of those cases to which Hooker's famous canon of interpretation most thoroughly applies, that "where a literal construction will stand, the farthest from the letter is commonly the worst" (*Eccl. Pol.*, v. lix. 2). This Hooker holds to be "a most infallible rule in expositions of sacred Scripture"; and although some persons may think that assertion somewhat too strong, of the soundness of the rule no reasonable student of Scripture can doubt. And it is worth our while to notice that it is in connexion with this very subject of baptismal regeneration that Hooker lays down this rule. He is answering those who perversely interpreted our Lord's words to Nicodemus, "Except a man be born of water and the Spirit" (John iii. 5), as meaning no more than "Except a man be born of the Spirit," "water" being (as they imagined) only a metaphor, of which "the Spirit" is the interpretation. On which Hooker remarks: "When the letter of the law hath two things plainly and expressly specified, Water, and the Spirit; Water as a duty required on our parts, the Spirit as a gift which God bestoweth; there is danger in presuming so to interpret it, as if the clause which concerneth ourselves were more than needeth. We may by such rare expositions attain perhaps in the end to be thought witty, but with ill advice." All which may be fitly applied to the passage before us, in which it is quite arbitrary and against all probability to contend that "the bath of regeneration" is a mere metaphor for regeneration without any bath, or for the Holy Spirit, or for the unmeasured bounty with which the Holy Spirit is poured upon the believer.

This might be tenable, if there had been no such rite as baptism by water enjoined by Christ and practised by the Apostles as the necessary and universal method of admission to the Christian Church. In Eph. v. 26 (the only other passage in the New Testament in which the word for "laver" or "bath" or "washing" occurs) the reference to baptism by water is indisputable, for the water is expressly mentioned. "Christ also loved the Church, and gave Himself up for it; that He might sanctify it, having *cleansed it by the washing of water* with the word." And in the passage in the First Epistle to the Corinthians which, like the one before us, contrasts the appalling wickedness of unbelievers with the spiritual condition of Christians, the reference to baptism is scarcely less clear. "And such were some of you: but *ye were washed* (lit. 'ye washed away'[82] your sins), but ye were sanctified, but ye were justified in the Name of the Lord Jesus Christ, and in the Spirit of our God" (1 Cor. vi. 11). In which passage, as here, the three Persons of the Trinity are named in connexion with the baptismal act.

And in speaking to the Jews at Jerusalem of his own admission to the Church, St. Paul uses the same forms of the same word as he uses to the Corinthians of their admission. The exhortation of Ananias to him, as he lay at Damascus, was "And now why tarriest thou? Arise, and *be baptized*, and *wash away thy sins*" (ἀπόλουσαι τὰς ἁμαρτίας σου), "calling on His Name" (Acts xxii. 16): words which are very parallel to the exhortation of St. Peter on the day of Pentecost: "Repent ye, and *be baptized, every one of you* in the Name of Jesus Christ *unto the remission of your sins*; and ye shall receive the gift of the Holy Ghost" (Acts ii. 38; comp. Heb. x. 23). In these passages we have a sacred rite described in which the human and the Divine elements are clearly marked. On man's side there is the washing with water; and on God's side there is the washing away of sin and pouring out of the Spirit. The body is purified, the soul is purified, and the soul is hallowed. The man is washed, is justified, is sanctified. He is regenerated: he is "a new creature." "The old things," his old principles, motives, and aims, then and there "passed away" (aorist tense, παρῆλθεν): "behold, they are become new" (2 Cor. v. 17). Can any one, with these passages before him, reasonably doubt, that, when the Apostle speaks of "the washing of regeneration" he means the Christian rite of baptism, in which, and by means of which, the regeneration takes place?

We are fully justified by his language here in asserting that it is *by means of* the baptismal washing that the regeneration takes place; for he asserts that God "saved us *through* the washing of regeneration." The laver or bath of regeneration is the instrument or means by which God saved us. Such is the natural, and almost the necessary meaning of the Greek construction (διά with the genitive). Nor is this an audacious erection of a comprehensive and momentous doctrine upon the narrow basis of a single preposition. Even if this passage stood alone, it would still be our duty to find a reasonable meaning for the Apostle's Greek: and it may be seriously doubted whether any more reasonable meaning than that which is here put forward can be found. But the passage does not stand alone, as has just been shown. And there are numerous analogies which throw light upon the question, proving to us that there is nothing exceptional in God (Who of course does not need any means or instruments) being willing to use them, doubtless because it is better for us that He should use them.

In illustration of the Greek construction we may compare that used by St. Peter of the event which he takes (and the Church of England in her baptismal service has followed him) as a type of Christian baptism. "When the long-suffering of God waited in the days of Noah, while the ark was a preparing, wherein few, that is, eight souls, were saved *through water*: which also after a true likeness doth now save you, even baptism." St. Peter says that Noah and his family "were saved *by means of water*" (δι' ὕδατος), just as St. Paul says that God "saved us *by means of the laver* of regeneration" (διὰ λουτροῦ παλιγγενεσίας). In each case the water is the *instrument* of salvation. And the analogy does not end with the identity of the instrument; that is the mere external resemblance between the flood and baptism. The main part of the likeness lies in this, that in both cases one of the same instrument both destroys and saves. The Flood destroyed the disobedient by drowning them, and saved Noah and his family by floating them into a new home. Baptism destroys the old corrupt element in man's nature by washing it away, and saves the regenerated soul by bringing it into a new life. And the other event which from the earliest days has been taken as a figure of baptism is of the same kind. At the crossing of the Red Sea, the water which destroyed the Egyptians saved the Israelites. In all these cases God was not tied to use water, or any other instrument. He could have saved Noah and the Israelites, and destroyed the disobedient and the Egyptians, just as He could have healed Naaman and the man born blind, without employing any means whatever. But for our edification He condescends to employ means, such as we can perceive and understand.

In what way is the employment of perceptible means a help to us? In two at least. It serves the double purpose of being both a *test* of faith and an *aid* to faith.

1. The acceptance of Divinely appointed means is necessarily a test of faith. Human intellect is apt to assume that Omnipotence is above using instruments. "Is it likely," we ask, "that the Almighty would employ these means? Are they not altogether beneath the dignity of the Divine Nature? Man needs tools and materials: but God needs neither. It is not credible that He has ordained these things as conditions of His own operation." All which is the old cry of the captain of the host of Syria. "Behold, I thought,

he will surely come out to me, and stand and call on the name of the Lord his God, and wave his hand over the place, and recover the leper." That is, why need he enjoin any instrument at all? But if he must, he might have enjoined something more suitable. "Are not Abanah and Pharpar, the rivers of Damascus, better than all the waters of Israel? may I not wash in them, and be clean?" In precisely the same spirit we ask still, "How can water wash away sin? How can bread and wine be Christ's body and blood? How can the laying on of a man's hand confer the gift of the Holy Spirit? Do not all such assumptions savour of magic rather than of Divine Providence?" Therefore humbly to accept the means which God has revealed as the appointed channels of His spiritual blessings is a real test of the recipient's faith. He is thus enabled to perceive for himself whether he does sincerely believe or not; whether he has the indispensable qualification for receiving the promised blessing.

2. The employment of visible means is a real aid to faith. It is easier to believe that an effect will be produced, when one can perceive something which might contribute to produce the effect. It is easier to believe when one sees means than when none are visible; and it is still easier to believe when the means seem to be appropriate. The man who was born blind would more readily believe that Christ would give him sight, when he perceived that Christ was using spittle and clay for the purpose; for at that time these things were supposed to be good for the eyes. And what element in nature is more frequently the instrument both of life and of death than water? What could more aptly signify purification from defilement? What act could more simply express a death to sin and a rising again to righteousness than a plunge beneath the surface of the water and a re-issuing from it? As St. Paul says in the Epistle to the Romans: "We were buried therefore with Him through baptism" (διὰ τοῦ βαπτίσματος) "into death; that like as Christ was raised from the dead through the glory of the Father, so we also might walk in newness of life" (vi. 4). And again to the Colossians: "Having been buried with Him in baptism, wherein ye were also raised with Him through faith in the working of God, Who raised Him from the dead" (ii. 12). Faith in the inward gift, promised by God to those who believe and are baptized, becomes more easy, when the outward means of conferring the gift, not only are readily perceived, but are recognized as suitable. In this way our faith is aided by God's employment of means.

Is the "renewing of the Holy Ghost" the same thing as the "washing of regeneration"? In this passage the two expressions refer to the same fact, but in their respective meanings they are not co-extensive. The Greek construction is ambiguous like the English; and we cannot be sure whether St. Paul means that God saved us by means of the washing and by means of the renewing, or that God saved us by means of a laver, which is both a laver of regeneration and a laver of renewal. The latter is more probable: but in either case the reference is to one and the same event in the Christian's life. The laver and the renewing refer to baptism; and the regeneration and the renewing refer to baptism; viz., to the new birth which is then effected. But, nevertheless, the two expressions are not co-extensive in meaning. The laver and the regeneration refer to one fact, and to one fact only; a fact which takes place once for all and can never be repeated. A man cannot have the new birth a second time, any more than he can be born a second time: and hence no one may be baptized twice. But the renewing of the Holy Spirit may take place daily. It precedes baptism in the case of adults; for it is only through a renewal which is the work of the Spirit that they can prepare themselves by repentance and faith for baptism. It takes place at baptism, as the Apostle clearly indicates here. And it continues after baptism; for it is by repeated quickening of the inward life through the action of the Spirit that the Christian grows in grace day by day. In the case of the adult, who unworthily receives baptism without repentance and faith, there is no spiritual renewal. Not that the sacred rite remains without effect: but the renewing of the Spirit is suspended until the baptized person repents and believes. Meanwhile the mysterious gift bestowed in baptism becomes a curse rather than a blessing; or at least a curse as well as a blessing. It may perhaps increase the possibilities of repentance: it certainly intensifies the guilt of all his sins. Such a person has thrust himself into a society without being qualified for membership. He has incurred the responsibilities of membership: if he desires the privileges, he must obtain the qualifications. [83]

It is God's gracious purpose that all should have the privileges in full. In baptism He washed us from our sins, He gave us a new birth, He poured out His Holy Spirit upon us richly, through Jesus Christ; "*in order that, being justified by His grace, we might be made heirs according to hope of eternal life.*"

FOOTNOTES:

[81] λουτρὸν παλιγγενεσίας. Comp. Eph. v. 26.

[82] Middle Voice, ἀπελούσασθε, on which see Professor Evans in the *Speaker's Commentary* iii., p. 282. And it is worth noticing that in both passages the principal verbs

are in the tense which in Greek commonly indicates some one particular occasion, "Ye were washed, were sanctified, were justified," are all in the aorist. So also here: "He saved us," and "He poured out upon us" are both in the aorist. And in both cases the natural reference is to the particular occasion of baptism in which we "were washed, sanctified, and justified," because God "saved us by the laver of regeneration and renewing of the Holy Spirit which He poured out upon us richly."

[83] See Waterland, *Regeneration Stated and Explained*: Works, Vol. vi. pp. 359—362. The whole tract may be commended for clearness and moderation.

CHAPTER XXVI
THE MEANING OF HERESY IN THE NEW TESTAMENT, AND THE APOSTLE'S DIRECTIONS RESPECTING THE TREATMENT OF HERETICAL PERSONS

"A man that is heretical after a first and second admonition refuse; knowing that such a one is perverted, and sinneth, being self-condemned"—Titus iii. 10, 11.

It is in connexion with this instruction respecting the treatment of heretical persons that we have some of the earliest testimonies to the genuineness of the Epistle to Titus. Thus Irenæus about a.d. 180 writes: "But as many as *fall away from*" (ἀφίστανται, 1 Tim. iv. 1) "the Church and give heed to these *old wives' fables*" (γραώδεσι μύθοις, 1 Tim. iv. 7), "are truly *self-condemned*" (αὐτοκατάκριτοι, Tit. iii. 1): "whom Paul charges us *after a first and second admonition to refuse*" (*Adv. Hær.*, I. xvi. 3). It will be observed that in this passage Irenæus makes an obvious allusion to the First Epistle to Timothy, and then quotes the very words of our text, attributing them expressly to St. Paul. And about ten or twelve years later, Tertullian, after commenting on St. Paul's words to the Corinthians, "For there must be also heresies among you, that they which are approved may be made manifest among you" (1 Cor. xi. 19), continues as follows: "But no more about that, seeing that it is the same Paul who elsewhere also in writing to the Galatians reckons heresies among sins of the flesh (Gal. v. 20), and who intimates to Titus that a *man who is heretical must after a first[84] admonition be refused, because he that is such is perverted and sinneth as being self-condemned.* But in almost every Epistle, when insisting on the duty of avoiding false doctrines, he censures heresies of which the practical results are false doctrines, called in Greek *heresies*, with reference to the *choice* which a man exercises, whether in instituting or in adopting them. For this reason he says that the heretical person is also self-condemned, because he has chosen for himself that in which he is condemned. We, however, may not allow ourselves anything after our own will; nor yet choose what any one has introduced of his own will. The Apostles of the Lord are our authorities: and even they did not choose to introduce anything of their own will, but faithfully consigned to the nations the instruction which they received from Christ. And so, even if an angel from heaven were to preach any other gospel, he would be called accursed by us" (*De Præs. Hær.*, vi). In this passage, which contains a valuable comment on the meaning of the word "heresy," it will be noticed that Tertullian not only quotes the text before us as coming from the Epistle to Titus, but, like Irenæus, his earlier contemporary, says expressly that the words are those of St. Paul. Thus, from both sides of the Mediterranean, men who had very large opportunities of knowing what books were accepted as Apostolic and what not, attribute our Epistle without hesitation to St. Paul. And in both cases this is done in treatises directed against heretics, who might be expected to reply with very telling effect, if it could be shown that what was quoted against them as the writing of an Apostle was of quite doubtful origin and authority.

But the testimony which these passages bear to the authenticity of this Epistle is not the main reason for their being quoted here. Their interest for us now consists in the light which they throw upon the history of the word "heresy," and upon the attitude of the primitive Church towards heretics.

"Heresy," as Tertullian points out, is a word of Greek origin, and the idea which lies at the root of it is *choice*.[85] Choosing for oneself what pleases oneself, independently of other considerations;—that is the fundamental notion on which later meanings of the term are based. Thus in the Septuagint it is used of a *free-will* offering, as distinct from what a man is bound to offer (Lev. xxii. 18; comp. 1 Macc. viii. 30). Then comes the notion of choice in reference to matters of opinion, without, however, necessarily implying that the chosen opinion is a bad one. And in this sense it is used quite as often for the party or school of thought which holds the particular opinion as for the body of opinion which is held. In this sense it is several times used in the Acts of the Apostles; as "the *sect* of the Sadducees" (v. 17), "the *sect* of the Pharisees" (xv. 5; xxvi. 5): and in this way Christianity itself was spoken of as a "heresy" or "sect"; that is, a party with chosen opinions (xxiv. 5, 14; xxviii. 22). And in profane literature we find Diogenes Laertius in the second or third century speaking of ten "heresies" or schools in moral philosophy (i. 19). But it will be seen from the passages in the Acts that the word is already acquiring somewhat of a bad meaning; and indeed this was almost inevitable, unless the original signification was entirely abandoned. In all spheres of thought and action, and especially in matters of belief, a tendency to choose for oneself, and to pursue one's own way independently, almost of necessity leads to separation from others, to divisions and factions. And factions in the Church readily widen into schisms and harden into heresies.

Outside the Acts of the Apostles the word heresy is found in the New Testament only in three passages: 1 Cor. xi. 19; Gal. v. 20; and 2 Pet. ii. 1. In the last of these it is used of the erroneous opinions themselves; in the other two the parties who hold them may be indicated. But in all cases the word is used of divisions inside the Church, not of separations from it or of positions antagonistic to it. Thus in 2 Pet. ii. 1 we have the prophecy that "there shall be false teachers, who shall privily *bring in* destructive *heresies*, denying even the Master that bought them." Here the false teachers are evidently inside the Church, corrupting its members; not outside, inducing its members to leave it. For the prophecy continues: "And many shall follow their lascivious doings; by reason of whom the way of the truth shall be evil spoken of." They could not cause "the way of the truth to be evil spoken of," if they were complete outsiders, professing to have no connexion with it. In Gal. v. 20 "heresies" are among "the works of the flesh" against which St. Paul warns his fickle converts, and "heresies" are there coupled with "factions" and "divisions." In 1 Cor. xi. 19 the Apostle gives as a reason for believing the report that there are divisions in the Church of Corinth the fact that (man's tendency to differ being what it is) divisions are inevitable, and have their use, for in this way those which are approved among Christians are made manifest. It is possible in both these passages to understand St. Paul as meaning the "self-chosen views," as in the passage in 2 Pet., rather than the schools or parties which have adopted the views. But this is not of much moment. The important thing to notice is, that in all three cases the "heresies" have caused or are tending to cause splits inside the Church: they do not indicate hostile positions outside it. This use of the word is analogous to that in the Acts of the Apostles, where it represents the Pharisees and Sadducees, and even the Christian Church itself, as parties or schools inside Judaism, not as revolts against it. We shall be seriously misled, if we allow the later meaning of "heresy," with all its medieval associations, to colour our interpretation of the term as we find it in the New Testament.

Another important thing to remember in reference to the strong language which St. Paul and other writers in the New Testament use with regard to "heresies" and erroneous doctrine, and the still stronger language used by early Christian writers in commenting on these texts, is the downright wickedness of a good many of the "self-chosen views" which had begun to appear in the Church in the first century, and which became rampant during the second. The peril, not only to faith, but to morals, was immense, and it extended to the very foundations of both. When Christians were told that there were two Creators, of whom one was good and one was evil; that the Incarnation was an impossibility; that man's body was so vile that it was a duty to abuse it; that his spirit was so pure that it was impossible to defile it; that to acquire knowledge through crime was estimable, for knowledge was good, and crime was of no moral significance to the enlightened;—then it was necessary to speak out, and tell men in plain terms what the persons who were inculcating such views were really doing, and what strong measures would be necessary, if they persisted in such teaching.

Unless we keep a firm grasp upon these two facts;—(1) the difference between the meaning of the word "heresy" as we find it in the New Testament and its usual meaning at the present time; and (2) the monstrous character of some of the views which many persons in the first century, and many more in the second, claimed to hold as part and parcel of the Christian religion;—we shall be liable to go grievously astray in drawing conclusions as to our own practice from what is said on the subject in Scripture.

"Woe unto the world," said our blessed Lord, "because of occasions of stumbling! For it must needs be that the occasions come; but woe to that man through whom the occasion cometh" (Matt. xviii. 7). Human nature being what it is, it is morally impossible that no one should ever lead another into sin. But that fact does not destroy the responsibility of the individual who leads his fellows into sin. St. Paul takes up the principle thus laid down by Christ and applies it in a particular sphere. He tells his Corinthian converts that "there must be heresies" among them, and that they serve the good purpose of sifting the chaff from the wheat. Wherever the light comes, it provokes opposition; there is at once antagonism between light and darkness. This is as true in the sphere of faith and morals as in that of the material world. Sooner or later, and generally sooner rather than later, truth and innocence are met and opposed by falsehood and sin; and it is falsehood, wilfully maintained in opposition to revealed and generally held truth, that constitutes the essence of heresy. There are many false opinions outside what God has revealed to mankind, outside the scope of the Gospel. However serious these may be, they are not heresies. A man may be fatally at fault in matters of belief; but, unless in some sense he accepts Christianity as true, he is no heretic. As Tertullian says, "In all cases truth precedes its copy; after the reality the likeness follows" (*De Præs. Hær.*, xxix). That is, heresy, which is the caricature of Christian truth, must be subsequent to it. It is a distortion of the original truth, which some one has arrogantly chosen as preferable to that of which it is the distortion. Error which has not yet come in contact with revelation, and which has had no opportunity of either submitting to it or rebelling against it, is not heretical. The heretical spirit is seen in that cold critical temper, that self-confident and self-willed attitude, which accepts and rejects opinions on principles of its own, quite independently of the principles which are the guaranteed and historical guides of the Church. But it cannot accept or reject what has never been presented to it; nor, until the Christian faith has to some extent been accepted, can the rejection of the remainder of it be accounted heresy. Heresy is "a disease of Christian knowledge." The disease may have come from without, or may have developed entirely from within; and in the former case the source of the malady may be far older than Christianity itself. But until the noxious elements have entered the Christian organism and claimed a home within the system, it is a misuse of language to term them heretical.

We have not exhausted the teaching of the Apostles respecting this plague of self-assertion and independent teaching, which even in their time began to afflict the infant Church, when we have considered all the passages in which the words "heresy" and "heretical" occur. There are other passages, in which the thing is plainly mentioned, although this name for it is not used. It has been said that "the Apostles, though they claimed disciplinary authority, had evidently no thought of claiming infallibility for any utterances of theirs."[86] But they certainly treated opposition to their teaching, or deviations from it, as a very serious matter. St. Paul speaks of those who opposed him in the Church of Corinth as "false apostles, deceitful workers" and "ministers of Satan" (2 Cor. xi. 13–15). He speaks of the Galatians as "bewitched" by those who would pervert the Gospel of Christ, and pronounces an anathema on those who should "preach any gospel other than that which he preached" (Gal. i. 7, 8; iii. 1). Of the same class of teachers at Philippi he writes: "Beware of the dogs, beware of the evil workers, beware of the concision" (iii. 2). He warns the Colossians against any one who may "make spoil of them through his philosophy and vain deceit, after the tradition of men, after the rudiments of the world, and not after Christ" (ii. 8); just as he warned the elders of the Church at Ephesus that after his departure "grievous wolves would enter in among them, not sparing the flock; and that from among themselves men would arise, speaking perverse things, to draw away the disciples after them" (Acts xx. 29, 30). And in the Pastoral Epistles we have several utterances of the same kind, including the one before us (1 Tim. i. 3–7, 19, 20; iv. 1–3; vi. 3, 4, 20, 21; Tit. i. 10–16; iii. 8–11; 2 Tim. ii. 16–18; iii. 8, 13).

Nor is St. Paul the only writer in the New Testament who feels bound to write in this strain. The same kind of language fills no inconsiderable portion of the Second Epistle of Peter and the Epistle of Jude (2 Pet. ii.; Jude 8–16). More remarkable still, we find even the Apostle of Love speaking in tones not less severe. The Epistles to the Seven Churches of Asia abound in such things (Rev. ii.; iii). In his General Epistle he asks, "Who is the liar but he that denieth that Jesus is the Christ? This is the antichrist, even he that denieth the Father and the Son" (1 John ii. 22: comp. ii. 26; iv. 1, 3). In his letter to "the elect lady and her children" he speaks of the "many deceivers" who "confess not that Jesus Christ cometh in the flesh." And, in a passage not unlike the direction to Titus which we are now considering, he says: "If any one cometh unto you, and bringeth not this teaching, receive him not into your house, and give him no greeting: for he that giveth him greeting partaketh in his evil works."

The impression which these passages produce on our minds is at least this;—that, whether or no the Apostles were conscious of being protected by the Holy Spirit from teaching anything that was doctrinally false, they were at any rate very stern in their condemnation of those Christians who deliberately contravened what an Apostle had taught. And this sternness is not confined to those who resisted the instructions of Apostles in matters of discipline. It is quite as clearly manifested against those who contradicted Apostolic teaching in matters of faith. The context of the passage before us shows that by "a man that is heretical" is meant one who wilfully takes his own line and thereby causes divisions in doctrine quite as much as one who does so as regards the order and discipline of the Church.

What, then, does St. Paul mean when he directs Titus to "refuse" such a person after once or twice admonishing him? Certainly not that he is to excommunicate him; the passage has nothing to do with formal excommunication. It is possible to maintain that the direction here given may *imply* excommunication; but it is also possible to maintain that it need not imply anything of the kind; and therefore that such an interpretation substitutes an uncertain inference for what is certainly expressed. The word translated in the r.v. "refuse," and in the a.v. "reject," is the same as that which is used in 1 Tim. v. 11 in the text, "Younger widows *refuse*" (παραιτοῦ). It means, "avoid, shun, excuse yourself from having anything to do with" (comp. Heb. xii. 25). It is also used of things as well as of persons, and in much the same sense: "*Refuse* profane and old wives' fables" (1 Tim. iv. 7), and "Foolish and ignorant questions *refuse*" (2 Tim. ii. 23). The meaning, then, here seems to be that, after a few attempts to induce the heretical person to desist from his perverse and self-willed conduct, Titus is to waste no more time on him, because now he knows that his efforts will be useless. At first he did not know this; but after having failed once or twice, he will see that it is vain to repeat what produces no effect. The man's self-will is incorrigible; and not only that, but inexcusable; for he stands self-condemned. He deliberately chose what was opposed to the received teaching; and he deliberately persists in it after its erroneous character has been pointed out to him. He "is perverted, and sinneth": that is, he not only has sinned, but goes on sinning: he continues in his sin, in spite of entreaty, exhortation, and reproof.

In what way are the directions here given to Titus to be used for our own guidance at the present time? Certain limitations as to their application have been already pointed out. They do not apply to persons who have always been, or who have ended in placing themselves, outside the Christian Church. They refer to persons who contend that their self-chosen views are part and parcel of the Gospel, and who claim to hold and teach such views as members or even ministers of the Church. Secondly, they refer to grave and fundamental errors with regard to first principles; not to eccentric views respecting matters of detail. And in determining this second point much caution will be needed; especially when inferences are drawn from a man's teaching. We should be on our guard with regard to assertions that a particular teacher *virtually* denies the Divinity of Christ, or the Trinity, or the personality of God. But when both these points are quite clear, that the person contradicts some of the primary truths of the Gospel, and that he claims to do so as a Christian, what is a minister to do to such a member of his flock? He is to make one or two efforts to reclaim him, and then to have as little to do with him as possible.

In all such cases there are three sets of persons to be considered:—the heretic himself, those who have to deal with him, and the Church at large. What conduct on the part of those who have to deal with him will be least prejudicial to themselves and to the Church, and most beneficial to the man himself? The supreme law of charity must be the guiding principle. But that is no true charity which shows tenderness to one person in such a way as to do grievous harm to others, or to do more harm than good to the person who receives it. Love of what is good is not only consistent with hatred of what is evil; it cannot exist without such hatred. What we have to consider, therefore, is this. Will friendliness confirm him in his error? Would he be more impressed by severity? Is intercourse with him likely to lead to our being led astray? Will it increase his influence and his opportunities of doing harm? Is severity likely to excite sympathy in other people, first for him, and then for his teaching? It is impossible to lay down a hard and fast rule that would cover all cases; and while we remember the stern instructions which St. Paul gives to Titus, and St. John to the "elect lady," let us not forget the way in which Jesus Christ treated publicans and sinners.

In our own day there is danger of mistaking lazy or weak indifferentism for Christian charity. It is a convenient doctrine that the beliefs of our fellow-Christians are no concern of ours, even when they try to propagate what contradicts the creed. And, while emphasis is laid upon the responsibility of accepting articles of faith, it is assumed that there is little or no responsibility in refusing to accept, or in teaching others to refuse also. To plead for tenderness, where severity is needed, is not charity, but Laodicean lukewarmness; and mistaken tenderness may easily end in making us "partakers in evil works." To be severe, when severity is imperatively called for, is not only charity to the offenders, it "is also charity towards all men besides. It is charity towards the *ignorant* as carrying instruction along with it; charity towards the *unwary*, as giving them warning to stand off from infection; charity towards the *confirmed* Christians, as encouraging them still more, and preserving them from insults; charity towards the *whole Church*, as supporting both their unity and purity; charity towards *all mankind*, towards them that are *without*, as it is recommending pure religion to them in the most advantageous light, obviating their most plausible calumnies, and giving them less occasion to blaspheme."[87]

FOOTNOTES:

[84] It is worth noting that Tertullian, with several other Latin writers, omits the second admonition: *hominem hæreticum post primam correptionem recusandum.* Similarly Cyprian: *hæreticum hominem post unam correptionem devita* (*Test.*, III. 78).

[85] αἵρεσις, from αἱρεῖν, αἱρεῖσθαι, "to choose": not from *hærere*, "to stick fast," as has been ignorantly asserted.

[86] T. Ll. Davies in a remarkable paper on "The Higher Life," in the *Fortnightly Review*, January, 1888.

[87] Waterland, *The Importance of the Doctrine of the Holy Trinity* iv. ii. 2; Works, vol. v. p. 96. Oxford, 1823.

THE SECOND EPISTLE TO TIMOTHY

CHAPTER XXVII
THE CHARACTER AND CONTENTS OF THE LAST EPISTLE OF ST. PAUL.—THE NEMESIS OF NEGLECTED GIFTS

"For the which cause I put thee in remembrance that thou stir up the gift of God, which is in thee through the laying on of my hands. For God gave us not a spirit of fearfulness; but of power and love and discipline."—2 Tim. i. 6, 7.

In the Second Epistle to Timothy we have the last known words of St. Paul. It is his last will and testament; his last instructions to his favourite disciple and through him to the Church. It is written with full consciousness that the end is at hand. His course in this world is all but over; and it will be closed by a violent, it may be by a cruel death. The letter is, therefore, a striking but thoroughly natural mixture of gloom and brightness. On the one hand, death throws its dark shadow across the page. On the other, there is the joyous thought that the realization of his brightest hopes is close at hand. Death will come with its pain and ignominy, to cut short the Apostle's still unfinished work, to take him away from the Churches which he has founded and which still sorely need his guidance, and from the friends whom he loves, and who still need his counsel and support. But death, while it takes him away from much to which he clings and which clings to him, will free him from toil, and anxiety, and neglect, and will take him to be with Christ until that day when he shall receive the crown of righteousness which is laid up for him.

If the shadow of impending death were the only source of gloom, the letter would be far more joyous than it is. It would be far more continuously a strain of thanksgiving and triumph. But the prospect of ending his life under the hand of the public executioner is not the thought which dominates the more sorrowful portion of the Epistle. There is the fact that he is almost alone; not because his friends are prevented from coming to him, but because they have forsaken him; some, it may be, for pressing work elsewhere;

others because the attractions of the world were too strong for them; but the majority of them, because they were afraid to stand by him when he was placed at the bar before Nero. The Apostle is heavy-hearted about this desertion of him, not merely because of the wound which it inflicts on his own affectionate spirit, but because of the responsibility which those who are guilty of it have thereby incurred. He prays that it "may not be laid to their account."

Yet the thought which specially oppresses him is "anxiety about all the Churches"—and about Timothy himself. Dark days are coming. False doctrine will be openly preached and will not lack hearers; and utterly un-Christian conduct and conversation will become grievously prevalent. And, while the godly are persecuted, evil men will wax worse and worse. This sad state of things has already begun; and the Apostle seems to fear that his beloved disciple is not altogether unaffected by it. Separation from St. Paul and the difficulties of his position may have told on his over-sensitive temperament, and have caused him to be remiss in his work, through indulgence in futile despondency. The words of the text strike the dominant chord of the Epistle and reveal to us the motive that prompts it. The Apostle puts Timothy in remembrance "that he stir up the gift of God which is in him." Again and again he insists on this and similar counsels. "Be not ashamed of the testimony of our Lord, nor of me His prisoner; but suffer hardships." "That good thing which was committed to thee guard through the Holy Ghost" (vv. 8, 13). "Suffer hardship with me, as a good soldier of Jesus Christ." "Give diligence to present thyself approved unto God, a workman that needeth not to be ashamed" (ii. 3, 15). "But abide thou in the things which thou hast learned and hast been assured of, knowing of whom thou hast learned them" (iii. 14). And then, as the letter draws to a close, he speaks in still more solemn tones of warning: "I charge thee in the sight of God, and of Christ Jesus, Who shall judge the quick and the dead, and by His appearing and His kingdom: be instant in season, out of season; reprove, rebuke, exhort, with all longsuffering and teaching." "Be thou sober in all things, suffer hardships, do the work of an evangelist, fulfil thy ministry" (iv. 1, 2, 5). Evidently the Apostle is anxious lest even the rich gifts with which Timothy is endowed should be allowed to rust through want of use. Timidity and weakness may prove fatal to him and his work, in spite of the spiritual advantages which he has enjoyed. The Apostle's anxiety about the future of the Churches is interwoven with anxiety about the present and future conduct of his beloved delegate and successor.

The Second Epistle to Timothy is more personal than either of the other Pastoral Epistles. It is less official in tone and contents, and is addressed more directly to the recipient himself, than through him to others. Three main subjects are treated in the letter; and first and foremost of these is the conduct of Timothy himself. This subject occupies about a third of the Epistle. The next and longest section treats of the present and future prospects of the Church (ii. 14–iv. 5). And lastly the Apostle speaks of himself.

It is not difficult to understand how even those who condemn the Pastoral Epistles as the product of a later writer, feel almost obliged to admit that at least some of this touching letter must be genuine. Whoever wrote it must have had some genuine letters of St. Paul to use as material. It may be doubted whether any of the writings of that age which have come down to us are more thoroughly characteristic of the person whose name they bear, or are more full of touches which a fabricator would never have thought of introducing. The person who forged the Second Epistle to Timothy in the name of St. Paul must indeed have been a genius. Nothing that has come down to us of the literature of the second century leads us to suppose that any such literary power existed. Whether we regard the writer, or the circumstances in which he is placed, or the person to whom he writes, all is thoroughly characteristic, harmonious, and in keeping. We have St. Paul with his exquisite sympathy, sensitiveness, and affection, his intense anxiety, his unflinching courage. We have the solemnity and importunity of one who knows that his days are numbered. And we have the urgency and tenderness of one who writes to a friend who has his faults and weaknesses, but who is trusted and loved in spite of them.

In encouraging Timothy to stir up the gift that is in him, and not suffer himself to be ashamed of the ignominy, or afraid of the hardships, which the service of Christ entails, the Apostle puts before him five considerations. There are the beautiful traditions of his family, which are now in his keeping. There is the sublime character of the Gospel which has been entrusted to him. There is the teaching of St. Paul himself, who has so often given him a "pattern of sound words" and a pattern of steadfast endurance. There is the example of Onesiphorus with his courageous devotion. And there is the sure hope of "the salvation which is in Christ Jesus with eternal glory." Any one of these things might suffice to influence him: Timothy cannot be proof against them all. St. Paul is persuaded that he is preserving the heritage of undissembled faith which his mother and his grandmother possessed before him. When he considers the character of the Gospel, of which he has become a minister, and the gifts of which he has thereby become a recipient, he cannot now become ashamed of bearing testimony for it. And has the teaching of his old master, separation from whom used once to make him weep, lost its hold upon him? Of the other disciples and friends of the master, some have turned away from him, showing coldness or dislike instead of sympathy and self-sacrifice; while others, at great personal inconvenience, and (it may be also) great personal danger, sought him out all the more diligently on account of his imprisonment, and ministered to him. Will Timothy take his stand with Phygelus and Hermogenes, or with Onesiphorus? And over and above all these considerations, which are connected with this world, there are the thoughts of the world to come. This is no mere question of expediency and opportuneness, or of personal loyalty and affection to a human teacher and friend. There is the whole of eternity at stake. To have shared Christ's martyr-death is to share His endless life. To share His endurance and service is to share His royalty. But to reject Him, is to ensure being rejected by Him. Were He to receive faithless followers among the faithful, He would be faithless to His promises and to Himself.

For all these reasons, therefore, the Apostle charges his disciple to "stir up the gift of God which is in him through the laying on of the Apostle's hands." And the fact that he uses so much argument and entreaty is evidence that he had grave anxiety about Timothy. Timothy's natural sensitiveness and tenderness of heart made him specially liable to despondency and timidity, especially when separated from friends and confronted by sturdy opposition.

"That thou stir up the gift of God which is in thee." Literally "that thou kindle up and fan into a flame." It does not *necessarily* imply that there has once been a bright flame, which has been allowed to die down, leaving only smouldering embers. But this is the natural meaning of the figure, and is possibly what St. Paul implies here. He does not explain what precise gift of God it is that Timothy is to kindle into a warmer glow; but, as it is one of those which were conferred upon him by the laying on of hands at the time of his ordination, we may reasonably suppose that it is the authority and power to be a minister of Christ. In the First Epistle St. Paul had given Timothy a similar charge (iv. 14); and by combining that passage with this we learn that both the Apostle and the elders laid their hands on the young evangelist: "Neglect not the gift that is in thee, which was given thee by prophecy, with the laying on of the hands of the presbytery."[88] This talent committed to his charge for use in God's service must not be allowed to lie idle; it must be used with vigour, and trust, and courage. The very character of the gift bestowed proves that it is to be used, and used freely. "For God gave us not a spirit of fearfulness; but of power and love and discipline." St. Paul includes himself in the statement. He, like his disciple, has received this gift from God, and he knows from long experience what its nature is. It is no "spirit of fearfulness;" no "spirit of bondage leading to fear" (Rom. viii. 15). It was never meant to produce in us a slavish fear of God, or a cowardly fear of men. To feel awe and reverence when dealing with God,—to feel responsibility when dealing with men,—is one thing. To abstain from action for fear of offending either, is quite another. It is sometimes possible to avoid criticism by refusing to commit oneself to anything; but such refusal may be a sinful neglect of opportunities: and no error of judgment in using the gifts committed to us can be worse than that of not using them at all. Those are not necessarily the most useful servants who make the fewest conspicuous mistakes.

The spirit with which we are endowed is a spirit of *power*, whereas a spirit of fearfulness is weak. Faintheartedness cannot be strong. The fainthearted mistrust themselves and others; and they discourage themselves and others. They anticipate dangers and difficulties, and thereby sometimes create them; and they anticipate failure, and thereby often bring it about. It is only by acting, and by acting vigorously and courageously, that we find out the full power of the spirit with which we have been blessed.

Again, the gift which God has bestowed upon us is a spirit of *love*: and more than anything else perfect love casts out the spirit of fear. Fear is the child of bondage; love is the child of freedom. If we love God, we shall not live in terror of His judgments: and if we love men, we shall not live in terror of their criticisms. Moreover, the spirit of love teaches us the nature of the gift of power. It is not force or violence; not an imposing of our own will on others. It is an affectionate striving to win others over to obedience to the will of God. It is the spirit of self-sacrifice; not of self-assertion.

Lastly, the spirit with which we are endowed by God is a spirit of *discipline*. By discipline that cowardly indolence, which the spirit of fearfulness engenders, can be kept down and expelled. If it be asked, whether the discipline be that which Timothy is to enforce in ruling others, or that which he is to practise in schooling himself, we may answer, "Both." The termination of the word which is here used (σωφρονισμός) seems to require the transitive meaning; and slackness in correcting others may easily have been one of the ways in which the despondency of Timothy showed itself. On the other hand the whole context here speaks of Timothy's treatment of himself. To take a more lively interest in the conduct of others would be discipline for himself and for them also. There may be as much pride as humility in indulging the thought that the lives of other people are so utterly bad, that it is quite out of the power of such persons as ourselves to effect a reformation. This is a subtle way of shirking responsibility. Strong in the spirit of power, glowing with the spirit of love, we can turn the faults of others, together with all the troubles which may befall us in this life, into instruments of discipline.

The words of the Apostle, though primarily addressed to ministers, in reference to the spiritual gifts bestowed on them at their ordination, must not be confined to them. They apply to the gifts bestowed by God upon every Christian, and indeed upon every human being. There is a terrible penalty attached to the neglect of the higher faculties, whether intellectual or moral; a penalty which works surely and unerringly by a natural law. We all of us have imagination, intellect, will. These wonderful powers must have an object, must have employment. If we do not give them their true object, viz., the glory of God, they will find an object for themselves. Instead of soaring upwards on the wings supplied by the glories of creation and the mercies of redemption, they will sink downwards into the mire. They will fasten upon the flesh; and in an atmosphere poisoned by debasing associations they will become debased also. Instead of raising the man who possesses them into that higher life, which is a foretaste of heaven, they will hurry him downwards with the accumulated pressure of an undisciplined intellect, a polluted imagination, and a lawless will. That which should have been for wealth, becomes an occasion of falling. Angels of light become angels of darkness. And powers which ought to be as priests, consecrating the whole of our nature to God, become as demons, shameless and ruthless in devoting us to the evil one. Not only every minister of Christ, but every thinking man, has need from time to time "to stir up the gift of God that is in him," to kindle it into a flame, and see that it is directed to holy ends and exercised in noble service. God's royal gifts of intellect and will cannot be flung away, cannot be left unused, cannot be extinguished. For good or for evil they are ours; and they are deathless. But, though they cannot be destroyed they can be neglected. They can be buried in the earth, till they breed worms and stink. They can be allowed to run riot, until they become as wild beasts, and turn again and rend us. Or in the spirit of power, or love, and of discipline, they may be chastened by lofty exercise and sanctified to heavenly uses, till they become more and more fit to be the equipment of one, who is for ever to stand "before the throne of God, and praise Him day and night in His temple."

FOOTNOTES:

[88] The assertion that this laying on of hands is a mark of an age subsequent to the Apostles, ignores the plain statements in Acts vi. 6 xiii. 3; comp. viii. 17; ix. 17; xix. 6; and Heb. vi. 2.

CHAPTER XXVIII
THE HEARTLESSNESS OF PHYGELUS AND HERMOGENES.—THE DEVOTION OF ONESIPHORUS.—PRAYERS FOR THE DEAD

"This thou knowest, that all that are in Asia turned away from me; of whom are Phygelus and Hermogenes. The Lord grant mercy unto the house of Onesiphorus: for he oft refreshed me, and was not ashamed of my chain; but, when he was in Rome, he sought me diligently and found me (the Lord grant unto him to find mercy of the Lord in that day); and in how many things he ministered at Ephesus, thou knowest very well."—2 Tim. i. 15–18.

We have here one of the arguments which St. Paul makes use of in urging his beloved disciple to stir up the gift of God that is in him through the laying on of hands, and not allow himself to be afraid of the ignominy and the sufferings, which the service of Jesus Christ involves. After reminding him of the holy traditions of his family, of the glorious character of the Gospel which has been committed to him, and of the character of the Apostle's own teaching, St. Paul now goes on to point out, as a warning, the conduct of those in Asia who had deserted him in his hour of need; and, as an example, in marked contrast to them, the affectionate courage and persistent devotion of Onesiphorus. Timothy is not likely to follow those in Asia in their cowardly desertion of the Apostle. He will surely bestir himself to follow an example, the details of which are so well known to him and so very much to the point. Timothy's special knowledge of both cases, so far as the conduct referred to lay not in Rome but in Asia, is emphatically insisted upon by St. Paul. He begins by saying, "This thou *knowest*, that all that are in Asia turned away from me:" and he concludes with the remark, "In how many things he ministered at Ephesus, thou *knowest* very well;" or, as the Greek comparative probably means, "thou knowest *better* than I do." And it is worth noticing that St. Paul uses a different word for "know" in the two cases. Of his desertion by those in Asia he uses a word of general meaning (οἶδας), which implies knowledge *about* the things or persons in question, but need not imply more than hearsay knowledge of what is notorious. Of the devoted service of Onesiphorus at Ephesus he uses a word (γινώσκεις), which implies *progressive personal experience.* Timothy had of course heard all about the refusal of Phygelus and Hermogenes and others to recognize the claim which St. Paul had upon their services; what he saw and experienced continually gave him intimate acquaintance with the conduct of Onesiphorus in the Church of which Timothy had the chief care.

There has been a great deal of discussion about the meaning of St. Paul's statements respecting these two contrasted cases, Phygelus and those like him on the one side, and Onesiphorus on the other: and with regard to both of them a variety of suggestions have been made, which are scarcely compatible with the language used, and which do not after all make the situation more intelligible. It must be admitted that the brevity of the statements does leave room for a certain amount of conjecture; but, nevertheless, they are clear enough to enable us to conjecture with a fair amount of certainty.

And first with regard to the case of those in Asia. They are in Asia at the time when this letter is being written. It is quite inadmissible to twist this plain language and force it to mean "those *from* Asia who are now in Rome." Οἱ ἐν τῇ Ἀσίᾳ cannot be equivalent to οἱ ἐκ τῆς Ἀσίας. If St. Paul meant the latter, why did he not write it? Secondly, it is the proconsular province of Asia that is meant, that is the western portion of Asia Minor, and not the continent of Asia. Thirdly, the "turning away" of these Christians in Asia Minor does not mean their apostasy from the faith, of which there is no hint either in the word or in the context. St. Paul would hardly have spoken of their abandonment of Christianity as turning away from *him*. It means that they turned their faces away from him, and refused to have anything to say to him. When he sought their sympathy and assistance, they renounced his acquaintance, or at any rate refused to admit his claim upon them. It is the very expression used by Christ in the Sermon on the Mount; "From him that would borrow of thee, *turn not thou away*" (Matt. v. 42). This was exactly what these Asiatic disciples had done: the Apostle had asked them to lend him their help and support; and they had "turned away from" him. But what is the meaning of the "all"? He says that "*all* that are in Asia turned away from" him. Obviously there is some qualification to be understood. He cannot mean that Timothy is well aware that every believer in Asia Minor had repudiated St. Paul. Some have supposed that the necessary qualification is to be found in what follows; viz., "of whom are Phygelus and Hermogenes." The meaning would then be that the whole of the party to which Phygelus and Hermogenes belong rejected the Apostle. But the arrangement of the sentence is quite against this supposition; and there is nothing either said or implied about these two men being the leaders or representatives of a party. The expression respecting them is exactly parallel to that in the First Epistle respecting those who "made shipwreck concerning the faith: of whom is Hymenæus and Alexander" (i. 19, 20). In each case, out of a class of persons who are spoken of in general terms, two are mentioned by name. What then is the qualification of the "all," which common sense requires? It means simply, "all whom I asked, all to whom I made an appeal for assistance."[89] At the time when this letter was written, there were several Christians in Asia Minor,—some of them known to Timothy,—to whom St. Paul had applied for help in his imprisonment; and, as Timothy was very well aware, they every one of them refused to give it. And this refusal took place in Asia Minor, not in Rome. Some have supposed that, although these unfriendly Christians were in Asia when St. Paul wrote about them, yet it was in Rome that they "turned away from" him. They had been in Rome, and instead of remaining there to comfort the prisoner, they had gone away to Asia Minor. On this supposition a difficulty has been raised, and it has been pressed as if it told against the genuineness of the Epistle. How, it is asked, could Timothy, who was in Ephesus, be supposed to be well aware of what took place in Rome? And to meet this objection it has been conjectured, that shortly before this letter was written some one had gone with news from Rome to Ephesus. But this is to meet an imaginary difficulty with an imaginary fact. Let us imagine nothing, and then all runs smoothly. Every one in Asia Minor, to whom application was made on behalf of St. Paul, "turned away from" him and refused to do what was asked. Of such a fact as this the overseer of the Church of Ephesus could not fail to have knowledge; and, distressing as it was, it ought not to make him sink down into indolent despondency, but stir him up to redoubled exertion. What the precise request was that Phygelus and Hermogenes and the rest had refused, we do not know; but very possibly it was to go to Rome and exert themselves on the Apostle's behalf. Of the two persons named nothing further is known. They are mentioned as being known to Timothy, and very possibly as being residents in Ephesus.

Now let us turn to the case of Onesiphorus, whose conduct is such a marked contrast to these others. In the most natural way St. Paul first of all tells Timothy what he experienced from Onesiphorus in Rome; and then appeals to Timothy's own experience of him in Ephesus. In between these two passages there is a sentence, inserted parenthetically, which has been the subject of a good deal of controversy. "The Lord grant unto him to find mercy of the Lord in that day." On the one side it is argued that the context shows that Onesiphorus is dead, and that therefore we have Scriptural authority for prayers for the dead: on the other that it is by no means certain that Onesiphorus was dead at the time when St. Paul wrote;

and that, even if he was, this parenthesis is more of the nature of a pious wish, or expression of hope, than a prayer. It need scarcely be said that on the whole the latter is the view taken by Protestant commentators, although by no means universally; while the former is the interpretation which finds favour with Roman Catholics. Scripture elsewhere is almost entirely silent on the subject; and hence this passage is regarded as of special importance. But it ought to be possible to approach the discussion of it without heat or prejudice.

Certainly the balance of probability is decidedly in favour of the view that Onesiphorus was already dead when St. Paul wrote these words. There is not only the fact that he here speaks of "the *house* of Onesiphorus" in connexion with the present, and of Onesiphorus himself only in connexion with the past: there is also the still more marked fact that in the final salutations, while greetings are sent to Prisca and Aquila, and from Eubulus, Pudens, Linus, and Claudia, yet it is once more "the *house* of Onesiphorus" and not Onesiphorus himself who is saluted. This language is thoroughly intelligible, if Onesiphorus was no longer alive, but had a wife and children who were still living at Ephesus; but it is not easy to explain this reference in two places to the *household* of Onesiphorus, if he himself was still alive. In all the other cases the individual and not the household is mentioned. Nor is this twofold reference to his family rather than to himself the only fact which points in this direction. There is also the character of the Apostle's prayer. Why does he confine his desires respecting the requital of Onesiphorus' kindness to the day of judgment? Why does he not also pray that he may be requited in this life? that he "may prosper and be in health, even as his soul prospereth," as St. John prays for Gaius (3 John 2)? This again is thoroughly intelligible, if Onesiphorus is already dead. It is much less intelligible if he is still alive. It seems, therefore, to be scarcely too much to say that there is no serious reason for questioning the now widely accepted view that at the time when St. Paul wrote these words Onesiphorus was among the departed.

With regard to the second point there seems to be equal absence of serious reason for doubting that the words in question constitute a prayer. It is difficult to find a term which better describes them than the word "prayer:" and in discussing them one would have to be specially careful in order to avoid the words "pray" and "prayer" in connexion with them. It does not much matter what meaning we give to "the Lord" in each case; whether both refer to Christ, or both to the Father, or one to Christ and the other to the Father. In any case we have a prayer that the Judge at the last day will remember those good deeds of Onesiphorus, which the Apostle has been unable to repay, and will place them to his account. Paul cannot requite them, but he prays that God will do so by showing mercy upon him at the last day.[90]

Having thus concluded that, according to the more probable and reasonable view, the passage before us contains a prayer offered up by the Apostle on behalf of one who is dead, we seem to have obtained his sanction, and therefore the sanction of Scripture, for using similar prayers ourselves. But what is a similar prayer? There are many kinds of intercessions which may be made on behalf of those who have gone before us into the other world: and it does not follow that, because one kind of intercession has Scriptural authority, therefore any kind of intercession is allowable. This passage may be quoted as reasonable evidence that the death of a person does not extinguish our right or our duty to pray for him: but it ought not to be quoted as authority for such prayers on behalf of the dead as are very different in kind from the one of which we have an example here. Many other kinds of intercession for the dead may be reasonable and allowable; but this passage proves no more than that some kinds of intercession for the dead are allowable, viz., those in which we pray that God will have mercy at the day of judgment on those who have done good to us and others during their life upon earth.

But is the right, which is also the duty, of praying for the departed limited by the amount of sanction which it is possible to obtain from this solitary passage of Scripture? Assuredly not. Two other authorities have to be consulted,—reason and tradition.

I. This pious practice, so full of comfort to affectionate souls, is *reasonable in itself*. Scripture, which is mercifully reticent respecting a subject so liable to provoke unhealthy curiosity and excitement, nevertheless does tell us plainly some facts respecting the unseen world. (2) Those whom we call the dead are still alive. God is still the God of Abraham, of Isaac, and of Jacob: and He is not the God of the dead, but of the living (Matt. xxii. 32). Those who believe that death is annihilation, and that there can be no resurrection, "do greatly err" (Mark xii. 27). And (2) the living souls of the departed are still conscious: their bodies are asleep in this world, but their spirits are awake in the other. For this truth we are not dependent upon the disputable meaning of the parable of Dives and Lazarus; although we can hardly suppose that that parable would ever have been spoken, unless the continued consciousness of the dead and their interest in the living were a fact. Christ's parables are never mere fables, in which nature is distorted in order to point a moral: His lessons are ever drawn from God's universe as it is. But besides the parable (Luke xvi. 19–31), there is His declaration that Abraham not only "exulted" in anticipation of the coming of the Messiah, but "he saw" that coming "and was glad" thereat (John viii. 56). And there is His promise to the penitent thief: "Verily I say unto thee, To-day shalt thou be with me in Paradise" (Luke xxiii. 43). Can we believe that this promise, given at so awful a moment with such solemn assurance ("Verily I say unto thee"), would have been made, if the robber's soul, when in Paradise, would be unconscious of Christ's companionship? Could Christ then have "preached unto the spirits in prison" (1 Pet iii. 19), if the spirits of those who had died in the Flood were deprived of consciousness? And what can be the meaning of "the souls of them that had been slain for the word of God" crying "How long, O Master the holy and true, dost Thou not judge and avenge our blood?" (Rev. vi. 10), if the souls of the slain slumber in the unseen world?

It is not necessary to quote Scripture to prove that the departed are not yet perfect. Their final consummation will not be reached until the coming of Christ at the last great day (Heb. xi. 40).

If, then, the dead are conscious, and are not yet perfected, they are capable of progress. They may increase in happiness, and possibly in holiness. May we not go farther and say, that they *must* be growing, *must* be progressing towards a better state; for, so far as we have experience, there is no such thing as conscious life in a state of stagnation? Conscious life is always either growing or decaying: and decay is incipient death. For conscious creatures, who are incapable of decay and death, growth seems to be a necessary attribute. We conclude, therefore, on grounds partly of Scripture and partly of reason, that the faithful departed are consciously progressing towards a condition of higher perfection.

But this conclusion must necessarily carry us still farther. These consciously developing souls are God's children and our brethren; they are, like ourselves, members of Christ and joint-heirs with us of His kingdom; they are inseparably united with us in "the Communion of Saints." May we not pray for them to aid them in their progress? And if, with St. Paul's prayer for Onesiphorus before us, we are convinced that we may pray for them, does it not become our bounden duty to do so? On what grounds can we accept the obligation of praying for the spiritual advancement of those who are with us in the flesh, and yet refuse to help by our prayers the spiritual advancement of those who have joined that "great cloud of witnesses" in the unseen world, by which we are perpetually encompassed (Heb. xii. 1)? The very fact that they witness our prayers for them may be to them an increase of strength and joy.

II. *Tradition* amply confirms us in the belief that this pious practice is lawful, and binding upon all who recognize its lawfulness. The remarkable narrative in 2 Maccabees xii. shows that this belief in a very extreme form was common among the Jews, and publicly acted upon, before the coming of Christ. It is highly improbable that prayers for the dead were omitted from the public worship of the synagogue, in which Jesus Christ so frequently took part. It is quite certain that such prayers are found in every early Christian liturgy, and to this day form part of the liturgies in use throughout the greater portion of Christendom. And, although the medieval abuses connected with such prayers induced the reformers of our own liturgy almost, if not quite, entirely to omit them, yet the Church of England has never set any bounds to the liberty of its members in this respect. Each one of us is free in this matter, and therefore has the responsibility of using or neglecting what the whole of the primitive Church, and the large majority of Christians throughout all these centuries, have believed to be a means of advancing the peace and glory of Christ's kingdom. About the practice of the primitive Church there can be no question. Doubt has been thrown upon the liturgies, because it has been said that some portions are certainly of much later origin than the rest, and therefore these prayers may be later insertions and corruptions. But that cannot be so; for liturgies do not stand alone. In this matter they have the support of a chain of Christian writers beginning with Tertullian in the second century, and also of early inscriptions in the catacombs. About the meagre allusions to the departed in our own liturgy there is more room for doubt: but perhaps the most that can safely be asserted is this;—that here and there sentences have been worded in such a way that it is possible for those, who wish to do so, to include the faithful departed in the prayer as well as the living. Bishop Cosin has given his authority to this interpretation of the prayer that "we and all Thy whole Church may obtain remission of our sins and all other benefits of His passion." By this, he says, "is to be understood, as well those that have been here before, and those that shall be hereafter, as those that are now members of it:" and as one of the revisers his authority is great. And the prayer in the Burial Service, "that we, with all those that are departed in the true faith of Thy holy name, may have our perfect consummation and bliss, both in body and soul," is equally patient of this meaning, even if it does not fairly demand it. For we do not pray that we may have our consummation and bliss with the departed; which might imply that they are enjoying these things now, and that we desire to join them; but we pray that we with the departed may have our consummation and bliss; which includes them in the prayer. And the petition in the Litany, "remember not, Lord, our offences, nor the offences of our forefathers," may, or may not, be a prayer for our forefathers, according to the way in which we understand it.

All this seems to show that neither Scripture nor the English Church forbids prayer for the departed; that, on the contrary, both of them appear to give a certain amount of sanction to it: and that what they allow, reason commends, and tradition recommends most strongly. It is for each one of us to decide for himself whether or no he will take part in the charitable work thus placed before him.[91]

FOOTNOTES:

[89] See below on "All forsook me," in No. XXXVII, p. 420.

[90] With the double use of Lord here, compare Exod. xxxiv. 9, where Moses prays, "O Lord, let the Lord, I pray Thee, go in the midst of us." Comp. also Gen. xix. 24.

[91] See J. M. Neale, *Liturgies of St. Mark, St. James, St. Clement, St. Chrysostom*, etc., 1859, pp. 216–224; C. E. Hammond, *Liturgies Eastern and Western*, 1878, pp. 45, 75, 113, 156, 183, 217, etc.; E. Burbridge, *Liturgies and Offices of the Church*, 1885, pp. 34, 222, 249; M. Plummer, *Observations on the Book of Common Prayer*, 1847, pp. 125–127; *Church Quarterly Review*, April 1880, pp. 1–25; H. M. Luckock, *After Death*, 1879: also various articles in the *Dict. of Christ. Antiquities*, 1875, 1880.

CHAPTER XXIX
THE NEED OF MACHINERY FOR THE PRESERVATION AND TRANSMISSION OF THE FAITH.—THE MACHINERY OF THE PRIMITIVE CHURCH

"Thou therefore, my child, be strengthened in the grace that is in Christ Jesus. And the things which thou hast heard from me among many witnesses, the same commit thou to faithful men, who shall be able to teach others also"—2 Tim. ii. 1, 2.

In this tenderly affectionate address we have a very early indication of the beginnings of Christian *tradition* and Christian *schools*, two subjects intimately connected with one another. St. Paul having pointed out as a warning to his "child" Timothy the cold or cowardly behaviour of those in Asia who had turned away from him, and as an example the affectionate courage of Onesiphorus, returns to the charge of which this letter is so full, that Timothy is "not to be ashamed of the testimony of our Lord," but be willing to "suffer hardship with the gospel according to the power of God" (i. 8). "*Thou therefore*, my child," with these instances in mind on the one hand and on the other, "be inwardly strengthened in the grace that is in Christ Jesus." In his own strength he will be able to do nothing; but in the grace which Christ freely bestows on all believers who ask it of Him, Timothy will be able to find all that he needs for the strengthening of his own character and for the instruction of others. And here St. Paul, in a way thoroughly natural in one who is writing a letter which is personal rather than official, diverges for a moment to give utterance to the idea which passes through his mind of securing permanence in the instruction of the faithful. Possibly it was in reference to this duty that he feared the natural despondency and sensitiveness of Timothy. Timothy would be likely to shrink from such work, or to do it in a half-hearted way. Or again the thought that this letter is to summon Timothy to come to him is in his mind (iv. 9, 21), and he forthwith exhorts him to make proper provision for continuity of sound teaching in the Church committed to his care. "The things which thou hast heard from me among many witnesses, the same commit thou to faithful men, who shall be able to teach others also." In other words, before leaving his flock in order to visit his spiritual father and friend, he is to secure the establishment of apostolic tradition. And in order to do this he is to establish a school,—a school of picked scholars, intelligent enough to appreciate, and trustworthy enough to preserve, all that has been handed down from Christ and His Apostles respecting the essentials of the Christian faith. There is only one Gospel,—that which the Apostles have preached ever since the Ascension. It is so well known, so well authenticated both by intrinsic sublimity and external testimony, that no one would be justified in accepting a different Gospel, even upon the authority of an angel from heaven. A second Gospel is an impossibility. That which is not identical with the Gospel which St. Paul and the other Apostles have preached would be no Gospel at all (Gal. i. 6–9). And this Divine and Apostolic Gospel is the Gospel which has been committed to Timothy's charge. Let him take all reasonable care for its preservation.

For in the first place, such care was commanded from the outset. Christ has promised that His truth shall continue and shall prevail. But He has not exempted Christians from the duty of preserving and propagating it. He, Who is the Truth, has declared that He is ever with His Church, even unto the end of the world (Matt. xxviii. 20); and in fulfilment of this promise He has bestowed the Spirit of truth upon it. But He has nowhere hinted that His Church is to leave the cause of His Gospel to take care of itself. On the contrary, at the very time that He promised to be alway with His disciples, He prefaced this promise with the command, "Go ye therefore, and make disciples of all the nations, ... teaching them to observe all things whatsoever I commanded you;" as if His promise were contingent upon their fulfilment of this charge. At the very moment when the Church received the truth, it was told that it had the responsibility of safeguarding it and making it known.

And, secondly, experience has proved how entirely necessary such care is. The Gospel cannot be superseded by any announcement possessing a larger measure of truth and authority. So far as the present dispensation goes, its claims are absolute and final. But it may be seriously misunderstood; it may be corrupted by large admixture of error; it may be partially or even totally forgotten; it may be supplanted by some meretricious counterfeit. There were Thessalonians who had supposed that the Gospel exempted them from the obligation of working to earn their bread. There were Christians at Corinth and Ephesus who had confounded the liberty of the Gospel with antinomian license. There was the Church of Sardis which had so completely forgotten what it had received, that no works of its doing were found fulfilled before God, and the remnant of truth and life which survived was ready to perish. And the Churches of Galatia had been in danger of casting on one side the glories of the Gospel and returning to the bondage of the Law. Through ignorance, through neglect, through wilful misrepresentation or interested opposition, the truth might be obscured, or depraved, or defeated; and there were few places where such disastrous results were more possible than at Ephesus. Its restless activity in commerce and speculation; its worldliness; the seductiveness of its forms of paganism;—all these constituted an atmosphere in which Christian truth, unless carefully protected, would be likely to become tainted or be ignored. Even without taking into account the proposal that Timothy should leave Ephesus for awhile and visit the Apostle in his imprisonment at Rome, it was no more than necessary precaution that he should endeavour to secure the establishment of a permanent centre for preserving and handing on in its integrity the faith once for all committed to the saints.

"The things which thou hast heard from me among many witnesses." The last three words are remarkable; and they are still more remarkable in the original Greek. St. Paul does not say simply *"in the presence of* many witnesses" (ἐνώπιον or παρόντων πολλῶν μαρτύρων) but *"by means of* many witnesses" (διὰ πολλῶν μαρτύρων). In the First Epistle (vi. 12) he had appealed to the good confession which Timothy had made "in the sight of many witnesses." As regards Timothy's confession these were witnesses and no more. They were able for ever afterwards to testify that he had made it; but they did not help him to make it. The confession was his, not theirs, although no doubt they assented to it and approved it; and their presence in no way affected its goodness. But here those who were present were something more than mere witnesses of what the Apostle said to Timothy; they were an integral part of the proceeding. Their presence was an element without which the Apostle's teaching would have assumed a different character. They were not a mere audience, able to testify as to what was said; they were guarantees of the instruction which was given. The sentiments and opinions which St Paul might express in private to his disciple, and the authoritative teaching which he delivered to him in public under the sanction of many witnesses, were two different things and stood on different grounds. Timothy had often heard from his friend his personal views on a variety of subjects; and he had often heard from the Apostle his official testimony, delivered solemnly in the congregation, as to the truths of the Gospel. It is this latter body of instruction, thus amply guaranteed, of which Timothy is to take such care. He is to treat it as a treasure committed to his charge, a precious legacy which he holds in trust. And in his turn he is to commit it to the keeping of trustworthy persons, who will know its value, and be capable of preserving it intact and of handing it on to others as trustworthy as themselves.

Some expositors interpret the passage as referring, not to the Apostle's public teaching as a whole, but to the instructions which he gave to Timothy at his ordination respecting the proper discharge of his office; and the aorist tense ἤκουσας favours the view that some definite occasion is intended (comp. 1 Tim. iv. 14; 2 Tim. i. 6). In that case the Apostle is here showing anxiety for the establishment of a sound tradition respecting the duties of ministers,—a very important portion, but by no means the main portion of the teaching which he had imparted. But the aorist does not compel us to confine the allusion to some one event, such as Timothy's ordination or baptism; and it seems more reasonable to understand the charge here given as a continuation of that which occurs towards the close of the first chapter. There he says, "Hold the pattern of sound words which thou hast heard" (ἤκουσας) "from me;" and here he charges Timothy not merely to hold this pattern of sound words fast himself, but to take care that it does not perish with him.

This, then, may be considered as the earliest trace of the formation of *a theological school,*—a school which has for its object not merely the instruction of the ignorant, but the protection and maintenance of a definite body of doctrine: That which the Apostle, when he was in Ephesus, publicly taught, under the sanction of a multitude of witnesses, is to be preserved and handed on without compromise or corruption as a pattern of wholesome doctrine. There are unhealthy and even deadly distortions of the truth in the air, and unless care is taken to preserve the truth, it may easily become possible to confuse weak and ignorant minds as to what are the essentials of the Christian faith.

The question as to the earliest methods of Christian instruction and the precautions taken for the preservation of Apostolic tradition is one of the many particulars in which our knowledge of the primitive Church is so tantalizingly meagre. A small amount of information is given us in the New Testament, for the most part quite incidentally, as here; and then the history runs underground, and does not reappear for a century or more. The first few generations of Christians did not contain a large number of persons who were capable of producing anything very considerable in the way of literature. Of those who had the ability, not many had the leisure or the inclination to write. It was more important to teach by word of mouth than with the pen; and where was the use of leaving records of what was being done, when (as was generally believed) Christ would almost immediately appear to put an end to the existing dispensation? Out of what was written much, as we know, has perished, including even documents of Apostolic origin (Luke i. 1, 2; 1 Cor. v. 9; 3 John 9). Therefore, much as we lament the scantiness of the evidence that has come down to us, there is nothing surprising about it. The marvel is, not that so little contemporary history has reached us, but that so much has done so. And what it behoves us to do is to make a sober use of such testimony as we possess.

We shall be doing no more than drawing a reasonable conclusion from the passage before us if we infer, that what St. Paul enjoins Timothy to do at Ephesus was done in many other Churches also, partly in consequence of this Apostolic injunction, and partly because what he enjoins would be suggested in many cases by necessity and common sense. This inference is confirmed by the fact that it is precisely to the continuity of doctrine secured by a regular succession of authorized and official teachers in the different Churches that appeal is continually made by some of the earliest Christian writers whose works have come down to us. Thus Hegesippus (c. a.d. 170) gives as the result of careful personal investigations at Corinth, Rome, and elsewhere, "But in every succession (of bishops) and in every city there prevails just what the Law and the Prophets and the Lord proclaim" (Eus., h.e., iv. xxii. 3). Irenæus, in his great work against heresies, which was completed about a.d. 185, says, "We can enumerate those who were appointed bishops by the Apostles themselves in the different Churches, and their successors down to our own day; and they neither taught nor acknowledged any such stuff as is raved by these men.... But since it would be a long business in a work of this kind to enumerate the successions in all the Churches," he selects as a primary example that of "the very great and ancient Church, well known to all men, founded and established by the two most glorious Apostles Peter and Paul." After giving the succession of Roman bishops from Linus to Eleutherus, he glances at Smyrna, presided over by St. John's disciple, Polycarp, whose letter to the Philippian Church shows what he believed, and at Ephesus, founded as a Church by St. Paul and presided over by St. John, until the times of Trajan (iii. iii. 1–3). Again he says, that, although there may be different opinions respecting single passages of Scripture, yet there can be none as to the sum total of its contents, viz. "that which the Apostles have deposited in the Church as the fulness of truth, and which has been preserved in the Church by the succession of bishops." And again, still more definitely, "The Church, though dispersed throughout the whole world even to the ends of the earth, has received from the Apostles and their disciples the belief in one God, Father Almighty, etc.... Having received this preaching and this belief, the Church, as we said before, although dispersed about the whole world, carefully guards it, as if dwelling in one house; and she believes these things, as if she had but one soul and one and the same heart, and with perfect concord she preaches them and teaches them and hands them down, as if she possessed but one mouth. For although the languages up and down the world are different, yet the import of the tradition is one and the same. For neither the Churches which are established in Germany believe anything different or hand down anything different, nor in Spain, nor in Gaul, nor throughout the East, nor in Egypt, nor in Libya, nor those established about the central regions of the earth.... And neither will he who is very mighty in word among those who preside in the Churches utter different [doctrines] from these (for no one is above the Master), nor will he who is weak in speaking lessen the tradition" (I. x. 1, 2). Clement of Alexandria (c. a.d. 200) tells us that he had studied in Greece, Italy, and the East, under teachers from Ionia, Cœlesyria, Assyria, and Palestine; and he writes of his teachers thus: "These men, preserving the true tradition of the blessed teaching directly from Peter and James, from John and Paul, the holy Apostles, son receiving it from father (but few are they who are like their fathers), came by God's providence even to us, to deposit among us those seeds which are ancestral and apostolic" (*Strom.*, I. p. 322, ed. Potter). Tertullian in like manner appeals to the unbroken tradition, reaching back to the Apostles, in a variety of Churches: "Run over the Apostolic Churches, in which the very chairs of the Apostles still preside in their places, in which their own authentic writings are read, uttering the voice and representing the face of each of them;" and he mentions in particular Corinth, Philippi, Thessalonica, Ephesus, and Rome. "Is it likely that Churches of such number and weight should have *strayed* into one and the same faith?" (*De Præs. Hær.*, xxviii., xxxvi.).

This evidence is quite sufficient to prove that what St. Paul charged Timothy to do at Ephesus was done not only there but at all the chief centres of the Christian Church: viz., that everywhere great care was taken to provide continuity of authoritative teaching respecting the articles of the faith. It indicates also that as a rule the bishop in each place was regarded as the custodian of the deposit, who was to be chiefly responsible for its preservation. But the precise method or methods (for there was probably different machinery in different places) by which this was accomplished, cannot now be ascertained. It is not until near the end of the second century that we begin to get anything like precise information as to the way in which Christian instruction was given, whether to believers or heathen, in one or two of the principal centres of Christendom; *e.g.*, Alexandria, Cæsarea, and Jerusalem.

St Paul himself had ruled that a bishop must be "apt to teach" (1 Tim. iii. 2; comp. Tit. i. 9); and although we have no reason to suppose that as a rule the bishop was the only or even the chief instructor, yet he probably selected the teachers, as Timothy is directed to do here. In the great Catechetical

School of Alexandria the appointment of what we should now call the Rector or senior professor was in the hands of the bishop. And, as we might expect, bishops selected clergy for this most important office. It forms one of the many contrasts between primitive Christianity and heathenism, that Christians did, and pagans did not, regard it as one of the functions of the priesthood to give instruction in the traditional faith. The heathen clergy, if consulted, would give information respecting the due performance of rites and ceremonies, and the import of omens and dreams; but of their giving systematic teaching as to what was to be believed respecting the gods, there is no trace.

It is more than probable that a great deal of the instruction both to candidates for baptism and candidates for the ministry was from very early times reduced to something like a formula; even before the dangers of corruption arising from Gnosticism rendered this necessary, we may believe that it took place. We know that the Gospel history was in the first instance taught orally; and the oral instruction very soon fell into something that approached to a stereotyped form. This would probably be the case with regard to statements of the essentials of the Christian faith. In Ignatius (*Philad.*, viii.), Justin Martyr (*Apol.*, I. 61, 66), and in Irenæus (*Hær.*, I. x. 1) we can trace what may well have been formulas in common use. But it is not until the middle of the fourth century that we get a complete example of the systematic instruction given by a Christian teacher, in the Catechetical Lectures of St. Cyril, Bishop of Jerusalem, delivered, however, before his episcopate.

But what is *certain* respecting the earliest ages of the Church is this; that in every Church regular instruction in the faith was given by persons in authority specially selected for this work, and that frequent intercourse between the Churches showed that the substance of the instruction given was in all cases the same, whether the form of words was identical or not. These facts, which do not by any means stand alone, are conclusive against the hypothesis, that between the Crucifixion and the middle of the second century, a complete revolution in the creed was effected; and that the traditional belief of Christians is not that which Jesus of Nazareth taught, but a perversion of it which owes its origin mainly to the overwhelming influence of His professed follower, but virtual supplanter, Saul of Tarsus.

CHAPTER XXX
THE CHRISTIAN'S LIFE AS MILITARY SERVICE; AS AN ATHLETIC CONTEST; AS HUSBANDRY

"Suffer hardships with me, as a good soldier of Christ Jesus. No soldier on service entangleth himself in the affairs of this life; that he may please him who enrolled him as a soldier. And if also a man contend in the games, he is not crowned, except he have contended lawfully. The husbandman that laboureth must be the first to partake of the fruits. Consider what I say; for the Lord shall give thee understanding in all things."—2 Tim. ii. 3–7.

St. Paul represents the Christian life and the Christian ministry under a variety of figures. Sometimes as *husbandry*; as when he tells the Galatians that "whatsoever a man soweth, that shall he also reap;" and that "in due season we shall reap, if we faint not" (Gal. vi. 7, 9); or when he reminds the Corinthians that "he that ploweth ought to plow in hope, and he that thresheth, to thresh in hope of partaking" (1 Cor. ix. 10). Sometimes as an *athletic contest*; as when he tells the Corinthians that "every man who striveth in the games is temperate in all things" (1 Cor ix. 25); or the Ephesians that "our wrestling is not against flesh and blood, but against the principalities, against the powers, against the world-rulers of this darkness, against the spiritual hosts of wickedness in the heavenly places" (Eph. vi. 12). Sometimes, and most frequently, as *military service*; as when he charges the Thessalonians to "put on the breastplate of faith and love, and for a helmet the hope of salvation" (1 Thess. v. 8); or when he writes to the Philippians of Epaphroditus as his "fellow-soldier" (Phil. ii. 25).

In the passage before us he makes use of all three figures: but the one of which he seems to have been most fond is the one which he places first,—that of military service. "Suffer hardships with me," or "take thy share in suffering," as a good soldier of Christ Jesus. No soldier on service entangleth himself in the affairs of this life; that he may please him who enrolled him as a soldier." He had used the same kind of language in the First Epistle, urging Timothy to "war the good warfare" and to "fight the good fight of faith" (i. 18; vi. 12). Every Christian, and especially every Christian minister, may be regarded as a soldier, as an athlete, as a husbandman; but of the three similitudes the one which fits him best is that of a soldier.

Even if this were not so, St. Paul's fondness for the metaphor would be very intelligible.

1. Military service was very familiar to him, especially in his imprisonments. He had been arrested by soldiers at Jerusalem, escorted by troops to Cæsarea, sent under the charge of a centurion and a band of soldiers to Rome, and had been kept there under military surveillance for many months in the first Roman imprisonment, and for we know not how long in the second. And we may assume it as almost certain that the place of his imprisonment was near the prætorian camp. This would probably be so ordered for the convenience of the soldiers who had charge of him. He therefore had very large opportunities of observing very closely all the details of ordinary military life. He must frequently have seen soldiers under drill, on parade, on guard, on the march; must have watched them cleaning, mending, and sharpening their weapons; putting their armour on, putting it off. Often during hours of enforced inactivity he must have compared these details with the details of the Christian life, and noticed how admirably they corresponded with one another.

2. Military service was not only very familiar to himself; it was also quite sufficiently familiar to those whom he addressed. Roman troops were everywhere to be seen throughout the length and breadth of the Empire, and nearly every member of society knew something of the kind of life which a soldier of the Empire had to lead.

3. The Roman army was the one great organization of which it was still possible, in that age of boundless social corruption, to think and speak with right-minded admiration and respect. No doubt it was often the instrument of wholesale cruelties as it pushed forward its conquests, or strengthened its hold, over resisting or rebelling nations. But it promoted discipline and *esprit de corps*. Even during active warfare it checked individual license; and when the conquest was over it was the representative and mainstay of order and justice against high-handed anarchy and wrong. Its officers several times appear in the narrative portions of the New Testament, and they make a favourable impression upon us. If they are fair specimens of the military men in the Roman Empire at that period, then the Roman army must have been indeed a fine service. There is the centurion whose faith excited even Christ's admiration; the centurion who confessed Christ's righteousness and Divine origin at the crucifixion; Cornelius, of the Italian cohort, to whom St. Peter was sent; C. Lysias, the chief captain or tribune who rescued St. Paul, first from the mob, and then from the conspiracy to

assassinate him; and Julius, who out of consideration for St. Paul prevented the soldiers from killing the prisoners in the shipwreck.

But the reasons for the Apostle's preference for this similitude go deeper than all this.

4. Military service involves self-sacrifice, endurance, discipline, vigilance, obedience, ready co-operation with others, sympathy, enthusiasm, loyalty. Tertullian in his *Address to Martyrs* draws with characteristic incisiveness the stern parallel between the severity of the soldier's life and that of the Christian. "Be it so, that even to Christians a prison is distasteful. We were called to active service under the Living God from the very moment of our response to the baptismal formula. No soldier comes to the war surrounded by luxuries, nor goes into action from a comfortable bed-room, but from the make-shift and narrow tent, where every kind of hardness and severity and unpleasantness is to be found. Even in peace soldiers learn betimes to suffer warfare by toil and discomforts, by marching in arms, running over the drill-ground, working at trench-making, constructing the tortoise, till the sweat runs again. In the sweat of the brow all things are done, lest body and mind should shrink at changes from shade to sunshine, and from sunshine to frost, from the dress of ease to the coat of mail, from stillness to shouting, from quiet to the din of war. In like manner do ye, O blessed ones, account whatever is hard in this your lot as discipline of the powers of your mind and body. Ye are about to enter for the good fight, in which the Living God gives the prizes, and the Holy Spirit prepares the combatants, and the crown is the eternal prize of an angel's nature, citizenship in heaven, glory for ever and ever. Therefore your trainer, Jesus Christ, Who has anointed you with the Spirit and led you forth to this arena, has seen good to separate you from a state of freedom for rougher treatment, that power may be made strong in you. For the athletes also are set apart for stricter discipline, that they may have time to build up their strength. They are kept from luxury, from daintier meats, from too pleasant drink; they are driven, tormented, distressed. The harder their labours in training, the greater their hopes of victory. And they do it, says the Apostle, that they may obtain a corruptible crown. We, with an eternal crown to obtain, look upon the prison as our training-ground, that we may be led to the arena of the judgment-seat well disciplined by every kind of discomfort: because virtue is built up by hardness, but by softness is overthrown" (*Ad Mart.*, iii). It will be observed that Tertullian passes by an easy transition from training for military service to training for athletic contests. The whole passage is little more than a graphic amplification of what St. Paul writes to Timothy.

5. But military service implies, what athletic contests do not, vigilant, unwearying, and organized opposition to a vigilant, unwearying, and

organized foe. In many athletic contests one's opponent is a rival rather than an enemy. He may defeat us; but he inflicts no injury. He may win the prizes; but he takes nothing of ours. And even in the more deadly conflicts of the amphitheatre the enemy is very different from an enemy in war. The combat is between individuals, not armies; it is the exception and not the rule; it is strictly limited in time and place, not for all times and all places; it is a duel and not a campaign,—still less a prolonged war. Military service is either perpetual warfare or perpetual preparation for it. And just such is the Christian life: it is either a conflict, or a preparation for one. The soldier, so long as he remains in the service, can never say, "I may lay aside my arms and my drill: all enemies are conquered: there will never be another war." And the Christian, so long as he remains in this world, can never think that he may cease to watch and to pray, because the victory is won, and he will never be tempted any more. It is for this reason that he cannot allow himself to be "entangled in the affairs of this life." The soldier on service avoids this error: he knows that it would interfere with his promotion. The Christian must avoid it at least as carefully; for he is always on service, and the loss of promotion is the loss of eternal life.

Observe that St. Paul does not suggest that Christians should keep aloof from the affairs of this life, which would be a flat contradiction of what he teaches elsewhere. The Christian is to "do his own business, and to work with his hands, that he may walk honestly toward them that are without, and may have need of nothing" (1 Thess. iv. 11, 12). He has a duty to perform "in the affairs of this life," but in doing it he is not to be *entangled* in them. They are means, not ends; and must be made to help him on, not suffered to keep him back. If they become entanglements instead of opportunities, he will soon lose that state of constant preparation and alertness, which is the indispensable condition of success.

The same thought is brought out in the second metaphor by the word "lawfully." The athlete who competes in the games does not receive a crown, unless he has contended *lawfully, i.e.*, according to rule (νομίμως, νόμος). Even if he seems to be victorious, he nevertheless is not crowned, because he has violated the well-known conditions. And what is the rule, what are the conditions of the Christian's contest? "If any man would come after Me, let him deny himself, and take up his cross, and follow Me." If we wish to share Christ's victory, we must be ready to share His suffering. No cross, no crown. To try to withdraw oneself from all hardship and annoyance, to attempt to avoid all that is painful or disagreeable, is a violation of the rules of the arena. This, it would appear, Timothy was in some respects tempted to do: and timidity and despondency must not be allowed to get the upper hand. Not that what is painful, or distasteful, or unpopular, is necessarily right; but it is certainly not necessarily wrong: and to try to avoid everything that one dislikes is to ensure being fatally wrong. So that, as Chrysostom says, "it behoves thee not to complain, if thou endurest hardness; but to complain, if thou dost not endure hardness."

Chrysostom and some modern commentators make the striving lawfully include not only the observance of the rules of the contest, but the previous training and preparation. "What is meant by *lawfully*? It is not enough that he is anointed, and even engages, unless he complies with all the regulations of training with respect to diet, temperance, and sobriety, and all the rules of the wrestling-school. Unless, in short, he go through all that is befitting a wrestler, he is not crowned." This makes good sense, if "is not crowned" be interpreted to mean "is not likely to be first," rather than "does not receive the crown, even if he is first." A victorious athlete is rightly deprived of the reward, if he has violated the conditions of the contest: but no one ever yet heard of a victor being refused the prize because he had not trained properly. Moreover, there are enough examples to show that "lawfully" (νομίμως) does sometimes include the training as well as the contest.

But this does not seem to be St Paul's meaning. In the first similitude he takes no account of the time which precedes the soldier's service, during which he may be supposed to be preparing himself for it. The Christian's life and the soldier's service are regarded as co-extensive, and there is no thought of any previous period. So also in the second similitude. The Christian's life and the athlete's contest are regarded as co-extensive, and no account is taken of anything that may have preceded. Baptism is entering the lists, not entering the training-school; and the only rules under consideration are the rules of the arena.

No doubt there are analogies between the training-school and Christian discipline, and St. Paul sometimes makes use of them (1 Cor. ix. 25, 27); but they do not seem to be included in the present metaphor.

But it is about the third similitude that there has been most discussion. "The husbandman that laboureth must be the first to partake of the fruits:" not, as the a. v., "must be first partaker of the fruits;" which seems to imply that he must partake of the fruits before he labours. What is the meaning of "first"? Some commentators resort to the rather desperate hypothesis that this word is misplaced, as it sometimes is in careless writing and conversation: and they suppose that what St. Paul means is, that "the husbandman, who labours first, must then partake of the fruits," or, more clearly, "the husbandman, who wishes to partake of the fruits, must first of all labour." The margin of the A. V. suggests a similar translation. But this is to credit the Apostle with great clumsiness of expression. And even if this transposition of the "first" could be accepted as probable, there still remains the fact that we have the present and not the aorist participle (κοπιῶντα and not κοπιάσαντα). Had St. Paul meant what is supposed, he would have said "The husbandman who *has* first *laboured*," not "who *labours* first." But there is no transposition of the "first." The order of the Greek shows that the emphatic word is "labours." "It is the *labouring* husbandman who must be the first to partake of the fruits." It is the man who works hard and with a will, and not the one who works listlessly or looks despondently on, who, according to all moral fitness and the nature of things, ought to have the first share in the fruits. This interpretation does justice to the Greek as it stands, without resorting to any manipulation of the Apostle's language. Moreover, it brings the saying into perfect harmony with the context.

It is quite evident that the three metaphors are parallel to one another and are intended to teach the same lesson. In each of them we have two things placed side by side,—a prize and the method to be observed in obtaining it. Do you, as a Christian soldier on service, wish for the approbation of Him who has enrolled you? Then you must avoid the entanglements which would interfere with your service. Do you, as a Christian athlete, wish for the crown of victory? Then you must not evade the rules of the contest. Do you, as a Christian husbandman, wish to be among the first to enjoy the harvest? Then you must be foremost in toil. And the Apostle draws attention to the importance of the lesson of self-devotion and endurance, inculcated under these three impressive figures, by adding, "Consider what I say; for the Lord shall give thee understanding in all things." That is, He has confidence that His disciple will be enabled to draw the right conclusion from these metaphors; and having done so, will have grace to apply it to his own case.

Timothy is not the only Christian, or the only minister, who is in danger of being disgusted, and disheartened, and dismayed, by the coldness and apathy of professing friends, and by the hostility and contempt of secret or open enemies. We all of us need at times to be reminded that here we have no abiding city, but that our citizenship is in heaven. And we all of us are at times inclined to murmur, because the rest for which we so often yearn, is not given us here;—a rest from toil, a rest from temptation, and a rest from sin. Such a sabbath-rest is the prize in store for us; but we cannot have it here. And if we desire to have it hereafter, we must keep the rules of the arena; and the rules are *self-control, self-sacrifice, and work.*

CHAPTER XXXI
THE POWER OF A BELIEF IN THE RESURRECTION AND THE INCARNATION.— THE GOSPEL OF ST. PAUL

"Remember Jesus Christ, risen from the dead, of the seed of David, according to my gospel: wherein I suffer hardship unto bonds, as a malefactor; but the word of God is not bound. Therefore I endure all things for the elects' sake, that they also may obtain the salvation which is in Christ Jesus with eternal glory."—2 Tim. ii. 8–10.

These words are a continuation of the same subject. They are additional thoughts supplied to the Apostle's beloved disciple to induce him to take courage and to bear willingly and thankfully whatever difficulties and sufferings the preaching of the gospel in all its fulness may involve. In the three metaphors just preceding, St. Paul has indicated that there is nothing amazing, nothing that ought to cause perplexity or despondency, in the fact that ministers of the word have to encounter much opposition and danger. On the contrary, such things are the very conditions of the situation; they are the very rules of the course. One would have to suspect that there was something seriously amiss, if they did not occur; and without them there would be no chance of reward. Here he goes on to point out that this hardship and suffering is very far from being mere hardship and suffering; it has its bright side and its compensations, even in this life.

Throughout this section it is well worth while to notice the very considerable improvements which the Revisers have made in it. One or two of these have been already noticed; but for convenience some of the principal instances are here collected together.

"Suffer hardship with me," or "Take thy part in suffering hardship," is better than "Thou therefore endure hardship," which while inserting a spurious "therefore," omits the important intimation that the hardship to which Timothy is invited is one which others are enduring, and which he is called upon, not to bear alone, but to share. "No soldier on service" is better than "No man that warreth," and "if also a man contend in the games" is more definite than the vague "if a man also strive for masteries."

The ambiguity of "must be first partaker of the fruits" is avoided in "must be the first to partake of the fruits." But perhaps none of these corrections are so important as those in the passage now before us. "Remember that Jesus Christ of the seed of David, was raised from the dead, according to my gospel," gives quite a wrong turn to St. Paul's language. It puts the clauses in the wrong order, and gives an erroneous impression as to what is to be remembered. Timothy is charged to "remember Jesus Christ;" and in remembering Him he is to think of Him as one Who is "risen from the dead," and Who is also "of the seed of David." These are central facts of the Gospel which St. Paul has always preached; they have been his support in all his sufferings; and they will be the same support to the disciple as they have been to the master.

"Remember Jesus Christ." Every Christian, who has to endure what seem to him to be hardships, will sooner or later fall back upon this remembrance. He is not the first, and not the chief sufferer in the world. There is One Who has undergone hardships, compared with which those of other men sink into nothingness; and Who has expressly told those Who wish to be His disciples, that they must follow Him along the path of suffering. It is specially in this respect that the servant is not above his Lord. And just in proportion as we are true servants will the remembrance of Jesus Christ help us to welcome what He lays upon us as proof that He recognizes and accepts our service.

But merely to remember Jesus Christ as a Master Who has suffered, and Who has made suffering a condition of service, will not be a permanently sustaining or comforting thought, if it ends there. Therefore St. Paul says to his perplexed and desponding delegate, "Remember Jesus Christ as one *risen from the dead.*" Jesus Christ has not only endured every kind of suffering, including its extreme form, death, but He has conquered it all by rising again. He is not only the sinless Sufferer, but also the triumphant Victor over death and hell. He has set us an example of heroic endurance in obedience to the will of God; but He has also secured for us that our endurance in imitation of Him shall be crowned with victory. Had Christ's mission ended on Calvary, He would but have given to the world a purified form of Stoicism, a refined "philosophy of suffering;" and His teaching would have failed, as Stoicism failed, because a mere philosophy of suffering is quickly proved by experience to be a "philosophy of despair." Renan remarks with truth, that the gospel of Marcus Aurelius fortifies, but does not console: and all teaching is doomed from the outset, which comes to a groaning and travailing humanity without any consolations to bestow. What is the thought which through long centuries has wrung, and is still wringing millions of human hearts with anguish? It is the thought of the existence and not only the existence but the apparent *predominance*, of evil. Everywhere experience seems to teach us that evil of every kind, physical, intellectual, and moral, holds the field and appears likely to hold it. To allow oneself to be mastered by this thought is to be on the road to doubting God's moral government of the world. What is the antidote to it? "Remember Jesus Christ as one risen from the dead." When has evil ever been so completely triumphant over good as when it succeeded in getting the Prophet of Nazareth nailed to the tree, like some vile and noxious animal? That was the hour of success for the malignant Jewish hierarchy and for the spiritual powers of darkness. But it was an hour to which very strict limits were placed. Very soon He Who had been dismissed to the grave by a cruel and shameful death, defeated and disgraced, rose again from it triumphant, not only over Jewish priests and Roman soldiers, but over death and the cause of death; that is, over every kind of evil—pain, and ignorance, and sin. It was for that very purpose that He laid down His life, that He might take it again: and it was for that reason that His Father loved Him, because He had received the commandment to lay it down and take it again from His Father (John x. 17, 18).

But "to remember Jesus Christ as one risen from the dead" does more than this. It not only shows us that the evil against which we have such a weary struggle in this life, both in others and in ourselves, is not (in spite of depressing appearances) permanently triumphant; it also assures us that there is another and a better life in which the good cause will be supreme, and supreme without the possibility of disaster, of even of contest. We talk in a conventional way of death as the country "from whose bourne no traveller returns:" but we are wrong. We do not mean it so; yet this saying, if pressed, would carry with it a denial of a fact, which is better attested than any fact in ancient history. One Traveller *has* returned; and His return is no extraordinary accident or exceptional and solitary success. It is a representative return and a typical success. What the Son of Man has done, other sons of men can do, and will do. The solidarity between the human race and the Second Adam, between the Church and its Head, is such, that the victory of the Leader carries with it the victory of the whole band. The breach made in the gates of death is one through which the whole army of Christ's followers may pass out into eternal life, free from death's power for evermore. This thought is full of comfort and encouragement to those who feel themselves almost overwhelmed by the perplexities, and contradictions, and sorrows of this life. However grievous this life may be, it has this merciful condition attached to it, that it lasts only for a short time; and then the risen Christ leads us into a life which is free from all trouble, and which knows no end. The miseries of this life are lessened by the knowledge that they cannot last long. The blessedness of the life to come is perfected by the fact that it is eternal.

Once more, to "remember Jesus Christ as one risen from the dead," is to remember One Who claimed to be the promised Saviour of the world, and Who *proved His claim*. By its countless needs, by many centuries of yearning, by its consciousness of failure and of guilt, the whole human race had been led to look forward to the coming of some great Deliverer, Who would rescue mankind from its hopeless descent down the path of sin and retribution, as a *possibility*. By the express promise of Almighty God, made to the first generation of mankind, and renewed again and again to patriarchs and prophets, the chosen people had been taught to look forward to the coming of a Saviour as a *certainty*. And Jesus of Nazareth had claimed to be this longed for and expected Deliverer, the Desire of all nations and the Saviour of the world. "I that speak unto thee am He" (John iv. 26). By His mighty works, and still more by His life-giving words, He had shown that He had Divine credentials in support of His claim: but not until He rose again from the dead was His claim absolutely proved. It was the proof which He Himself volunteered. "Destroy this temple and in three days I will raise it up" (John ii. 19). "There shall no sign be given but the sign of Jonah the prophet: for as Jonah was three days and three nights in the belly of the whale, so shall the Son of man be three days and three nights in the heart of the earth" (Matt. xii. 39, 40), and then return again to the light of day as Jonah did. He had raised others from the dead; but so had Elijah and Elisha done. That proved no more than that He was a prophet as mighty as they. But no one before Jesus had ever raised Himself. If His Messiahship was doubtful before, all doubt vanished on Easter morning.

And this leads St. Paul on to the second point which his downcast disciple is to remember in connexion with Jesus Christ. He is to remember Him as "of the seed of David." He is not only truly God, but truly man. He was risen from the dead, and yet He was born of flesh and blood, and born of that royal line of which Timothy, who "from a babe had known the sacred writings," had many times heard and read. The Resurrection and the Incarnation;—those are the two facts on which a faltering minister of the Gospel is to hold fast, in order to comfort his heart and strengthen his steps.

It is worth noting that St. Paul places the Resurrection before the Incarnation, a fact which is quite lost in the transposed order of the A. V. St. Paul's order, which at first sight seems to be illogical, was the usual order of the Apostles' preaching. They began, not with the miraculous birth of Christ, but with His resurrection. They proved by abundant testimony that Jesus had risen from the dead, and thence argued that He must have been more than man. They did not preach His birth of a virgin, and thence argue that He was Divine. How was His miraculous birth to be proved, to those who were unwilling to accept His mother's word for it? But thousands of people had seen Him dead upon the Cross, and hundreds had seen Him alive again afterwards. No matter of fact was more securely established for all those who cared to investigate the evidence. With the Resurrection proved, the foundations of the faith were laid. The Incarnation followed easily after this, especially when combined with the descent from David, a fact which helped to prove His Messiahship. Let Timothy boldly and patiently preach these great truths in all their grand simplicity, and they will bring comfort and strength to him in his distress and difficulty, as they have done to the Apostle.

This is the meaning of "according to my gospel." These are the truths which St. Paul has habitually preached, and of the value of which he can speak from full experience. He knows what he is talking about, when he affirms, that these things are worth remembering when one is in trouble. The Resurrection and the Incarnation are facts on which he has ceaselessly insisted, because in the wear and tear of life he has found out their worth.

There is no emphasis on the "my," as the Greek shows. An enclitic cannot be emphatic. The Apostle is not contrasting his Gospel with that of other preachers, as if he would say, "Others may teach what they please, but this is the substance of *my* Gospel." And Jerome is certainly mistaken, if what is quoted as a remark of his is rightly assigned to him by Fabricius, to the effect that whenever St. Paul says "according to my Gospel" he means the written Gospel of his companion St. Luke, who had caught much of his spirit and something of his language. It would be much nearer the truth to say that St. Paul never refers to a written Gospel. In every one of the passages in which the phrase occurs the context is quite against any such interpretation (Rom. ii. 16; xvi. 25; cf Tim. 1. i. 11). In this place the words which follow are conclusive: "Wherein I suffer hardship unto bonds, as a malefactor." How could he be said to suffer hardship unto bonds in the Gospel of St. Luke?

A word of protest may be added against the strange and impossible theory that the third Gospel and the Acts of the Apostles were written by St. Paul himself. If there is one thing which is certain with regard to the authorship of the Books of the New Testament, it is that the Acts was written by a companion of St. Paul. Even destructive critics who spare little else, admit this of portions of the Acts; and the Book must be accepted or rejected as a whole. Moreover, it is admitted by both defenders and assailants that the writer of the Acts did not know the Epistle to the Galatians; and it is highly probable that when he wrote he had not seen the Epistles to the Romans and to the Corinthians.[92] How then can he have been St. Paul? And why should the Apostle write sometimes in the third person of what *Paul* said and did, and sometimes in the first person of what *we* did? All this is quite natural, if the writer is a companion of the Apostle, who was sometimes with him and sometimes not; it is most extraordinary if the Apostle himself is the writer. And of course if the Acts is not by St. Paul, the third Gospel cannot be; for it is impossible to assign them to different writers. Moreover, not to mention other difficulties, it may be doubted whether, more than two years (Acts xxviii. 30) before the death of St. Paul, there would have been time for "*many*" to "have taken in hand to draw up a narrative concerning those matters which have been fulfilled among us" (Luke i. 1), and then for him to have collected material for the third Gospel and to have written it, and then, after an interval, for him to have written the Acts. All the arguments in favour of the Pauline authorship of the third Gospel and of the Acts are satisfied by the almost universally accepted view, that these two works were written by a companion of the Apostle, who was thoroughly familiar with his modes of thought and expression.

The preaching of this Gospel of the Resurrection and the Incarnation had caused the Apostle (as he here tells us) to suffer much evil, as if he had done much evil, even to the extent of a grievous imprisonment. He is bound as a malefactor; but his Gospel "is not bound," because it is "the word of God." He perhaps changes the expression from "my Gospel" to "the word of God" in order to indicate why it is that, although the preacher is in prison, yet his Gospel is free;—because the word which he preaches is not his own, but God's.

"The word of God is not bound." The Apostle is imprisoned; but his tongue and his companion's pen are free. He can still teach those who come to him; can still dictate letters for others to Luke and the faithful few who visit him. He can still, as in his first Roman imprisonment, see that what has befallen him may "have fallen out rather unto the progress of the gospel; so that his bonds became manifest in Christ throughout the whole praetorian guard, and to all the rest" (Phil. i. 12, 13). He has been able to influence those whom, but for his imprisonment, he would never have had an opportunity of reaching,—Roman soldiers, and warders, and officials, and all who have to take cognisance of his trial before the imperial tribunal.

"The word of God is not bound." While he is in prison, Timothy, and Titus, and scores of other evangelists and preachers, are free. Their action is not hampered because a colleague is shut up. The loss of him might have a depressing and discouraging effect on some; but this ought not to be so, and he hopes will not be so. Those who are left at large ought to labour all the more energetically and enthusiastically, in order to supply whatever is lost by the Apostle's want of freedom, and in order to convince the world that this is no contest with a human organization or with human opinion, but with a Divine word and a Divine Person.

"The word of God is not bound," because His word is the truth, and it is the truth that makes men free. How can that of which the very essence is freedom, and of which the attribute is that it confers freedom, be itself kept in bondage? Truth is freer than air and more incompressible than water. And just as men must have air and must have water, and you cannot keep them long from either; so you cannot long keep them from the truth or the truth from them. You may dilute it, or obscure it, or retard it, but you cannot bury it or shut it up. Laws which are of Divine origin will surely and irresistibly assert themselves, and truth and the mind of man will meet.

FOOTNOTES:

[92] It is not credible that a writer who was very familiar with the incidents and persons mentioned and alluded to in Gal. i. 17; ii. 1–5, 11–14; Rom. xv. 19, 28; xvi. 1–3, 23; 1 Cor. i. 11–16; v. 1; xi. 30; xvi. 15; 2 Cor. ii. 12; vii. 5; xi. 24; xii. 3, 7, 18, should make no mention of them or reference to them. The silence respecting Titus would be most extraordinary if the Apostle himself were the author of the Acts. See Bishop Lightfoot's article on the Acts in the new edition of the *Dict. of the Bible*.

CHAPTER XXXII
THE NEED OF A SOLEMN CHARGE AGAINST A CONTROVERSIAL SPIRIT, OF DILIGENCE FREE FROM SHAME, AND OF A HATRED OF THE PROFANITY WHICH WRAPS UP ERROR IN THE LANGUAGE OF TRUTH

"Of these things put them in remembrance, charging them in the sight of the Lord, that they strive not about words, to no profit, to the subverting of them that hear. Give diligence to present thyself approved unto God, a workman that needeth not to be ashamed, handling aright the word of truth. But shun profane babblings: for they will proceed further in ungodliness, and their word will eat as doth a gangrene; of whom is Hymenæus and Philetus; men who concerning the truth have erred, saying that the resurrection is passed already, and overthrow the faith of some." —2 Tim. ii. 14–18.

We here enter upon a new section of the Epistle, which continues down to the end of the chapter. It consists in the main of directions as to Timothy's own behaviour in the responsible post in which he has been placed. And these are both positive and negative; he is told what to aim at, and what to avoid.

As to the meaning of "these things," of which he is to put his flock in remembrance, it seems most natural to refer the expression to the "faithful saying" with which the previous section closes. He is to remind others (and thereby strengthen his own courage and faith), that to die for Christ is to live with Him, and to suffer for Christ is to reign with Him, while to deny Him is to involve His denying us; for, however faithless we may be, He must abide by what He has promised both of rewards and punishments. The fact that the Apostle uses the expression "put them in remembrance," implying that they already know it, is some confirmation of the view that the "faithful saying" is a formula that was often recited in the congregation; a view which the rhythmical character of the passage renders somewhat probable.

Having reminded them of what they already know well, Timothy is to "charge them in the sight of the Lord, that they strive not about words." This phrase "charge them in the sight of the Lord" is worthy of notice. The Apostle twice uses it in addressing Timothy himself. "I charge thee in the sight of God, and Christ Jesus, and the elect angels, that thou observe these things without prejudice" (1 Tim. v. 21); and "I charge thee in the sight of God, and of Christ Jesus, Who shall judge the quick and dead, and by His appearing and His kingdom; preach the word" (2 Tim. iv. 1). The word for "charge" (διαμαρτύθεσθαι) indicates the interposition (διά) of two parties, and hence comes to mean to "call heaven and earth to witness;" in other words, to "testify solemnly" or "adjure;" and from this latter meaning it easily becomes employed for a solemn charge or exhortation. In translating, it would be quite legitimate to insert an adverb to express this: "*solemnly* charging them in the sight of God." In dealing with these pestilent disputes and perilous opinions Timothy, both for his own sake and for that of his hearers, is to remember, and to remind them, in Whose presence he is speaking. God's eye is upon both preacher and congregation; and in pleading the cause of truth and sobriety the preacher is in fact pleading before the Divine tribunal. This will make the teacher wary in his words, and will lead his hearers to listen to them in a spirit of sobriety.

It has been debated whether St. Paul has in his mind those "faithful men" to whom Timothy is to commit the substance of the Apostle's teaching (ver. 2), or whether he is not now taking a wider view and including the whole of the disciple's flock. It is impossible to determine this with certainty; and it is not a question of much moment. One thing is clear; viz., that the whole section is applicable to ministers throughout the Church in all ages; and the words under consideration seem to be well worthy of attention at the present time, when so many unworthy topics and so much unworthy language may be heard from the pulpit. One is inclined to think that if ministers always remembered that they were speaking "in the sight of God," they would sometimes find other things to say, and other ways of saying them. We talk glibly enough of another man's words and opinions, when he is not present. We may be entirely free from the smallest wish to misrepresent or exaggerate; but at the same time we speak with great freedom and almost without restraint. What a change comes over us, if, in the midst of our glib recital of his views and sayings, the man himself enters the room! At once we begin to measure our words and to speak with more caution. Our tone becomes less positive, and we have less confidence that we are justified in making sweeping statements on the subject. Ought not something of this circumspection and diffidence to be felt by those who take the responsibility of telling others about the mind of God? And if they remembered constantly that they speak "in the sight of the Lord," this attitude of solemn circumspection would become habitual.

"That they strive not about words." The spirit of controversy is a bad thing in itself; but the evil is intensified when the subject of controversy is a question of words. Controversy is necessary; but it is a necessary evil: and that man has need of searchings of heart who finds that he enjoys it, and sometimes even provokes it, when it might easily have been avoided. But a fondness for strife about words is one of the lowest forms which the malady can take. Principles are things worth striving about, when opposition to what we know to be right and true is unavoidable. But disputatiousness about words is something like proof that love of self has taken the place of love of truth. The word-splitter wrangles, not for the sake of arriving at the truth, but for the sake of a dialectical victory. He cares little as to what is right or wrong, so long as he comes off triumphant in the argument. Hence the Apostle said in the first Epistle, that the natural fruit of these disputes about words is "envy, strife, and railings" (vi. 4). They are an exhibition of dexterity in which the object of the disputants is not to investigate, but to baffle; not to enlighten, but to perplex. And here he says that they are worse than worthless. They tend "to no profit:" on the contrary they tend "to the subverting of those who listen to them." This subversion or overthrow (καταστροφή) is the exact opposite of what ought to be the result of Christian discussion, viz., edification or building up (οἰκοδομή). The audience, instead of being built up in faith and principle, find themselves bewildered and lowered. They have a less firm grasp of truth and a less loyal affection for it. It is as if some beautiful object, which they were learning to understand and admire, had been scored all over with marks by those who had been disputing as to the meaning and relation of the details. It has been a favourite device of the heretics and sceptics of all ages to endeavour to provoke a discussion on points about which they hope to place an opponent in a difficulty. Their object is not to settle, but to unsettle; not to clear up doubts but to create them: and hence we find Bishop Butler in his Durham Charge recommending his clergy to avoid religious discussions in general conversation, because the clever propounder of difficulties will find ready hearers, while the patient answerer of them will not do so. To dispute is to place truth at an unnecessary disadvantage.

"Give diligence to present thyself approved unto God, a workman that needeth not to be ashamed." In the previous section St. Paul exhorted Timothy to be ready to suffer for Christ: here he charges him to work for Him; and in the language which he uses he indicates that such work is a serious matter;—"Give diligence." The word which he uses (σπουδάζειν) is one which scarcely occurs in the New Testament except in the writings of St. Paul. And the corresponding substantive (σπουδή) is also much more common in his Epistles than it is elsewhere. It indicates that ceaseless, serious, earnest zeal, which was one of his chief characteristics. And certainly if the proposed standard is to be reached, or even seriously aimed at abundance of this zeal will be required. For the end proposed is not the admiration or affection of the congregation, or of one's superiors, nor yet success in influencing and winning souls; but that of presenting oneself to God in such a way as to secure His approval, without fear of incurring the reproach of being a workman who has shirked or scamped his work. The Apostle's charge is a most wholesome one: and if it is acted upon, it secures diligence without fussiness, and enthusiasm without fanaticism. The being "approved" (δόκιμος) implies being tried and proved as precious metals are proved before they are *accepted* (δέχομαι) as genuine. It is the word used of the *"pure* gold" with which Solomon overlaid his ivory throne (2 Chron. ix. 17). In the New Testament it is always used of persons, and with one exception (James i. 12) it is used by no one but St. Paul. He uses it of being approved both of men (Rom. xiv. 18) and of God (2 Cor. x. 18).

The single word which represents "that needeth not to be ashamed" (ἀνεπαίσχυντος) is a rare formation, which occurs nowhere else in the New Testament. Its precise meaning is not quite certain. The more simple and frequent form (ἀναίσχυντος) means "shameless," *i.e.*, one who does not feel shame when he ought to do so. Such a meaning, if taken literally, would be utterly unsuitable here. And we then have choice of two interpretations, either (1) that which is adopted in both A. V. and R. V., who *need* not feel shame, because his work will bear examination, or (2) who *does* not feel shame, although his work is of a kind which the world holds in contempt. The latter is the interpretation which Chrysostom adopts, and there is much to be said in its favour. Three times already in this letter has the Apostle spoken of not being ashamed of the Gospel. He says "Be not ashamed of the testimony of our Lord, nor of me His prisoner." Again, "I suffer these things; yet I am not ashamed." And again of Onesiphorus, "He oft refreshed me, and was not ashamed of my chain" (i. 8, 12, 16). Does he not, therefore, mean here also, "Present thyself to God as a workman who is not ashamed of being in His service and of doing whatever work may be assigned to him"? This brings us very close to what would be the natural meaning of the word, according to the analogy of the simpler form. "If you are to work for God," says Paul, "you must be in a certain sense *shameless*. There are some men who set public opinion at defiance, in order that they may follow their own depraved desires. The Christian minister must be prepared sometimes to set public opinion at defiance, in order that he may follow the commands of God." The *vox populi*, even when taken in its most comprehensive sense, is anything but an infallible guide. Public opinion is nearly always against the worst forms of selfishness, dishonesty, and sensuality; and to set it at defiance in such matters is to be "shameless" in the worst sense. But sometimes public opinion is very decidedly against some of the noblest types of holiness; and to be "shameless" under such circumstances is a necessary qualification for doing one's duty. It is by no means certain that this is not St. Paul's meaning. If we translate, "A workman that feeleth no shame," we shall have a phrase that would cover either interpretation.

"Handling aright the word of truth," or "Rightly dividing the word of truth." There is some doubt here also as to the explanation of the word rendered "handling aright" or "rightly dividing" (ὀρθοτομεῖν). Once more we have a word which occurs nowhere else in New Testament. Its radical meaning is to "cut aright" or "cut straight," especially of driving a straight road through a district, or a straight furrow across a field. In the LXX. it is twice used of making straight or directing a person's path. "In all thy ways acknowledge Him, and He shall direct thy paths;" and "The righteousness of the perfect shall direct his way" (Prov. iii. 6; xi. 5). The idea of rightness seems to be the dominant one; that of cutting quite secondary; so that the Revisers are quite justified in following the example of the Vulgate (*recte tractantem*), and translating simply "rightly handling." But this right handling may be understood as consisting in seeing that the word of truth moves in the right direction and progresses in the congregation by a legitimate development. The word, therefore, excludes all fanciful and perilous deviations and evasions, such as those in which the false teachers indulged, and all those "strivings about words," which distract men's minds and divert them from the substance of the Gospel. It may be doubted whether the word contains any idea of *distribution*, as that the word of truth is to be preached according to the capacity of the hearers,—strong meat to the strong, and milk to those who are still but babes in the faith. We may feel sure that the expression has nothing to do with the cutting up of victims in sacrifices, or with cutting straight to the heart of a thing, as if the word of truth had a kernel which must be reached by cleaving it down the middle. Yet both these explanations have been suggested. Clement of Alexandria and Eusebius use the substantive derived from St. Paul's verb (ὀρθοτομία) in the sense of orthodoxy; which seems to imply that they understood the verb in the sense of handling aright (*Strom.*, VII. xvi.; *H. E.*, IV. iii.).

Once more (1 Tim. vi. 20) the Apostle warns his disciple against "profane babblings." He is (according to St. Paul's graphic word) to make a circuit in order to avoid such things, to "give them a wide berth" (περιίστασο; comp. Tit. iii. 9). These empty profanities, with their philosophic pretentiousness, had done much harm already, and would do still more; for the men who propagate them would certainly go still greater lengths in impiety; and they must receive no encouragement. Their teaching is of a kind that will spread rapidly, and it is deadly in its effects. It "will eat as doth a gangrene."

The substitution of "gangrene" for "cancer" is an improvement, as giving the exact word used in the original, which expresses the meaning more forcibly than "cancer." Cancer is sometimes very slow in its ravages, and may go on for years without causing serious harm. Gangrene poisons the whole frame and quickly becomes fatal. The Apostle foresees that doctrines, which really ate out the very heart of Christianity, were likely to become very popular in Ephesus and would do incalculable mischief. The nature of these doctrines we gather from what follows. They are preached by the kind of people (οἵτινες) who miss their aim as regards the truth. They profess to be aiming at the truth, but they go very wide of the mark. For instance, some of them say that it is quite a mistake to look forward to a resurrection of the body, or indeed to any resurrection at all. The only real resurrection has taken place already and cannot be repeated. It is that intellectual and spiritual process which is involved in rising from degrading ignorance to a recognition and acceptance of the truth. What is commonly called death, viz., the separation of soul and body, is not really death at all. Death in the true sense of the word means ignorance of God and of Divine things; to be buried is to be buried in error. Consequently the true resurrection is to be reanimated by the truth and to escape from the sepulchre of spiritual darkness; and this process is accomplished once for all in every enlightened soul. We learn from the writings of Irenaeus (*Hær.*, II. xxxi. 2) and of Tertullian (*De Res. Carn.*, xix.) that this form of error was in existence in their day: and Augustine in a letter to Januarius (lv. iii. 4) shows how such false notions might have grown out of St. Paul's own teaching. The Apostle insisted so frequently upon the fact of our being dead with Christ and raised together with Him, that some persons jumped to the conclusion that this was the whole of the Christian doctrine of the resurrection. The resurrection of the body was a great stumbling-block to Greeks and Orientals, with their low notions of the dignity of the human body; and therefore any interpretation of the resurrection which got rid of the difficulty of supposing that in the world to come also men would have bodies, was welcome. It was calamity enough to be burdened with a body in this life: it was appalling to think of such a condition being continued in eternity. Hence the obnoxious doctrine was explained away and resolved into allegory and metaphor.

Of Hymenæus and Philetus nothing further is known. Hymenæus is probably the same person as is mentioned in the first Epistle with Alexander, as having made shipwreck of the faith, and been delivered unto Satan by the

Apostle, to cure him of his blasphemies. We are told here that much mischief had been done by such teaching: for a number of persons had been seduced from the faith. "Some," in the English phrase "overthrow the faith of *some*," conveys an impression, which is not contained in the Greek (τινων), that the number of those who were led astray was small. The Greek indicates neither a large nor a small number; but what is told us leads to the conclusion that the number was not small. It is probably to this kind of teaching that St. John alludes, when he writes some twenty or more years later than this, and says, "Even now there have arisen *many* antichrists" (1 John ii. 18). Teaching of this kind was only too likely to be popular in Ephesus.

It is by no means unknown among ourselves. At the present time also there is a tendency to retain the old Christian terms and to deprive them of all Christian meaning. Not only such words as "miracle," "Church," "catholic," and "sacrament" are evaporated and etherealized, until they lose all definite meaning; but even such fundamental terms as "atonement," "redemption," and "immortality." Nay it is quite possible to find even the word "God" used to express a Being which is neither personal nor conscious. And thus language, which has been consecrated to the service of religion for a long series of centuries, is degraded to the unworthy purpose of insinuating pantheism and agnosticism. This perversion of well established phraseology is to be condemned on purely literary grounds: and on moral grounds it may be stigmatized as dishonest. If Hymenæus and Philetus wish to deny the resurrection, let them also surrender the word which expresses it. They have abundance of words wherewith to express mental and moral enlightenment. Let them not so handle a word of truth as to make it suggest a lie.

CHAPTER XXXIII
THE LAST DAYS.—THE BEARING OF THE MENTION OF JANNES AND JAMBRES ON THE QUESTION OF INSPIRATION AND THE ERRORS CURRENT IN EPHESUS

"But know this, that in the last days grievous times shall come. For men shall be lovers of self, lovers of money, boastful, haughty, railers, disobedient to parents, unthankful, unholy.... And like as Jannes and Jambres withstood Moses, so do these also withstand the truth; men corrupted in mind, reprobate concerning the faith."—2 Tim. iii. 1, 2, 8.

In the first chapter the Apostle looks back over the past; in the second he gives directions about the present; in the third he looks forward into the future. These divisions are not observed with rigidity throughout, but they hold good to a very considerable extent. Thus in the first division he remembers Timothy's affectionate grief at parting, his faith and that of his family, and the spiritual gift conferred on him at his ordination. And respecting himself he remembers his teaching Timothy, his being deserted by those in Asia, his being ministered to by Onesiphorus. In the second chapter he charges Timothy to be willing to suffer hardships with him, and instructs him how to conduct himself in the manifold difficulties of his present position. And now he goes on to forewarn and forearm him against dangers and troubles which he foresees in the future.

There are several prophecies in the New Testament similar to the one before us. There is that of St. Paul to the Ephesian Church some ten years before, just before his final departure for the bonds and afflictions which awaited him at Jerusalem. "I know that after my departing grievous wolves shall enter in among you, not sparing the flock; and from your own selves shall men arise, speaking perverse things, to draw away disciples after them" (Acts xx. 29, 30). The Epistles to Timothy show that this prediction was already being fulfilled during the Apostle's lifetime. There is, secondly, the prophecy respecting the great falling away and the revealing of the man of sin, which is somewhat parallel to the one before us (2 Thess. ii. 3–7).

Thirdly, there is the similar prediction in the First Epistle to Timothy (iv. 1–3). And besides these three by St. Paul, there are those contained in 2 Peter ii. 1, 2 about the rise of false teachers, and in the First Epistle of St. John (ii. 18 and iv. 3) about the coming of antichrist. Those in 2 Thessalonians and 2 Peter should be compared with the one before us, as containing a mixture of present and future. This mixture has been made the basis of a somewhat frivolous objection. It has been urged that the shifting from future to present and back again indicates the hand of a writer who is contemporary with the events which he pretends to foretell. Sometimes he adopts the form of prophecy and uses the future tense. But at other times the influence of facts is too strong for him. He forgets his assumed part as a prophet, and writes in the present tense of his own experiences. Such an objection credits the feigned prophet with a very small amount of intelligence. Are we seriously to suppose that any one would be so stupid as to be unable to sustain his part for half a dozen verses, or less, without betraying himself? But, in fact, the change of tense indicates nothing of the kind. It is to be explained in some cases by the fact that the germs of the evils predicted were already in existence, in others by the practice (especially common in prophecy) of speaking of what is certain to happen as if it were already a fact. The prophet is often a *seer*, who sees as present what is distant or future; and hence he naturally uses the present tense, even when he predicts.

The meaning of the "last days" is uncertain. The two most important interpretations are: (1) the *whole* time between Christ's first and second coming, and (2) the portion *immediately* before Christ's second coming. Probability is greatly in favour of the latter; for the other makes the expression rather meaningless. If these evils were to come at all, they *must* come between the two Advents; for there is no other time: and in that case why speak of this period as the "last days"? It might be reasonable to call them "*these* last days," but not "last days" without such specification. At the present time it would not be natural to speak of an event as likely to happen in the last days, when we meant that it would happen between our own time and the end of the world. The expression used in 1 Tim. iv. 1 very probably does mean no more than "in future times; hereafter" (ἐν ὑστέροις καιροῖς). But here and in 2 Pet. iii. 3 the meaning rather is "in the last days; when the Lord is at hand." It is then that the enemy will be allowed to put forth all his power, in order to be more completely overthrown. Then indeed there will be perilous, critical, grievous times (καιροὶ χαλεποί). The Apostle treats it as possible, or even probable, that Timothy will live to see the troubles which will mark the eve of Christ's return. The Apostles shared, and contributed to produce, the belief that the Lord would come again soon, within the lifetime of some who were then alive. Even at the close of a long life we find the last surviving Apostle pointing out to the Church that "it is the last hour" (1 John ii. 18), obviously meaning by that expression, that it is the time immediately preceding the return of Christ to judge the world. And some twenty years later we find Ignatius writing to the Ephesians "These are the last times (ἔσχατοι καιροί). Henceforth let us be reverent; let us fear the longsuffering of God, lest it turn into a judgment against us. For either let us fear the wrath which is to come, or let us love the grace which now is" (*Eph.* xi.). Only by the force of experience was the mind of the Church cleared so as to see the Kingdom of Christ in its true perspective. The warning which Jesus had given, that "of that day or that hour knoweth no one, not even the angels in heaven, neither the Son, but the Father," seems to have been understood as meaning no more than the declaration "in an hour that ye think not the Son of man cometh." That is, it was understood as a warning against being found unprepared, and not as a warning against forming conjectures as to how near Christ's return was. Therefore we need not be at all surprised at St. Paul writing to Timothy in a way which implies that Timothy will probably live to see the evils which will immediately precede Christ's return, and must be on his guard against being amazed or overwhelmed by them. He is to "turn away from" the intense wickedness which will then be manifested, and go on undismayed with his own work.

"Like as Jannes and Jambres withstood Moses, so do these also withstand the truth." The Apostle is obviously referring to the Egyptian magicians mentioned in Exodus. But in the Pentateuch neither their number nor their names are given; so that we must suppose that St. Paul is referring to some Jewish tradition on the subject. The number two was very possibly suggested by the number of their opponents:—Moses and Aaron on one side, and two magicians on the other. And on each side it is a pair of brothers; for the Targum of Jonathan represents the magicians as sons of Balaam, formerly instructors of Moses, but afterwards his enemies. The names vary in Jewish tradition. Jannes is sometimes Johannes, and Jambres is sometimes either Mambres or Ambrosius. The tradition respecting them was apparently widely spread. It was known to Numenius, a Platonic philosopher of Apameia in Syria, who is mentioned by Clement of Alexandria (*Strom.*, I. xxii.), and quoted by Origen and Eusebius as giving an account of Jannes and Jambres (*Con. Cels.*, IV. li.; *Præp. Evang.*, IX. viii.). In Africa we find some knowledge of the tradition exhibited by Appuleius, the famous author of the *Golden Ass*, who like Numenius flourished in the second century. And in the previous century another Latin writer, Pliny the Elder, shows a similar knowledge. Both of them mention Jannes as a magician in connexion with Moses, who is also in their eyes a magician; but Pliny appears to think that both Moses and Jannes were Jews.[93] It is highly improbable that any of these writers derived their knowledge of these names from the passage before us; in the case of Pliny this would scarcely have been possible. His *Natural History* was published about a.d. 77, and at that time the Second Epistle to Timothy must have been known to but few, even among Christians. The author of the apocryphal Gospel of Nicodemus very possibly did derive his knowledge of the names from St. Paul; yet he may have had independent sources of information. He represents Nicodemus as pleading before Pilate that Jannes and Jambres worked miracles before Pharaoh; "but because they were not from God, what they did was destroyed." Whereas "Jesus raised up Lazarus, and he is alive" (chap. v.).

One of the ablest of English commentators on these Epistles remarks upon this passage, "It is probable that the Apostle derived these names from a current and (being quoted by him) *true* tradition of the Jewish Church." And in a similar spirit a writer in the *Dictionary of the Bible* thinks that it would be "inconsistent with the character of an inspired record for a baseless or incorrect current tradition to be cited."

Let us look at the phenomena of the case and see whether the number and the names appear to be trustworthy or otherwise, and then consider the question of inspiration. To drag in the latter question in order to determine the former, is to begin at the wrong end.

That there should be a pair of brothers to oppose a pair of brothers, has been pointed out already as a suspicious circumstance. The jingling pairing of the names is also more like fiction than fact. Thirdly, the names appear to be in formation, not Egyptian, but Hebrew; which would naturally be the case if Jews invented them, but would be extraordinary if they were genuine names of Egyptians. Lastly, Jannes might come from a Hebrew root which means "to seduce," and Jambres from one which means "to rebel." If Jews were to invent names for the Egyptian magicians, what names would they be more likely to fasten on them than such as would suggest seductive error and rebellious opposition? And is it probable that a really trustworthy tradition, on such an unimportant fact as the names of the enchanters who opposed Moses, would have survived through so many centuries? Sober and unbiassed critics will for the most part admit that the probabilities are very decidedly against the supposition that these names are true names, preserved from oblivion by some written or unwritten tradition outside Scripture.

But is it consistent with the character of an inspired writer to quote an incorrect tradition? Only those who hold somewhat narrow and rigid theories of inspiration will hesitate to answer this question in the affirmative.

No one believes that inspired persons are in possession of all knowledge on all subjects. And if these names were commonly accepted as authentic by the Jews of St. Paul's day, would his inspiration necessarily keep him from sharing that belief? Even if he were well aware that the tradition respecting the names was untrustworthy, there would be nothing surprising in his speaking of the magicians under their commonly accepted names, when addressing one to whom the tradition would be well known. And if (as is more probable) he believed the names to be genuine, there is still less to surprise us in his making use of them to add vivacity to the comparison. Nothing in God's dealings with mankind warrants us in believing that He would grant a special revelation to an Apostle, in order to preserve him from so harmless a proceeding as illustrating an argument by citing the incorrect details which tradition had added to historical facts. And it is worth noting that nothing is *based* upon the names; they occur in what is mere illustration. And even in the illustration it is not the names that have point, but the persons, who are supposed to have borne them; and the persons are real, although the names are probably fictitious. Still less are we warranted in believing, as Chrysostom suggests, that St. Paul by inspiration had supernatural knowledge of the names. As we have seen, the names were known even to Gentiles who cannot well have derived their knowledge from him; and why should he have received a revelation about a trifle which in no way helps his argument? Such views of inspiration, although the product of a reverential spirit, degrade rather than exalt our conceptions of it. The main point of the comparison between the two cases appears to be opposition to the truth. But there is perhaps more in it than that. The magicians withstood Moses by professing to do the same wonders that he did; and the heretics withstood Timothy by professing to preach the same gospel as he did. This was frequently the line taken by heretical teachers; to disclaim all intention of teaching anything new, and to profess substantial, if not complete, agreement with those whom they opposed. They affirmed that their teaching was only the old truth looked at from another point of view. They used the same phraseology as Apostles had used: they merely gave it a more comprehensive (or, as would now be said, a more *catholic*) meaning. In this way the unwary were more easily seduced, and the suspicions of the simple were less easily aroused. But such persons betray themselves before long. Their mind is found to be tainted; and when they are put to the proof respecting the faith, they cannot stand the test (ἀδόκιμοι).

There is nothing improbable in the supposition that St. Paul mentions the magicians who withstood Moses as typical opponents of the truth, because the false teachers at Ephesus used magic arts; and the word which he uses for impostors (γόητες) in ver. 13 fits in very well with such a supposition, although it by no means makes it certain. Ephesus was famous for its charms and incantations (Ἐφέσια γράμματα), and around the statue of its goddess Artemis were unintelligible inscriptions, to which a strange efficacy was ascribed. The first body of Christians in Ephesus had been tainted by senseless wickedness of this kind. After accepting Christianity they had secretly retained their magic. The sons of the Jew Sceva had tried to use the sacred name of Jesus as a magical form of exorcism; and this brought about the crisis in which numbers of costly books of incantations were publicly burned (Acts xix. 13–20). The evil would be pretty sure to break out again, especially among new converts; just as it does among negro converts at the present day. Moreover we know that in some cases there was a very close connexion between some forms of heresy and magic: so that the suggestion that St. Paul has pretensions to miraculous power in his mind, when he compares the false teachers to the Egyptian magicians, is by no means improbable.

The connexion between heresy and superstition is a very real and a very close one. The rejection or surrender of religious truth is frequently accompanied by the acceptance of irrational beliefs. People deny miracles and believe in spiritualism; they cavil at the efficacy of sacraments and accept as credible the amazing properties of an 'astral body.' There is such a thing as the nemesis of unbelief. The arrogance which rejects as repugnant to reason and morality truths which have throughout long centuries satisfied the highest intellects and the noblest hearts, is sometimes punished by being seduced into delusions which satisfy nothing higher than a grovelling curiosity.

FOOTNOTES:

[93] Est et alia Magices factio a Moyse, et Janne, et Jotape Judæis pendens (Plin. *Hist. Nat.*, XXX. ii.).

Si quamlibet emolumentum probaveritis, ego ille sim Carinondas, vel Damigeron, vel is Moses, vel Jannes [*al. l.* Johannes], vel Apollonius, vel ipse Dardanus, vel quieunque post Zoroastren et Hostanen inter Magos celebratus est (Appul., *Apologia*, 544, p. 580 ed. Oudendorp).

CHAPTER XXXIV
THE PERILS OF RATIONALISM AND THE RESPONSIBILITIES OF A LIFELONG CONTACT WITH TRUTH.—THE PROPERTIES OF INSPIRED WRITINGS

> "But abide thou in the things which thou hast learned and hast been assured of, knowing of whom thou hast learned them; and that from a babe thou hast known the sacred writings, which are able to make thee wise unto salvation through faith which is in Christ Jesus. Every scripture inspired of God is also profitable for teaching, for reproof, for correction, for instruction which is in righteousness: that the man of God may be complete, furnished completely unto every good work."—2 Tim. iii. 14–17.

For the second time in this paragraph the Apostle puts his faithful disciple in marked contrast to the heretical teachers. A few lines before, after comparing the latter to the Egyptian magicians, he continues, "But *thou* (σὺ δέ) didst follow my teaching." And in the passage before us, after saying that "evil men and impostors shall wax worse and worse," he continues, "But abide *thou* (σὺ δὲ μένε) in the things which thou hast learned." Here there is a double contrast; first between Timothy and the impostors, and secondly between his abiding in the truth and their going away from it, and so from bad to worse, first as deceivers and then as being deceived. They begin by being seducers and end in being dupes, and the dupes (very often) of their own deceptions; for deceit commonly leads to self-deceit. Such a result may well act as a warning to Timothy and those committed to his charge of the peril of trifling with the fundamentals of religious truth.

The articles of the Christian faith are not like the commodities in a bazaar from which one can pick and choose at pleasure, and of which one can take three or four without in any way affecting one's relation to the remainder, or reject three or four, without in any way affecting the security of one's hold upon those which one decides to take. With regard to the truths of religion, our right to pick and choose has very strict limits. When the system as a whole has presented its credentials to the reason and the conscience, and these have decided that the bearer of such credentials must be the representative of a Divine Being, then the attempt to pick and choose among the details of the system becomes perilous work. To reject this or that item, as being mere fringe and setting rather than a constituent element, or as being at any rate unessential, may be to endanger the whole structure. We may be leaving an impregnable position for an exposed and untenable one, or be exchanging a secure platform for an inclined plane, on which we shall find no lasting resting place until the bottom is reached. And this was what the men, against whom Timothy is warned, had done. They had left the sure position, and were sometimes sliding, sometimes running, further and further away from the truth.

In other words, there is a right and a wrong use of reason in matters of faith. The wrong use is sometimes spoken of as "Rationalism," and (adopting that term as convenient) the following clear statement, borrowed from another writer, will show in a striking way where it was that St. Paul wished Timothy to part company with the principles of his opponents. "As regards Revealed Truth," wrote J. H. Newman in 1835, "it is *not* Rationalism to set about to ascertain, by the exercise of reason, what things are attainable by reason, and what are not; nor, in the absence of an express Revelation, to inquire into the truths of Religion, as they come to us by nature; nor to determine what proofs are necessary for the acceptance of a Revelation, if it be given; nor to reject a Revelation on the plea of insufficient proof; nor, after recognising it as Divine, to investigate the meaning of its declarations, and to interpret its language; nor to use its doctrines, as far as they can be fairly used, in inquiring into its divinity; nor to compare and connect them with our previous knowledge, with a view of making them parts of a whole; nor to bring them into dependence on each other, to trace their mutual relations, and to pursue them to their legitimate issues. This is not Rationalism. But it is Rationalism to accept the Revelation, and then to *explain it away*; to speak of it as the Word of God, and to treat it as the word of man; to refuse to let it speak for itself; to claim to be told the *why* and the *how* of God's dealings with us, as therein described, and to assign to Him a motive and a scope of our own; to stumble at the partial knowledge which He may give us of them; to put aside what is obscure, as if it had not been said at all; to *accept one half of what has been told us, and not the other half*; to assume that the contents of Revelation are also its proof; to frame some gratuitous hypothesis about them, and then to garble, gloss, and colour them, to trim, clip, pare away and twist them, in order to bring them into conformity with the idea to which we have subjected them."[94]

Timothy is to abide in those things which he has "learned and been assured of." He has experienced the result which St. Luke wished to produce in Theophilus when he wrote his Gospel: he has attained to "full knowledge of the certainty concerning the things wherein he had been instructed" (Luke i. 4). And he is not to allow the wild teaching of his opponents, thoroughly discredited as it is and will be by equally wild conduct, to shake his security. Not everything that is disputed is disputable, nor everything that is doubted doubtful. And if the fruits of the two kinds of teaching do not fully convince him of the necessity of abiding by the old truths rather than by the suggestions of these innovators, let him remember those from whom he first learnt the truths of the Gospel,—his grandmother Lois, his mother Eunice, and the Apostle himself. When it comes to a question of the authority of the teachers, which group will he choose? Those who established him in the faith, or those who are trying to seduce men away from it?

There is a little doubt about the word "of *whom* thou hast learned them." The "whom" is probably plural (παρὰ τίνων); but a reading which makes it singular (παρὰ τίνος) is strongly supported. The plural must include all Timothy's chief instructors in the faith, especially the earliest, as is clear from the nature of the case and from what follows. If the singular is adopted, we must refer it to St. Paul, in accordance with "the things which thou hast heard from me ... the same commit thou to faithful men" (ii. 2). It is possible that the words just quoted have influenced the reading in the passage under consideration, and have caused the substitution of the singular for the plural.

But there is a further consideration. There is not only the *character* of the doctrine on each side, and the *fruits* of the doctrine on each side, and the *teachers* of whom Timothy has had personal experience, and about whose knowledge and trustworthiness he can judge; there is also the fact that from his tenderest infancy he has had the blessing of being in contact with the truth, first as it is revealed in the Old Testament, and then as it is still further revealed in the Gospel. The responsibilities of those who from their earliest days have been allowed to grow in the knowledge of God and of His government of the world, are far greater than the responsibilities of those who have had no opportunity of acquiring this knowledge until late in life. Old habits of thought and conduct are not extinguished by baptism; and the false opinion and vicious behaviour of many of those who are vexing, or will hereafter vex, the Church in Ephesus, may be traced to influences which had become dominant in them long before they came into contact with God's revealed law. No such allowance can be made for Timothy. He has had the inestimable privilege of knowing the sacred writings from his earliest childhood. It will be his own fault if they do not "make him wise unto salvation through faith which is in Christ Jesus."

The expression "sacred writings" (ἱερὰ γράμματα) occurs nowhere else in the New Testament. The usual expression is "the scriptures" (αἱ γραφαί); and once (Rom. i. 2) we have "holy scriptures" (γραφαὶ ἅγιαι). Here both substantive and adjective are unusual. The adjective occurs in only one other passage in the New Testament, a passage which throws light upon this one. "Know ye not that they who perform the sacred rites, from the sacred place get their food?" (*Speaker's Commentary*, on 1 Cor. ix. 13.) And just as in that passage "the sacred rites" are the Jewish sacrifices, and "the sacred place" the Jewish Temple, so here "the sacred writings" are the Jewish Scriptures. It is utterly improbable that any Christian writings are included. How could Timothy have known any of these from infancy? Even at the time when St. Paul wrote this farewell letter, there was little Christian literature, excepting his own Epistles; and he was not likely to speak of them as "sacred writings," or to include them under one expression with the Old Testament Scriptures. The suggestion that Christian writings are included, or are mainly intended, seems to be made with the intention of insinuating that this letter cannot have been written by the Apostle, but by some one of a later age. But would even a writer of the second century have made such a blunder as to represent Timothy as knowing Christian literature from his childhood?

With the use of the substantive "writings" (γράμματα) in this passage, should be compared the use of the same word in Christ's discourse at Jerusalem after the miracle at the pool of Bethesda, where he shows the Jews how hopeless their unbelief is, and how vain their appeal to Moses, who is really their accuser. "But if ye believe not *his* writings (γράμματα), how shall ye believe *My* words?" The Jews had had two opportunities of knowing and accepting the truth; the writings of Moses, and the words of Jesus. So also Timothy had had two sets of instructors; the holy women who had brought him up, whose work had been completed by the Apostle, and the sacred writings. If the authority of the former should seem to be open to question, there could be no doubt of the sufficiency of the latter. They "are able to make him wise unto salvation through faith which is in Christ Jesus."

It must be observed that the Apostle uses the present tense and not the past (δυνάμενα) in expressing the power of the sacred writings in communicating a saving wisdom to him who uses them aright. This power was not exhausted when the young Timothy was brought to the ampler truths of the Gospel. However far advanced he may be in sacred knowledge, he will still find that they are able to make him increase in the wisdom which enlightens and saves souls.

But Scripture confers this life-giving wisdom in no mechanical manner. It is not a charm, which has a magical effect upon every one who reads it. The most diligent study of the sacred writings will do nothing for the salvation of a man who does not prosecute his researches in something more than the mere spirit of curious enquiry. Therefore St. Paul adds, "through faith which is in Christ Jesus." It is when this is added to the soul of the enquirer that the sacred writings of the Old Covenant have their illuminating power; without it, so far from leading to the salvation won for us by Christ, they may keep those who study them away from the truth, as in the case of the Jews to this day. The pillar of fire becomes a pillar of cloud, and what should have been for wealth becomes an occasion of falling.

"Every scripture inspired of God is also profitable for teaching, for reproof, for correction, for instruction which is in righteousness." This is the Revisers' rendering. Besides one or two smaller changes, they have made two important alterations of the A. V. (1) They have substituted "every scripture" for "all scripture," without allowing the old rendering even a place in the margin. (2) They have inserted the "is" (which *must* be supplied somewhere in the sentence) *after* instead of *before* "inspired by God;" thus making "inspired by God" an epithet of Scripture and not something stated respecting it. "Every scripture inspired by God *is also* profitable," instead of "*is* inspired of God *and* profitable:" but they allow the latter rendering a place in the margin.

This treatment of the passage appears to be very satisfactory, so far as the second of these two points are concerned. Certainty is not attainable in either. Yet, as regards the second, the probabilities are greatly in favour of the Apostle's meaning that "inspired scripture is also profitable," rather than "scripture is inspired and profitable." But, with regard to the first point, it may be doubted whether the balance is so decidedly against the translation "all scripture" as to warrant its exclusion. No doubt the absence of the article in the Greek (πᾶσα γραφή, and not πᾶσα ἡ γραφή) is against the old rendering; but it is by no means conclusive, as other instances both in the New Testament and in classical Greek prove.[95] Nevertheless, there is the further fact that in the New Testament "the scripture" generally means a particular passage of Scripture (Mark xii. 10; Luke iv. 21; John xix. 24, 28, 36, 37; Acts viii. 32, 35). When Scripture as a whole is meant, the word, is commonly used in the plural, "the scriptures" (Matt. xxi. 42; Mark xii. 24; John v. 39). In the passage before us the meaning is not seriously affected by the change. It matters little whether we say "the whole of scripture," or "every passage of scripture."

"Every scripture inspired by God is also profitable for teaching, for reproof, for correction, for discipline (παιδεία) which is in righteousness:" *i.e.*, is of use both for doctrinal and for practical purposes, for informing both faith and conduct. It is because it is "inspired by God," because God's Spirit breathes through the whole of it, making every passage of it to be a portion of a living whole, that Scripture possesses this unique utility. And if the Apostle can say this of the Old Testament, much more may we affirm it of the New Testament. From the two together, everything that a Christian ought to believe, everything that a Christian ought to do, may be learned.

But while this declaration of the Apostle assures us that there is no passage in Holy Writ, which, when properly handled, does not yield Divine instruction for the guidance of our minds, and hearts, and wills, yet it gives no encouragement to hard and fast theories as to the *manner* in which the Spirit of God operated upon the authors of the sacred writings. Inspiration is no mechanical process. It is altogether misleading to speak of it as Divine *dictation*, which would reduce inspired writers to mere machines. There are certain things which it clearly does *not* do.

1. While it governs the substance of what is written, it does not govern the language word by word. We have no reasons for believing in *verbal* inspiration, and have many reasons for not believing in it. For no one believes that copyists and printers are miraculously preserved from making verbal mistakes. Is it, then, reasonable to suppose that God would work a miracle to produce what He takes no care to preserve. Of the countless various readings, which are the words which are inspired?

2. Inspiration does not preserve the inspired writers from *every* kind of mistake. That it guards them from error in respect to matters of faith and morality, we may well believe; but whether it does more than this remains to be proved. On the other hand it can be proved that it does not preserve them from mistakes in *grammar*; for there is plenty of unquestionably bad grammar in the Bible. Look for instance at the Greek of Mark vi. 8, 9; Acts xv. 22; xix. 34; Eph. iv. 2; Col. iii. 16; Rev. vii. 9; etc., etc. And it may be doubted whether inspiration preserves the inspired writer from all possibility of error as regards matters of fact, as to whether there were two men healed or only one; as to whether the healing took place as Christ entered the city or as He left it; as to whether the prophecy quoted comes from Jeremiah or Zechariah, and the like. Can there be any reasonable doubt

that St. Matthew has made a slip in writing "Zechariah the son of Barachiah" instead of "Zechariah the son of Jehoiada"? And is there any honest method of bringing St. Stephen's speech into complete harmony with statements in the Old Testament respecting all the facts mentioned? Must we not suppose that there is error on one side or the other? If, as is quite certain, inspiration does not make a man a grammatical scholar, or give him a perfect literary style, ought we to conclude that it will make him a faultless historian or chronologer? A Divine Revelation through a series of inspired writers has been granted in order to save our souls. We have no right to assume that it has been granted in order to save us trouble. Those saving truths about God and our relations to Him, which we could never have discovered without a revelation, we may expect to find set forth without taint of error in the sacred writings. But facts of geology, or history, or physiology, which our own intelligence and industry can discover, we ought not to expect to find accurately set forth for us in the Bible: and we ought to require very full evidence before deciding that in such matters inspired writers may be regarded as infallible. St. Luke tells us in the Preface to his Gospel that he took great pains to obtain the best information. Need he have done so, if inspiration protected him from all possibility of mistake?

3. Inspiration does not override and overwhelm the inspired writer's personal characteristics. There appears to be no such thing as an inspired style. The style of St. John is as different from that of St. Paul as the style of Bishop Butler is from that of Jeremy Taylor. Each inspired writer uses the language, and the illustrations, and the arguments that are natural and familiar to him. If he has an argumentative mind, he argues his points; if he has not, he states them without argument. If he has literary skill, he exhibits it; if he has none, inspiration does not give it to him. "No inspiration theory can stand for a moment which does not leave room for the personal agency and individual peculiarities of the sacred authors and the exercise of their natural faculties in writing" (Schaff, *Apostolic Christianity*, p. 608).

What inspiration has *not* done in these various particulars is manifest to every one who studies the sacred writings. What it *has* done is scarcely less manifest, and is certainly much more generally recognized. It has produced writings which are absolutely without a parallel in the literature of the world. Even as regards literary merits they have few rivals. But it is not in their literary beauty that their unique character consists. It lies rather in their lofty spirituality; their inexhaustible capacities for instruction and consolation; their boundless adaptability to all ages and circumstances; above all, in their ceaseless power of satisfying the noblest cravings and aspirations of the human heart. Other writings are profitable for knowledge, for advancement, for amusement, for delight, for wealth. But these "make wise unto salvation." They produce that discipline which has its sphere in righteousness. They have power to instruct the ignorant, to convict the guilty, to reclaim the fallen, to school all in holiness; that all may be complete as men of God, "furnished completely unto every good work."

FOOTNOTES:

[94] "Rationalism in Religion," in *Tracts for the Times*, republished in *Essays Critical and Historical*, vol. i. p. 32.

[95] See the quotations given in Alford's note on πᾶσα οἰκοδομὴ in Eph. ii. 21, which might be increased, if necessary: *e.g.* πᾶν σῶμα, in Arist., *Nic. Eth.*, I. xiii. 7, which must = "the whole body."

CHAPTER XXXV
THE PARADOXICAL EXULTATION OF THE APOSTLE.—HIS APPARENT FAILURE AND THE APPARENT FAILURE OF THE CHURCH.—THE GREAT TEST OF SINCERITY

"But be thou sober in all things, suffer hardship, do the work of an evangelist, fulfil thy ministry. For I am already being offered, and the time of my departure is come. I have fought the good fight, I have finished the course, I have kept the faith: henceforth there is laid up for me the crown of righteousness, which the Lord, the righteous judge, shall give to me at that day: and not only to me, but also to all them that have loved His appearing."—2 Tim. iv. 5–8.

St. Chrysostom tells us that this passage was for a long time a source of perplexity to him. "Often," he says, "when I have taken the Apostle into my hands and have considered this passage, I have been at a loss to understand why Paul here speaks so loftily: *I have fought the good fight*. But now by the grace of God I seem to have found it out. For what purpose then does he speak thus? He writes to console the despondency of his disciple; and he therefore bids him be of good cheer, since he was going to his crown, having finished all his work and obtained a glorious end. Thou oughtest to rejoice, he says; not to grieve. And why? Because *I have fought the good fight*. Just as a son, who was sitting bewailing his orphan state, might be consoled by his father saying to him, Weep not, my son. We have lived a good life; we have reached old age; and now we are leaving thee. Our life has been free from reproach; we are departing with glory; and thou mayest be held in honour for what we have done.... And this he says not boastfully;—God forbid;—but in order to raise up his dejected son, and to encourage him by his praises to bear firmly what had come to pass, to entertain good hopes, and not to think it a matter grievous to be borne."

Chrysostom's explanation is no doubt part of the reason why the Apostle here speaks in so exalted a key. This unusual strain *is* partly the result of a wish to cheer his beloved disciple and assure him that there is no need to grieve for the death which now cannot be very far off. When it comes, it will be a glorious death and a happy one. A glorious death, for it will crown with the crown of victory struggles in a weary contest which is now ending triumphantly. And a happy death; for Paul has for years had the longing "to depart and be with Christ, which is far better." The crown is one which will not wither; for it is not made of olive, bay, or laurel. And it is not one of which the glory is doubtful, or dependent upon the fickle opinions of a prejudiced crowd; for it is not awarded by a human umpire, nor amid the applauses of human spectators. The Giver is Christ, and the theatre is filled with angels. In the contests of this world men labour many days and suffer hardships; and for one hour they receive the crown. And forthwith all the pleasure of it passes away. In the good fight which St. Paul fought a crown of righteousness is won, which continues for ever in brightness and glory.

But besides wishing to console Timothy for the bereavement which was impending, St. Paul also wished to encourage him, to stimulate him to greater exertion and to a larger measure of courage. "Be *thou* sober in all things, suffer hardship, do the work of an Evangelist, fulfil thy ministry. For *I* am already being poured out as a drink-offering, and the time of my departure is at hand." That is: *You* must be more vigorous, more enduring, more devoted; for *I* am going away, and must leave you to carry on to perfection that which I have begun. My fighting is over; therefore do you fight more bravely. My course is finished; therefore do you run more perseveringly. The faith entrusted to me has been preserved thus far inviolate: see to it, that what has been entrusted to you be kept safe. The crown which righteousness wins is waiting now for me: so strive that such a crown may await you also. For this is a contest in which all may have crowns, if only they will live so as to feel a longing for the appearing of the righteous Judge who gives them.

But there is more in this passage than the desire to comfort Timothy for the approaching loss of his friend and instructor, and the desire to spur him on to greater usefulness, not merely in spite of, but because of, that loss. There is also the ecstatic joy of the great Apostle, as with the eye of faith he looks back over the work which he has been enabled to perform, and balances the cost of it against the great reward.

As has been already pointed out in an earlier passage, there is nothing in this touching letter which is more convincingly like St. Paul than the way in which conflicting emotions succeed one another and come to the surface in perfectly natural expression. Sometimes it is anxiety that is uppermost; sometimes it is confidence. Here he is overflowing with affection; there he is stern and indignant. One while he is deeply depressed; and then again becomes triumphant and exulting. Like the second Epistle to the Corinthians this last letter to the beloved disciple is full of intense personal feelings, of a different and apparently discordant character. The passage before us is charged with such emotions, beginning with solemn warning and ending in lofty exultation. But it is the warning, not of fear, but of affection; and it is the exultation, not of sight, but of faith.

Looked at with human eyes the Apostle's life at that moment was a failure,—a tragic and dismal failure. In his own simple but most pregnant language, he had been "the *slave* of Jesus Christ." No Roman slave, driven by whip and goad, could have been made to work as Paul had worked. He had taxed his fragile body and sensitive spirit to the utmost, and had encountered lifelong opposition, derision, and persecution, at the hands of those who ought to have been his friends, and had been his friends until he entered the service of Jesus Christ. He had preached and argued, had entreated and rebuked, and in doing so had rung the changes on all the chief forms of human suffering. And what had been the outcome of it all? The few Churches which he had founded were but as handfuls in the cities in which he had established them; and there were countless cities in which he had established nothing. Even the few Churches which he had succeeded in founding had in most cases soon fallen away from their first faith and enthusiasm. The Thessalonians had become tainted with idleness and disorder, the Corinthians with contentiousness and sensuality, the Galatians, Colossians, and Ephesians with various forms of heresy; while the Roman Church, in the midst of which he was suffering an imprisonment which would almost certainly end in death, was treating him with coldness and neglect. At his first defence no one took his part, but all forsook him; and in his extremity he was almost deserted. As the results of a life of intense energy and self-devotion, all these things had the appearance of total failure.

And certainly if the work of his life seemed to have been a failure with regard to others, it did not bear any resemblance to success as regards himself. From the world's point of view he had given up much, and gained little, beyond trouble and disgrace. He had given up a distinguished position in the Jewish Church, in order to become the best hated man among that people of passionate hatreds. While his efforts on behalf of the Gentiles had ended for a third time in confinement in a Gentile prison, from which, as he saw clearly, nothing but death was likely to release him.

And yet, in spite of all this, St. Paul is exultingly triumphant. Not at all because he does not perceive, or cannot feel, the difficulties and sorrows of his position. Still less because he wishes to dissemble either to himself or others the sufferings which he has to endure. He is no Stoic, and makes no profession of being above human infirmities and human emotions. He is keenly sensitive to all that affects his own aspirations and affections and the well-being of those whom he loves. He is well aware of the dangers both of body and soul which beset those who are far dearer to him than life. And he gives strong expression to his trouble and anxiety. But he measures the troubles of time by the glories of eternity. With the eye of faith he looks across all this apparent failure and neglect to the crown of righteousness which the righteous Judge has in store for him, and for thousands upon thousands of others also,—even for *all* those who have learned to look forward with longing to the time when their Lord shall appear again.

In all this we see in miniature the history of Christendom since the Apostle's death. His career was a fore-shadowing of the career of the Christian Church. In both cases there appears to be only a handful of real disciples with a company of shallow and fickle followers, to set against the stolid, unmoved mass of the unconverted world. In both cases, even among the disciples themselves, there is the cowardice of many, and the desertions of some. In both cases those who remain true to the faith dispute among themselves which of them shall be accounted the greatest. St. Paul was among the first to labour that Christ's ideal of one holy catholic Church might be realized. Eighteen centuries have passed away, and the life of the Church, like that of St. Paul, looks like a failure. With more than half the human race still not even nominally Christian; with long series of crimes committed not only in defiance, but in the name, of religion; with each decade of years producing its unwholesome crop of heresies and schisms;— what has become of the Church's profession of being catholic, holy, and united?

The failure, as in St. Paul's case, is more apparent than real. And it must be noted at the outset that our means of gauging success in spiritual things are altogether uncertain and inadequate. Anything at all like scientific accuracy is quite out of our reach, because the data for a trustworthy conclusion cannot be obtained. But the case is far stronger than this. It is impossible to determine even roughly where the benefits conferred by the Gospel end; what the average holiness among professing Christians really is; and to what extent Christendom, in spite of its manifold divisions, is really one. It is more than possible that the savage in central Africa is spiritually the better for the Incarnation of which he knows nothing, and which his whole life seems to contradict; for at least he is one of those for whom Christ was born and died. It is probable that among quite ordinary Christians there are many whom the world knows as sinners, but whom God knows as saints. And it is certain that a belief in a Triune God and in a common Redeemer unites millions far more closely than their differences about ministers and sacraments keeps them apart. The Church's robe is tattered and travel-stained; but she is still the Bride of Christ, and her children, however much they may quarrel among themselves, are still one in Him.

And where the failure of St. Paul and of those who have followed him can be shown to be unquestionably real, it can generally be shown to be thoroughly intelligible. Although Divine in its origin, the Gospel has from the first used human instruments with all the weaknesses,—physical, intellectual, and moral,—which characterize humanity. When we remember what this implies, and also remember the forces against which Christianity has had to contend, the marvel rather is that the Gospel has had so large a measure of success, than that its success is not yet complete. It has had to fight against the passions and prejudices of individuals and nations, debased by long centuries of immorality and ignorance, and strengthened in their opposition to the truth by all the powers of darkness. It has had to fight, moreover, with other religions, many of which are attractive by their concessions to human frailty, and others by the comparative purity of their rites and doctrines. And against them all it has won, and continues to win, man's approbation and affection, by its power of satisfying his highest aspirations and his deepest needs. No other religion or philosophy has had success so various or so far reaching. The Jew and the Mahometan, after centuries of intercourse, remain almost without influence upon European minds; while to Western civilization the creed of the Buddhist remains not only without influence, but without meaning. But the nation has not yet been found to which Christianity has been proved to be unintelligible or unsuitable. To whatever quarter of the globe we look, or to whatever period of history during the Christian era, the answer is still the same. Multitudes of men, throughout eighteen centuries, under the utmost variety of conditions, whether of personal equipment or of external circumstance, have made trial of Christianity, and have found it satisfying. They have testified as the result of their countless experiences that it can stand the wear and tear of life; that it can not only fortify but console; and that it can rob even death of its sting and the grave of its victory by a sure and certain hope of the crown of righteousness, which the righteous Judge prepares for all those who love, and have long loved, His appearing.

"Who have loved and do love His appearing."[96] That is the full force of the Greek perfect (τοῖς ἠγαπηκόσιν), which expresses the present and permanent result of past action; and therein lies the test whereby to try the temper of our Christianity. St. Paul, who had long yearned to depart and be with Christ, could not easily have given a more simple or sure method of finding out who those are who have a right to believe that the Lord has a crown of righteousness in store for them. Are we among the number? In order to answer this question we must ask ourselves another. Are our lives such that we are longing for Christ's return? Or are we dreading it, because we know that we are not fit to meet Him, and are making no attempt to become so. Supposing that physicians were to tell us, that we are smitten with a deadly disease, which must end fatally, and that very soon,—what would be our feeling? When the first shock was over, and we were able to take a calm view of the whole case, could we welcome the news as the unexpected fulfilment of a long cherished wish that Christ would deliver us out of the miseries of this sinful world and take us to Himself? The Bible sets before us the crown of righteousness which fadeth not away, and the worm which never dieth. Leaning upon God's unfailing love let us learn to long for the coming of the one; and then we shall have no need to dread, or even to ask the meaning of, the other.

FOOTNOTES:

[96] The somewhat unusual word here used for Christ's second coming (ἐπιφάνεια) has been condemned as un-Pauline; but it occurs 2 Thess. ii. 8, and the cognate verb φανεροῦν is found Col. iii. 4. Cf. 2 Tim. i. 10; iv. 1; Tit. ii. 13; 1 Tim. vi. 14.

CHAPTER XXXVI
THE PERSONAL DETAILS A GUARANTEE OF GENUINENESS

"Do thy diligence to come shortly unto me: For Demas forsook me, having loved this present world, and went to Thessalonica; Crescens to Galatia, Titus unto Dalmatia. Only Luke is with me. Take Mark, and bring him with thee: for he is useful to me for ministering. But Tychicus I sent to Ephesus. The cloke that I left at Troas with Carpus, bring when thou comest, and the books, especially the parchments. Alexander the coppersmith did me much evil: the Lord will render to him according to his works: of whom be thou ware also; for he greatly withstood our words."—2 Tim. iv. 9–15.

"Salute Prisca and Aquila, and the house of Onesiphorus. Erastus abode at Corinth: but Trophimus I left at Miletus sick. Do thy diligence to come before winter. Eubulus saluteth thee, and Pudens, and Linus, and Claudia, and all the brethren." vv. 19–21.

It would scarcely be exceeding the limits of legitimate hyperbole to say that these two passages prove the authenticity and genuineness of the Pastoral Epistles; that they are sufficient to show that these letters are an authentic account of the matters of which they treat, and that they are genuine letters of the Apostle Paul.

In the first of these expositions it was pointed out how improbable it is that a portion of one of these letters should be genuine, and not the remainder of it; or that one of the three should be genuine, and not the other two; and *a fortiori*, that two of the three should be genuine, and not the remaining one.

The passages before us are among those of which it has been truly said that they "cling so closely to Paul that it is only by tearing the letter to pieces that any part can be dissociated from that Apostle."[97] The internal evidence is here too strong even for those critics who deny the Pauline authorship of the Pastoral Epistles as a whole. Thus Renan and Weisse are disposed to admit that we have here embedded in the work of a later writer portions of a genuine letter of the Apostle; while Ewald, Hausrath, and Pfleiderer accept not only these verses, but the earlier passage about Phygelus, Hermogenes, and Onesiphorus as genuine also. Similar views are advocated by Hitzig, Krenkel, and Immer, of whom the two first admit that the Epistle to Titus also contains genuine fragments. And quite recently (1882) we have Lemme contending that only the central portion of 2 Timothy (ii. 11 to iv. 5) is an interpolation.

These concessions amount to a concession of the whole case. It is impossible to stop there. Either much more must be conceded or much less. For, (1) we cannot without very strong evidence indeed accept so improbable a supposition as that a Christian long after the Apostle's death was in possession of letters written by him, of which no one else knew anything, that he worked bits of these into writings of his own, which he wished to pass off as Apostolic, and that he then destroyed the genuine letters, or disposed of them in such a way that no one knew that they had ever existed. Such a story is not absolutely impossible, but it is so unlikely to be true, that to accept it without clear evidence would be most uncritical. And there is not only no clear evidence; there is no evidence at all. The hypothesis is pure imagination. (2) The portions of this letter which are allowed by adverse critics to be genuine are precisely those in which a forger would be pretty sure to be caught tripping. They are full of personal details, some of which admit of being tested, and all of which can be criticized, as to whether they are natural and consistent or not. Would a forger be likely to risk detection by venturing on such dangerous ground? He would put into the letter those doctrines for which he wished to appear to have St. Paul's authority; and, if he added anything else, he would take care not to go beyond vague generalities, too indefinite to be caught in the meshes of criticism. But the writer of this letter has done the reverse of all this. He has given an abundance of personal detail, such as can be found in only one other place in the New Testament, and that in the concluding portion of the Epistle to the Romans, one of the indisputable writings of St. Paul.

And he has not been caught tripping. Hostile writers have subjected these details to the most searching criticism; and the result, as we have seen, is that many of them are constrained to admit that these portions of the letter are genuine productions of the Apostle. That is, those portions of the Epistle which can be subjected to a severe test, are allowed to be by St. Paul, because they stand the test; while those which do not admit of being thus tested are rejected, not because there is any proof of their being spurious, but because critics think that the style is not like the Apostle's. Would they not be the first to deride others for such an opinion? Supposing that these details had contained absurdities or contradictions, which *could* not have been written by St. Paul, would they not have maintained, and reasonably maintained, that it was monstrous to surrender as spurious those sections of the letter which had been tested and found wanting, and to defend as genuine the other sections, which did not admit of being tested?

Let us look at the details a little more closely. Besides St. Paul and Timothy, twenty-three Christians of the Apostolic age are mentioned in this short letter. A considerable number of these are persons of whom we read in the Acts or in St. Paul's other letters; but the majority are new names, and in most of these cases we know nothing about the bearers of the names beyond what is told us here. Would a forger have given us this mixture of known and unknown? If he ventured upon names at all, would he not either have given us imaginary persons, whose names and actions could not be checked by existing records, or else have kept closely to the records, so that the checking might tell in his favour? He has done neither. The new names do not look like those of imaginary persons, and the mention of known persons is by no means a mere reproduction of what is said of them elsewhere.

"Demas forsook me, having loved this present world.... Take Mark and bring him with thee: for he is useful to me for ministering." A forger with the Acts and the Epistles to the Colossians and Philemon before him would have made Mark forsake Paul, and Demas be commended as useful to him; for in the Acts (xv. 38) Paul had to condemn Mark for slackness, and in the Epistles to the Colossians (iv. 14) and to Philemon (24) Demas with Luke is waiting on the Apostle in his imprisonment. And yet how natural that the Apostle's condemnation should rouse Mark to greater earnestness, and that the Apostle should recognize that earnestness in this farewell letter? And how consistent with human frailty also that Demas should have courage enough to stand by St. Paul during his first Roman imprisonment, and yet should quail before the greater risks of the second! That the Apostle's complaint respecting him means more than this, is unlikely. Yet some have exaggerated it into a charge of heresy, or even utter apostasy. We are simply to understand that Demas preferred comfort and security away from Rome to the hardship and danger of a Roman prison; and therefore went to Thessalonica. Why he selected that town we are not told, but there being a Christian community there would be one reason.

"Titus to Dalmatia." Why should a forger send Titus to Dalmatia? The Pastoral Epistles, whether a forgery or not, are all by one hand, and seem to have been written within a short time of one another. Would not a forger have sent Titus either to Crete (Tit. i. 5), or to Nicopolis (Tit. iii. 12)? But if Titus went to Nicopolis, and failed to find Paul there, owing to his having been meanwhile arrested, what more probable than that he should go on into Dalmatia? The forger, if he had thought of this, would have called attention to it, to ensure that his ingenuity was not overlooked.

"But Tychicus I sent to Ephesus." The meaning of the "but" is not quite clear. Perhaps the most probable supposition is that it indicates the reason why the Apostle needs a useful person like Mark. "I had such a person in Tychicus; but he is gone on a mission for me to Ephesus." How natural all this is! And what could induce a forger to put it in? We are told in the Acts that Tychicus belonged to the Roman province of Asia (xx. 4), and that he was with St. Paul at the close of his third missionary journey about nine years before the writing of this letter to Timothy. Three or four years later we find Tychicus once more with St. Paul during the first Roman imprisonment; and he is sent with Onesimus as the bearer of the Epistle to the Colossians (iv. 7) and to the Ephesians (vi. 21). And we learn from the sentence before us, as well as from Titus iii. 12, that he still enjoys the confidence of the Apostle, for he is sent on missions for him to Crete and to Ephesus. All these separate notices of him hang together consistently representing him as "the beloved brother," and also as a "faithful minister and fellow-servant in the Lord," whom St. Paul was accustomed to entrust with special commissions. If the mission to Ephesus mentioned here is a mere copy of the other missions, would not a forger have taken some pains to ensure that the similarity between his fiction and previous facts should be observed?

"The cloke that I left at Troas with Carpus, bring when thou comest, and the books, especially the parchments." Here the arguments against the probability of forgery reach a climax; and this verse should be remembered side by side with "Be no longer a drinker of water, but use a little wine for thy stomach's sake" in the First Epistle (v. 23). What writer of a fictitious letter would ever have dreamed of inserting either passage? To an unbiassed mind they go a long way towards producing the impression that we are dealing with real letters and not with inventions. And this argument holds good equally well, whatever meaning we give to the word (φελόνη) which is rendered "cloke." It probably means a cloke, and is a Greek form of the Latin *penula*. It appears to have been a circular garment without sleeves, but with a hole in the middle for the head. Hence some persons have made the astounding suggestion that it was a eucharistic vestment analogous to a chasuble, and have supposed that the Apostle is here asking, not for warm clothing "before winter," but for a sacerdotal dress for ritualistic purposes. But since Chrysostom's day there has been a more credible suggestion that the word means a bag or case for books. If so, would the Apostle have mentioned both the book-bag and the books, and would he have put the bag before the books? He might naturally have written, "Bring the book-bag," — of course with the books in it; or, "Bring the books and the bag also." But it seems a strange way of putting the request to say, "The book-bag that I left at Troas with Carpus, bring when thou comest; the books also, especially the parchments," as if the bag were the chief thing that he thought about. It seems better to abide by the old rendering "cloke;" and, if this is correct, then it fits in well with "Do thy diligence to come *before winter.*" Yet the writer in no way draws our attention to the connexion between the need of the thick cloke and the approach of winter: and the writer of a real letter would have no need to do so. But would a forger have left the connexion to chance?[98]

Whether Alexander the coppersmith is the person of that name who was put forward by the Jews in the riot raised by Demetrius (Acts xix. 33), is not more than a possibility. The name Alexander was exceedingly common; and we are not told that the Jew in the riot at Ephesus was a smith, or that Alexander the smith was a Jew. In what way the coppersmith "showed much ill-treatment" to the Apostle, we are not told. As St. Paul goes on immediately afterwards to speak of his "first defence," it seems reasonable to conjecture that Alexander had seriously injured the Apostle's cause in some way. But this is pure conjecture; and the ill-treatment may refer to general persecution of St. Paul and opposition to his teaching. On the whole the latter hypothesis appears to be safer.

The reading, "The Lord *will* render to him" (ἀποδώσει), is shown by an overwhelming balance of evidence to be preferable to "The Lord reward him (ἀποδώη) according to his works." There is no malediction. Just as in ver. 8 the Apostle expresses his conviction that the Lord will render (ἀποδώσει) a crown of righteousness to all those who love His appearing, so here he expresses a conviction that He will render a just recompense to all those who oppose the work of His kingdom. What follows in the next verse, "may it not be laid to their account," seems to show that the Apostle is in no cursing mood. He writes in sorrow rather than in anger. It is necessary to put Timothy on his guard against a dangerous person; but he leaves the requital of the evil deeds to God.

"Salute Prisca and Aquila." A forger with the Apostle's indisputable writings before him, would hardly have inserted this; for he would have concluded from Rom. xvi. 3, 4, that these two well-known helpers of St. Paul were in Rome at this very time. Aquila was a Jew of Pontus who had migrated from Pontus to Rome, but had had to leave the capital again when Claudius expelled the Jews from the city (Acts xviii. 2). He and his wife Prisca or Priscilla then settled in Corinth, where St. Paul took up his abode with them, because they were Jews and tent-makers, like himself. And in their workshop the foundations of the Corinthian Church were laid. Thenceforward they became his helpers in preaching the Gospel, and went with him to Ephesus, where they helped forward the conversion of the eloquent Alexandrian Jew Apollos. After much service to the Church they returned once more to Rome, and were there when St. Paul wrote the Epistle to the Romans. Either the persecution under Nero, or possibly missionary enterprise, induced them once more to leave Rome and return to Asia. The Apostle naturally puts such faithful friends, "who for his life laid down their necks" (Rom. xvi. 3), in the very first place in sending his personal greetings; and they are equally naturally coupled with the household of Onesiphorus, who had done similar service in courageously visiting St. Paul in his imprisonment (ver. 16). The double mention of "the *household* of Onesiphorus" (not of Onesiphorus himself) has been commented upon in a former exposition (see No. XXVIII.).

Of the statements, "Erastus abode at Corinth: but Trophimus I left at Miletus sick," no more need be said than to point out how lifelike and natural they are in a real letter from one friend to another who knows the persons mentioned; how unlikely they are to have occurred to a writer who was inventing a letter in order to advocate his own doctrinal views. That Trophimus is the same person as the Ephesian, who with Tychicus accompanied St. Paul on his third missionary journey (Acts xx. 4; xxi. 29), may be safely assumed. Whether Erastus is identical with the treasurer of Corinth (Rom. xvi. 23), or with the Erastus who was sent by Paul with Timothy to Macedonia (Acts xix. 22), must remain uncertain.

"Eubulus saluteth thee, and Pudens, and Linus, and Claudia." With this group of names our accumulation of arguments for the genuineness of this portion of the letter, and therefore of the whole letter, and therefore of all three Pastoral Epistles, comes to an end. The argument is a cumulative one, and this last item of the internal evidence is by no means the least important or least convincing. About Eubulus, Pudens, and Claudia we know nothing beyond what this passage implies, viz., that they were members of the Christian Church in Rome; for the very bare possibility that Pudens and Claudia may be the persons of that name who are mentioned by Martial, is not worth more than a passing reference. But Linus is a person about whom something is known. It is unlikely that in the Apostolic age there were two Christians of this name in the Roman Church; and therefore we may safely conclude that the Linus who here sends greeting is identical with the Linus, who, according to very early testimony preserved by Irenæus (*Hær.*, III. iii. 3), was first among the earliest bishops of the Church of Rome. Irenæus himself expressly identifies the first Bishop of Rome with the Linus mentioned in the Epistles to Timothy, and that in a passage in which (thanks to Eusebius) we have the original Greek of Irenæus as well as the Latin translation. From his time (c. a.d. 180) to the present day, Linus, Anencletus or Anacletus or Cletus (all three forms of the name are used), and Clement have been commemorated as the three first Bishops of Rome. They must all of them have been contemporaries of the Apostle. Of these three far the most famous was Clement; and a writer at the end of the first century, or beginning of the second, inventing a letter for St. Paul, would be much more likely to put Clement into it than Linus. Again, such a writer would know that Linus, after the Apostle's death, became the presiding presbyter of the Church of Rome, and would place him before Eubulus and Pudens. But here Linus is placed after the other two. The obvious inference is, that, at the time when this letter was written, Linus was not yet in any position of authority. Like the other persons here named, he was a leading member of the Church in Rome, otherwise he would hardly have been mentioned at all; but he has not yet been promoted to the chief place, otherwise he would at least have been mentioned first, and probably with some epithet or title. Once more one asks, what writer of fiction would have thought of these niceties? And what writer who thought of them, and elaborated them thus skilfully, would have abstained from all attempt to prevent their being overlooked and unappreciated?

The result of this investigation is greatly to increase our confidence in the genuineness of this letter and of all three Pastoral Epistles. We began by treating them as veritable writings of the great Apostle, and a closer acquaintance with them has justified this treatment. Doubts may be raised about everything; but reasonable doubts have their limits. To dispute the authenticity of the Epistles to the Corinthians, Romans, and Galatians is now considered to be a sure proof that the doubter cannot estimate evidence; and we may look forward to the time when the Second Epistle to Timothy will be ranked with those four great Epistles as indisputable. Meanwhile let no student of this letter doubt that in it he is reading the touching words in which the Apostle of the Gentiles gave his last charge to his beloved disciple, and through him to the Christian Church.

FOOTNOTES:

[97] Salmon's *Historical Introduction to the New Testament*, p. 426, 3rd ed., to which the writer of this exposition is under great obligations. The book should be in the hands of every student of the N. T.

[98] The striking parallel to this request afforded by that of William Tyndale is pointed out in Farrar's *St. Paul*, ii. p. 571. Tyndale writes from his prison in the Castle of Vilvorden to ask, "idque per Dominum Jesum," for warmer clothing, and above all for his Hebrew Bible, grammar, and dictionary.

CHAPTER XXXVII
THE APOSTLE FORSAKEN BY MEN BUT STRENGTHENED BY THE LORD.—THE MISSION TO THE GENTILES COMPLETED.—THE SURE HOPE, AND THE FINAL HYMN OF PRAISE

"At my first defence no man took my part, but all forsook me: may it not be laid to their account. But the Lord stood by me and strengthened me; that through me the message might be fully proclaimed, and that all the Gentiles might hear: and I was delivered out of the mouth of the lion. The Lord will deliver me from evil work, and will save me unto His heavenly kingdom: to whom be the glory for ever and ever. Amen."—2 Tim. iv. 16–18.

There is a general agreement at the present time that Eusebius is in error, when, in a well-known passage in his Ecclesiastical History (II. xxii. 2–7), he refers this "first defence" and the "deliverance out of the lion's mouth" to the first Roman imprisonment and the release which put an end to it, probably a.d. 63. The deliverance does not mean release from prison following upon acquittal, but temporary rescue from imminent danger. Eusebius makes a second mistake in this chapter which is the result of the first error; but an avoidance of the second would have preserved him from the first. He says that the Apostle shows in the Second Epistle to Timothy that only Luke was with him when he wrote, but at his former defence not even he. Now during the first Roman imprisonment St. Paul was not alone, and one of the persons who was with him was Timothy himself, as we see from the opening of the letter to the Philippians. It is, therefore, highly improbable that the Apostle would think it worth while to tell Timothy what took place at the trial which ended the first imprisonment, seeing that Timothy was then in Rome. And even if Timothy had left Rome before the trial came on, which is not very likely, he would long since have heard what took place, both from others and from the Apostle himself. It is obvious that in the present passage St. Paul is giving his disciple information respecting something which has recently taken place, of which Timothy is not likely to have heard.

The value of the witness of Eusebius is not, however, seriously diminished by this twofold mistake. It is clear that he was fully convinced that there were two Roman imprisonments; one early in Nero's reign, when the Emperor was more disposed to be merciful, and one later; and that he was convinced of this on independent grounds, and not because he considered that the genuineness of the Pastoral Epistles would be untenable without the hypothesis of a second imprisonment.

Another confirmation of the view of Eusebius is found in the statement respecting Trophimus, that Paul had left him sick at Miletus. It is impossible to place the Apostle at Miletus with Trophimus prior to the first imprisonment. Consequently some who deny the second imprisonment, and yet maintain the genuineness of this letter, resort to the desperate method of making the verb to be third person plural instead of first person singular (ἀπέλειπον or ἀπέλιπον), and translating "Trophimus *they* left at Miletus sick."

"At my first defence no man took my part, but all forsook me." He had no *patronus*, no *advocatus*, no *clientela*. Among all the Christians in Rome there was not one who would stand at his side in court either to speak on his behalf, or to advise him in the conduct of his case, or to support him by a demonstration of sympathy. The expression for "no one took my part" (οὐδείς μοι παρεγένετο) literally means "no one came to my side," or "became present on my behalf." The verb is specially frequent in the writings of St. Luke. And the word which is rendered "forsook" (ἐγκατέλιπον) is still more graphic. It signifies "leaving a person *in* a position," and especially in a *bad* position; leaving him in straits. It is almost the exact counterpart of our colloquial phrase "to leave in the lurch." St. Paul uses it elsewhere of those who with him are "pursued, but not *forsaken*" (2 Cor. iv. 9). And both St. Mark and St. Luke, following the LXX., use it in translating Christ's cry upon the cross: "Why hast thou *forsaken* Me?" Hence it signifies not merely desertion (καταλείπειν), but desertion at a time when help and support are needed.

What is the meaning of the "all"? "*All* forsook me." Does it include Luke, whom he has just mentioned as being the only person with him? And, if so, is it meant as an indirect reproach? Some would have it that we have here an indication of the spurious character of the letter. The forger is unable consistently to maintain the part which he has assumed. In writing "all forsook me" he has already forgotten what he has just written about Luke: and he forgets both statements when a few lines further on he represents Eubulus, Pudens, Linus, Claudia, and others as sending greetings.

But, like so many of these objections, this criticism turns out, when reasonably examined, to be an argument for the genuineness of the letter.

These apparent inconsistencies are just the things which a forger could and would have avoided. Even a very blundering forger would have avoided three glaring contradictions in about thirty lines: and they *are* glaring contradictions, if they are interpreted as they must be interpreted for the purposes of this criticism. "Only Luke is with me." "Every one has forsaken me." "All the brethren salute thee." Any one of these statements, if forced to apply to the same set of circumstances, contradicts the other two. But then this meaning is forced upon them, and is not their natural meaning: and these are just the apparent inconsistencies which the writer of a real letter takes no pains to avoid, because there is not the smallest danger of his being misunderstood.

"All forsook me" is exactly a parallel to "all that are in Asia turned away from me" (see pp. 321, 322.) The "all" in both cases means "all who might have been expected to help." It refers to those who could have been of service, who in many cases had been asked to render service, by being witnesses in Paul's favour and the like, and who abstained from doing anything for him. The Apostle's "first defence" probably took place some weeks, or even months, before the writing of this letter. From our knowledge of the delays which often took place in Roman legal proceedings, there would be nothing surprising if a whole year had elapsed since the first opening of the case. It is quite possible, therefore, that at the time when it began St. Luke was not yet in Rome, and consequently had no opportunity of aiding his friend. And it is also possible that he was not in a position to render any assistance, however anxious he may have been to do so. There is no reason whatever for supposing that the Apostle includes him among those for whom he prays that God will forgive them their desertion of him, even as he himself forgives it.

Nor is there any contradiction between "Only Luke is with me," and the salutations sent by Eubulus and others. There were various members of the Church in Rome who occasionally visited St. Paul in his imprisonment, or at least kept up a certain amount of communication with him. But Luke was the only *outsider* who was with him, the only one who had come to him from a distance and been both able and willing to *remain* with him. Others both in Rome and from other Churches had paid visits to the prisoner; but they had been unable or unwilling to stay with him. Luke was the only person who had done that. Therefore the fact that various Roman Christians were ready to send greetings to Timothy is in no way inconsistent with the special commendation bestowed upon St. Luke for being his friend's sole companion in prison.

For the cowardly or unkind abstention of the rest the Apostle has no stronger word of condemnation than "may it not be laid to their account." No one knew better than himself how weak-hearted many of these disciples were, and how great were the dangers of his own position and of all those who ventured to associate themselves with him. It was otherwise in his first imprisonment. Then Nero was not quite the monster that he had since become. At that time the burning of Rome had not yet taken place, nor had the cruel outcry against the Christians, of which the conflagration was made the occasion, as yet been raised. It was quite otherwise now. To be known as a Christian might be dangerous; and to avow oneself as the associate of so notorious a leader as Paul could not fail to be so. Therefore, "May it not be laid to their account" (μὴ αὐτοῖς λογισθείη). This is the very spirit which the Apostle himself years before had declared to be a characteristic of Christian charity; "it taketh not account of evil" (οὐ λογίζεται τὸ κακόν): and of God Himself, Who in dealing with mankind, "lays not to their account their trespasses" (μὴ λογιζόμενος αὐτοῖς τὰ παραπτώματα αὐτῶν).[99]

"But," in contrast to these timid friends, "*the Lord* stood by me and strengthened me." Christ did not desert His faithful servant in the hour of need, but gave him courage and strength to speak out bravely before the court all that it was right that he should say. The contrast which the Apostle here makes between the many who forsook him and the One who stood by him reminds us of a similar contrast made by the Lord Himself. "Behold, the hour cometh, yea is come, that ye shall be scattered, every man to his own, and shall leave Me alone: and yet I am not alone, because the Father is with Me" (John xvi. 32). In this respect also the saying remains true "A servant is not greater than his lord" (John xv. 20); and Apostles must expect no better treatment than their Master received. If they are deserted by their disciples and friends in the hour of danger, so also was He. But in each case those who are deserted are not alone, because, although human help fails, Divine support is always present.

"The Lord" in this passage, both here and a few lines further on, means Christ rather than the Father. This is in accordance with St. Paul's usage. "Lord" here has the article (ὁ κύριος): and when that is the case it commonly means Jesus Christ (comp. ii. 7, 14, 22; iii. 11; iv. 14, 22; 1 Tim. i. 2, 12, 14; vi. 3, 14; 1 Cor. iv. 5; vi. 13; vii. 10, 12, 34; etc., etc. In Titus the word does not occur). Where "Lord" has no article in the Greek (κύριος) St. Paul usually means God and not Christ. Some would assert that, excepting where he quotes from the Old Testament (*e.g.*, 1 Cor. x. 26), this usage is invariable; but that is probably too sweeping an assertion. Nevertheless, there is no reason for doubting that in this passage "the Lord" means Jesus Christ. We may compare our own usage, according to which "our Lord" almost invariably means Christ, whereas "the Lord" more commonly means God the Father.

The word for "strengthen" (ἐνδυναμοῦν) means literally "to infuse power into" a person. It is one of which the Apostle is rather fond; and outside his writings it occurs in the New Testament only in the Acts and in Hebrews, once in each (Rom. iv. 20; Eph. vi. 10; Phil. iv. 13; 1 Tim. i. 12; 2 Tim. ii. 1). It is worth while to compare the passage in which he speaks to Timothy of Christ having given him power to turn to Him and become His servant; and still more the passage in which, during his first Roman imprisonment, he tells the Philippians "I can do all things in Him that strengthened me." The same thing was true in the second imprisonment.

The special purpose for which Christ stood by His Apostle and put strength and power into him is stated. "That through me the message might be fully proclaimed, and that all the Gentiles might hear." Those who follow Eusebius in the mistake of supposing that the "first defence" refers to the trial which ended in St. Paul's release after the first imprisonment, understand this proclamation of the message to the Gentiles as referring to the missionary work which St. Paul was enabled to do during the few years of interval (c. a.d. 63–66) before he was again arrested. But if the proclamation of the message took place in consequence of the Apostle's release, then it would have been placed after, and not before, the mention of deliverance out of the mouth of the lion. It is not said that he was *delivered* in order that through him the message might be proclaimed, but that he was *strengthened* in order that it might be proclaimed. And the special strengthening by Christ took place in reference to the first hearing of the case in court, when all human friends forsook him, while Christ stood by him. It was in court, therefore, that the proclamation of the message was made, and that through the instrumentality of the Apostle the preaching of the Gospel reached its culmination (τὸ κήρυγμα πληροφορηθῇ). This was the climax;—that in the metropolis of the world, in open court, before the imperial tribunal, the Gospel proclamation should be made with all solemnity and power. It is quite possible that this event, which the Apostle of the Gentiles regards as the completing act of his own mission and ministry, took place in the forum itself. Here Tiberius had caused a tribunal to be erected for causes which he had to hear as Emperor. But Claudius sometimes heard such cases elsewhere; and his successors probably followed his example. So that in the reign of Nero we cannot be certain that such a case as St. Paul's would be heard in the forum. But at any rate it would be held in a court to which the public had access; and the Roman public at this time was the most representative in the world. The Apostle is fully justified, therefore, in the language which he uses. This opportunity and power were granted "in order that through me the message might be fully proclaimed, and *that all the Gentiles might hear.*" In that representative city and before that representative audience he preached Christ; and through those who were present and heard him the fact would be made known throughout the civilized world that in the imperial city and before the imperial bench the Apostle of Christ had proclaimed the coming of His Kingdom.

And the result of it was that he was "delivered out of the mouth of the lion." This was a second consequence of the Lord's standing by him and strengthening him. He was enabled to speak with such effect, that the sentence of condemnation, which had been feared, was for the present averted. He was neither acquitted nor convicted; but the court, being unable to arrive at a satisfactory decision, granted an extension of time (*ampliatio*); that is an adjournment. In technical phraseology the *actio prima* ended in a verdict of *non liquet,* and an *actio secunda* became necessary; and as this second trial might have a similar result, the amount of delay that was possible was almost boundless.

To ask who is meant by the lion is a futile question. Whom did the Psalmist mean by the lion, when he prayed "Save me from the lion's mouth"? (Ps. xxii. 21.) He meant no one by the lion; but by the lion's mouth he meant some great and imminent danger. And that is what we must understand here. All kinds of gratuitous conjectures have been made by those who have insisted on identifying the lion;—the lion of the amphitheatre, to whom the Apostle might have been thrown, had he been condemned; the Emperor Nero, or, as he was possibly in Greece at this time, his prefect and representative Helius; or, the chief accuser; or again, Satan, whom St. Peter describes as "a roaring lion." All these are answers to a question which does not arise out of the text. The question is not, "Who is the lion?" but, "What is the meaning of the lion's mouth?" And the answer to that is, "a terrible danger," and especially "peril of death."

The goodness of the Lord does not end with this welcome, but temporary deliverance. "The Lord will deliver me from every evil work, and will save me unto His heavenly kingdom." Paul's enemies are not likely to be idle during the extension of time granted by the court. They will do their utmost to secure a sentence of condemnation at the second hearing of the case, and thus get the man whom they detest removed from the earth. Whether they will succeed in this or not, the Apostle does not know. But one thing he knows;—that whatever is really evil in their works against him will be powerless to harm him. The Lord will turn their evil into good. They may succeed in compassing his death. But, even if they do so, the Lord will make their work of death a work of salvation; and by the severing of the thread which still binds Paul to this life "will save him unto," that is, will translate him safe into, "His heavenly kingdom."

It is utterly improbable that by "every evil work," St. Paul means any weakness or sin into which he himself might be betrayed through want of courage and steadfastness. Even if the lion's mouth could mean Satan, this would not be probable; for it would be Satan's attacks from without, by means of opposition and persecution, and not his attempts from within by means of grievous temptations, that would be meant. What is said above about Alexander the coppersmith shows what kind of "evil" and what kind of "works" is intended in "every evil work." The expression evidently refers to the machinations of Paul's enemies.

It is also highly improbable that "will save me unto His heavenly kingdom" means "will keep me alive until He returns in glory." There was a time when the Apostle expected, like most other Christians of that day, to live to behold the second coming of Christ. But what we have already seen in this Epistle shows that in St. Paul's mind that expectation is extinct. He no longer thinks that he will be one of those "that are alive, that are left unto the coming of the Lord" (1 Thess. iv. 15, 17); that he will be among the living, who "shall be changed," rather than among the dead, who "shall be raised" at the sounding of the last trump (1 Cor. xv. 53). He does not repeat, what seems almost to have been a familiar watchword among the Christians of that day,—"Maran atha"; "the Lord is at hand" (1 Cor. xvi. 22; Phil. iv. 5). On the contrary, it is his own hour that is at hand: "I am already being offered, and the time of my departure is come." He is fully persuaded now that he will not live to see Christ's return in glory; and he does not expect that return to come speedily; for, as we have seen, one of his chief anxieties is that there should be a permanently organized ministry in the Churches, and that provision should be made for handing on the faith intact from generation to generation (Tit. i, 5; 2 Tim. ii. 2). There can be little doubt, therefore, that when the Apostle expresses a conviction that the Lord will save him unto His heavenly kingdom, he is not expecting to reach that kingdom without first passing through the gate of death. What he is sure of is this,—that the evil works of his adversaries will never be allowed to prevent him from reaching that blessed resting place. Christ's kingdom is twofold; He has a kingdom on earth and a kingdom in heaven. The saints who are in the kingdom on earth are still exposed to many kinds of evil works; and the Apostle is persuaded that in his case such works will be overruled by the Lord to further his progress from the earthly to the heavenly kingdom.

"To whom be the glory for ever and ever. Amen."

If what was said above about "the Lord" is correct, then here we have a doxology which manifestly is addressed to Christ. It is possible that in Rom. ix. 5 and xvi. 27 we have other examples, as also in Heb. xiii. 21; but in all these three cases the construction is open to question. Here, however, there can be no doubt that "the glory for ever and ever" is ascribed to the Lord Who stood by Paul at his trial and will deliver him from all evil works hereafter; and the Lord is Jesus Christ. As Chrysostom pointedly remarks without further comment: "Lo, here is a doxology to the Son." And it is word for word the same as that which in Gal. i. 5 is addressed to the Father.

With these words of praise on his lips we take our leave of the Apostle. He is a wearied worker, a forlorn and all but deserted teacher, a despised and all but condemned prisoner; but he knows that he has made no mistake. The Master, Who seems to have requited His servant so ill, is a royal Master, Who has royal gifts in store. He has never failed His servant in this life, in which His presence, though but dimly reflected, has always brightened suffering; and He will not fail in His promises respecting the life which is to come. The Apostle has had to sustain him, not merely Divine truth wherewith to enlighten his soul, and Divine rules, wherewith to direct his conduct; he has had also a Divine Person, wherewith to share his life. He has kept the faith in the Divine truth; he has finished his course according to the Divine rules; yet these things he has done, not in his own strength, but in Christ Who lives in him. It is this gracious indwelling which made the victory that has been won possible; and it is this which gives it its value. The faith which has been kept is faith in Him Who is the Truth. The course which has been finished is according to Him Who is the Way. And the life which has been shared has been united with Him Who is the Life. That union will never end. It began here; and it will be continued throughout eternity in "the life which is life indeed." And therefore, with a heart full of thankfulness to the Master Who has shared his sufferings and will share his bliss, he leaves us as his last address to Christ, "To Him be the glory for ever and ever. Amen."

FOOTNOTES:

[99] 1 Cor. xiii. 5; 2 Cor. v. 19.

INDEX

Abecedarians

Acts of the Apostles not written by Titus, nor by St. Paul

Adornment, The nature of

Alexander

Ambrose

Anacletus

Ananias and Sapphira

Anarchy in the Church

Angels

Antinomian doctrine

Apocalypse

Apollos

Apostles

Apostolic Constitutions

Appuleius

Aquila

Aratus

Aristotle

Army, Roman

Artemis, Temple of

Article, The Greek

Asceticism

Athenagoras

Athleticism

Aurelius, M.

Augustine

Authenticity of the Pastoral Epistles

Authority, Divine origin of

Avarice, Dangers of

Baptism

Basilides

Bauer

Blandina

Bodily exercise profitable

Bretschneider

Butler's Durham Charge

Carpus

Cathari

Celsus

Cellini

Certainty, Nature of historical

Children, Care of

Chrysostom

Circumcision of Timothy

Claudia

Claudius

Cleanthes

Clement of Alexandria

Clement of Rome

Clergy and laity from the first distinct

Cloke

Collection for Jewish Christians

Conscientious disobedience

Contentment

Continuity of doctrine

Controversial spirit

Controversial violence

Corinth, Case of incest at

Corinth, Timothy at

Corinth, Titus at

Cosin, Bishop

Credner

Crete, The Church in

Cynicism, Evils of

Cyril of Jerusalem

Davies, T. Ll.

Deaconesses

Dead, Prayers for the

Delivering to Satan

Demas

Devil, Personality of the

Diogenes Laertius

Discipline necessary to the Church

Divinity of Christ

Divorce

Doctrinal statements in the Pastoral Epistles

Doctrine, Continuity of

Doctrine of the Twelve Apostles

Döllinger

Doxology addressed to Christ

Dress of women

Ecstasy

Elders or presbyters

Elymas

Emotion in religion

Ephesus, Timothy at

Epimenides

Epiphanies of Christ

Episcopacy

Erastus

Evans, T. S.

Eunice

Eubulus

Eusebius

Ewald

Excommunication

Extempore prayer

Failure, Apparent, of the Gospel

Faith, Test of

Farrar, F. W.

Flood, The, a type of baptism

Free will

Freedom of the Gospel

Friendship of Paul and Timothy

Genealogies

Genuineness of the Pastoral Epistles

Gessius Florus

Gladiatorial shows

Gnosticism, its rapid progress, its problem, its moral teaching

Godet

Gœthe

Golden ages of the Church

Grammatical errors in Scripture

Gregory the Great

Gregory of Tours

Hadrian

Handling aright

Hands, Imposition of

Hands lifted in prayer

Hausrath

Hegesippus

Helius

Heresy, Meaning of in New Testament

Heresy and magic

Heretical teachers

Hermas

Hermogenes

Hippolytus

Hitzig

Hooker

Husband of one wife

Huxley

Hymenæus, The punishment of

Hymns, Ancient Christian

Ideal Church

Ignatius

Immer

Imposition of hands

Imprisonments of St. Paul

Imprisonment of Timothy

Incarnation, The

Inspiration of Scripture

Intercession

Irenæus

Jannes and Jambres

Jerome

Jewish Gnosticism

Job

Julian the Apostate

Justin Martyr

Kölling

Krenkel

Lambeth Conferences

Last days

Latin Fathers and Pagan culture

Laver of regeneration

Lemme

Lightfoot, Bishop

Linus

Lion's mouth

Liturgical forms in New Testament

Lois

Lord, when used of Christ

Luke

Lystra

Magic

Mahometanism and slavery

Maine

Manumission of slaves

Marcion's rejection of the Pastoral Epistles

Mark

Marriages, Second

Mill, J. S.

Milligan

Missions

Money, Love of

Montanus

Mouth of the lion

Muratorian Canon

Mystery, Meaning of in New Testament

Nero

Newman, J. H.

Nicodemus, Gospel of

Numenius

Obedience, Duty of

Onesimus

Onesiphorus

Ordination

Origen

Origin of the Christian ministry

Pastoral Epistles, Character of

Paul III., Pope

Pedanius Secundus

Persecution

Peshitto

Pfleiderer

Philetus

Phraseology of the Pastoral Epistles

Phygelus

Plato

Pliny the Elder

Pliny the Younger

Polycarp

Polygamy

Prayer, Forms of

Prayers for the dead

Presbyters or elders

Priesthood, The idea of

Prisca

Prophecies on Timothy

Prophet, Meanings of the term

Prophets in New Testament, in the Primitive Church

Public worship

Pudens

Punishment of Hymenæus and Alexander

Rationalism

Red Sea, Passage of the, a type of baptism

Regeneration, Laver of

Religious emotion, the use of

Renan

Resurrection, Belief in the

Reunion of Christendom

Reuss

Revisers, Changes made by the

Roman Church, Its neglect of St. Paul

Salmon

Satan, Delivering unto

Satan, Personality of

Schaff

Schleiermacher

Second Advent, Nearness of the

Second Roman imprisonment of St. Paul

Second marriages

Shamelessness in serving God

Slavery

Sobriety in religion

Socialism

Solidarity of Christendom

Strauss

Superstition and heresy

Tatian's rejection of 1 and 2 Tim.

Tertullian

Thanksgivings for all men

Theophilus of Antioch
Threefold ministry
Tiberius
Tigellinus
Timothy compared with St. John
Timothy at Corinth
Titus compared with Timothy
Titus at Corinth
Titus in Dalmatia
Trinitarian doctrine
Trophimus
Trullo, Council in
Tychicus
Tyndale
Verbal inspiration
Visible means an aid to faith
Washing of regeneration
Waterland
Weiss
Weisse
Widows
Will, Freedom of the
Women, Social position of
Women's dress
Worship, Public
Wordsworth, Bishop C.
Zenas
Zwickau prophets